LIVE FROM YC

EVERYTHING I LEARNED ABOUT TEACHING, I LEARNED FROM WORKING AT
SATURDAY NIGHT LIVE

JAMIE MASON COHEN

Cardinal Rules
—— PRESS ——

GET FREE DOWNLOADABLE TEACHERS' RESOURCES AND WORKSHEETS BELOW THAT WILL HELP YOU:

Winner of the *TED-Huff Post* International Teaching Award, The SOLE Challenge

INSPIRE CURIOSITY AND WONDER IN YOUR STUDENTS

The Simple and Practical High School Teacher's Guide to Create Self Organized Learning Environments (SOLES)

Jamie Mason Cohen

DOWNLOAD

WWW.JAMIEMASONCOHEN.COM/RESOURCES/

- Create Simple Self-Organized Learning Environments (SOLES) Your Students Will Love in Just 5 Minutes

- Gain immediate access to a SOLE Lesson Plan Template that you can use today! Get your students asking meaningful questions about the subject you're teaching (with over 20 Examples!)

- Improve engagement by 50% in just one class by creating a teen-centered learning environment that reaches your most challenging students.

Praise for LIVE FROM YOUR CLASS

"Everyone can tell you to inject some humour into your teaching to engage students, but few can help you understand how to do it! Jamie Mason Cohen has written the go to handbook on exactly how and why you need to get them laughing when they are learning. When an award winning teacher from an award winning comedy show has some help on how to bring a lightness to the classroom that brings results… you'd surely be playing the fool to not listen!"

—**Mark Bowden,** *best-selling author, Tame the Primitive Brain, TED speaker, presentation trainer for The Kellogg-Schulich Executive MBA ranked #1 in the world by The Economist*

"Jamie Mason Cohen cares deeply about helping you become a better educator. If you're interested in building a trust-filled relationship with your students, this book is a golden resource. Jamie has an ability to glean valuable lessons from his experience-rich life and translate them for your use in the classroom. He's gone to unexpected sources to find nuggets of wisdom and powerful techniques that will transform how you teach."

-**Dan Trommater,** *Toronto keynote speaker and magician*

"In this engaging, powerful and practical book, based on over a decade of front-line teaching experience together with his time at Saturday Night Live, Jamie Mason Cohen shares the secrets to using stories and humour in a compelling and relevant way to dramatically increase student engagement."

—**John Tighe,** *host of iTunes top ranked podcast, Publish Position Profit*

"I felt like a Baptist reading this book, as I caught myself saying 'Amen' multiple times. Cohen says it best when he says, "If you're laughing, you're learning." Not only does he provide a wealth of strategies that any teacher could benefit from; he also shows the vital role humour plays in building relationships with students. This book is an essential playbook for educators dedicated to creating meaningful learning connections for students."

—**Dr. Danny Brassell,** *(www.dannybrassell.com), "America's Leading Reading Ambassador," internationally-acclaimed speaker & top-selling author of Leadership Begins with Motivation*

"Jamie Mason Cohen is a man and a teacher of rare vision and insight, who I've gotten to know and collaborate with on multiple projects over the past fifteen years. Reading his book reinforces the importance of how fundamental teachers are in impacting young lives while reminding you not to take yourself too seriously in the process."

—**Jack Healey,** *executive director, Human Rights Action Center, former director, Amnesty International, author of Create Your Future*

"Jamie places the students first. This is why students connect with him and his approaches to learning. He is one of the top three teachers I have taught or observed in over four decades in education."

—**Jim Barry,** *veteran high school English teacher, teacher of teachers, author and editor of several books on education including, Themes on the Journey: Reflections in Poetry*

"When Jamie Cohen worked at Broadway Video and *Saturday Night Live*, he absorbed the environment and wore it well. As evidenced so clearly in his work, time and again Jamie has given back the gifts of his experience in the person of teacher, mentor and colleague."

—**Cristina McGinniss,** *senior producer, Broadway Video (Lorne Michaels' Production Company)*

"Brilliant book...really great! The ability to engage students and inspire a classroom is a 'requisite' to teaching...which makes this book mandatory reading. I will provide this book to our faculty."

—**Dirk L. Daenen,** *TEDxOrganizer, dean, United Business Institutes*

"The learning environment in Mr. Cohen's class could not be more positive; it is based on addressing multiple intelligences. Students are excited about their tasks and are totally involved. His lessons are academic excellence delivered creatively at their best; his work is outstanding."

—**Ray Buchowski,** *former vice-principal, TanenbaumCHAT*

"When I came into your class, I was dead inside. After your teaching, I feel alive."

—**Jacob,** *grade 10 student, CALC school in the Toronto District School Board, survivor of the Sudanese genocide*

"In LIVE FROM YOUR CLASS, Jamie unlocks the mystery of how to design and facilitate a meaningful and dynamic classroom atmosphere."

—**Grant Reimer,** *retired principal, Toronto District School Board*

"LIVE FROM YOUR CLASS practically bombards you with ideas and strategies, all of them extremely well thought out and the product of an insanely creative approach to education."

—**Dr. Nicholas Maes,** *professor, high school teacher, author*

"The skills Cohen proposes teaching in LIVE FROM YOUR CLASS derive from professional life – the art of entertainment, skill in business presentation, digital literacy – while preparing both pupil (and teacher) for the working world."

—**Louis Jebb,** *founder and chief executive at Immersivly Ltd, a virtual reality news app.*

"What I discovered is that in addition to the humour there is a ton of practical, cutting-edge tips on how to engage both young and adult learners."

—**James Muir,** *business trainer and coach*

"LIVE FROM YOUR CLASS is filled with practical advice in education and reads like a novel with a touch of glamour, struggle and so much needed solution. Jamie found his home, his domain, his passion and his nobility. Every single teacher and student should read it."

—**Nenad Bach,** *musician and human rights activist*

ABOUT THE AUTHOR

Jamie Mason Cohen is Co-Director, Student Activities and a High School English Teacher at TanenbaumCHAT, an independent school in Maple, Ontario. Cohen is the recipient of "The SOLE Challenge," an international teaching award sponsored by TED Youth Conference and The Huffington Post, and is a TEDx speaker. His work is featured in the upcoming issue of Ontario College of Teachers' magazine, *Professionally Speaking* as well in *TED.com*, the JW Foundation's, The Art of Learning Project, and the scholarly journal, *Jewish Educational Leadership.*

After years of working behind the scenes for *Saturday Night Live* creator Lorne Michaels in New York, Jamie created synergy between his knowledge of entertainment, arts, media, and education to generate unconventional teaching strategies for educators.

With over a decade of classroom experience, Jamie's professional passion is to find creative ways to instill in his students a love of learning and to help them develop real-world skills as well as give teachers inspiring and practical tools to make their jobs easier, more fun, and increasingly effective.

Cohen's credits include the design and implementation of teacher training workshops for schools in the Toronto District School Board, York Region District School Board, the Canadian Pre-University Programme in Malaysia, Tanenbaum Community Hebrew Academy of Toronto and education seminars such as RAVSAK Day School Conference and the Digital J Learning Network's Webinar series. He lives in Maple, Ontario with his wife, Karen and their two children.

Cataloging-in-Publication data for this book is available from the
ISBN-13: 978-1530777914
ISBN-10: 1530777917

Published in Canada

Cover design by Zeljka Kojic
Interior design and production by Artful Publications
Editing by Jim Barry, Estelle Cohen and Marley Gibson
Photographs by Matthew Liteplo, Ch.4 and Ch.15
Kindle Edition digital book design by Mehboob Sam

DISCLAIMER

I have tried to recreate events, locales and conversations from my memories of them. In order to maintain their anonymity in some instances I have changed the names of individuals and places, I may have changed some identifying characteristics and details such as physical properties, occupations and places of residence.

THIS BOOK IS DEDICATED TO:

The most important person in my life, my beautiful and compassionate wife, Karen. Thank you for creating a home full of unconditional love, warmth and laughter and for making me smile every day. You read my first draft and gave brilliant editing notes at every stage, encouraging me every step of this project. I included several stories about my life in teaching and working at Saturday Night Live in this book but the greatest story of my life began five years ago when I met you. You are my world.

To my children, Koby and Maya. You make me want to be a better dad, a better man, and create things you'll be proud of someday.

To my dad, Hushy Cohen, who had the vision before I did to push me to seek out the adventure of living and working in New York City. Your quiet pride, wisdom and unconditional belief in me has helped me through challenging times along this path.

To my mom, Estelle Cohen, who taught me a love of learning long before I thought of becoming a teacher. You are the greatest role model and teacher of my life.

To my sister, Carly Cohen, whose constant encouragement and career intervention convinced me to apply to Teachers' College. You played a key role in my decision to go down this road and did not let me leave the house until I filled out the application forms.

To my Bubbie, my closest confidante growing up, who believed in me before I believed in myself. Eleven years ago, I was sitting at your feet at a low point in my life in the convalescent home and you predicted where I am today.

To Becky Cohen, my late grandmother, who believed in my dream to work with *Saturday Night Live* in New York. You opened your home to the kids in your neighbourhood, one of whom turned out to be Lorne Michaels.

To my late grandfather, Max "Popeye" Cohen, an ingenious self-made entrepreneur and a strong and gentle man with a Zen-like presence. I adored and admired you. I always loved your smile.

To my late grandfather, Lou Gross, whose legend lives on through my mother and uncle Morty; the stories of you making people feel good with a compliment, of making them laugh, and your inspired charcoal portraits are gifts and images that surround me in my teaching and my life.

To my late uncle Stan and my uncle Morty and aunt Bonnie, who made living and working for Saturday Night Live in New York possible through your encouragement, advice and assistance.

To Reuven and Smadar for your love, support and generosity. Thank you for taking an interest in where my teaching journey takes me.

To Kevin, our late brother, who passed before we had a chance to laugh together. Your memory is infused in all we do.

Table of Contents

PART 3: RESOURCES

INTRODUCTION

WHAT IF YOU COULD BRING THE CREATIVE ENVIRONMENT OF *SATURDAY NIGHT LIVE* TO YOUR CLASSROOM?

THIS BOOK WILL GIVE YOU SPECIFIC STRATEGIES AND RESOURCES THAT CAN BE ADAPTED TO ANY SUBJECT TO IMPACT ALL OF YOUR STUDENTS THROUGH HUMOUR.

You'll learn how to:

☑ Use humour to grab your students' attention within the first 60 seconds and get full engagement until the bell goes.

☑ Effectively deal with the class clown and solve other classroom management problems without them stressing you out.

☑ Add humour to your class to build trust with your students even if you don't see yourself standing up there like a comedian.

☑ Effortlessly tell a story with humour and connect it to your lesson which enhances students' understanding of the content.

☑ Create an easy-going, creative and fun learning environment.

☑ Apply simple, unconventional student-centered resources your students will love, appreciate and be inspired to learn.

☑ Discover the humour in boring material.

☑ 3 Resources to encourage humour through play.

☑ The #1 strategy using humour to reach tactile learners.

☑ This book is about teaching and what it means to impact teenagers' lives. It will help you shift from the sage on the stage to the guide on the side.

LIVE FROM YOUR CLASS has three parts: The first two parts of the book provide real-world anecdotes, strategies, tips, tactics and lesson ideas, some of which were inspired by my experiences in

New York. The third part of the book offers humour-infused, blank lesson plans, worksheets, video-taped classroom examples and links to simple, practical project-based, experiential lessons for every classroom. You can find these lesson plans in the Resources section in the back of the book.

You ask yourself questions like:

- ☑ How can I become great at creating epic classroom environments in which my students are passionate about learning?
- ☑ What are some compelling ideas for my course?
- ☑ What are some real ideas I can use right now to develop intriguing and significant lessons?
- ☑ How do I help my students fulfill their creative potential?
- ☑ What's one new teaching strategy or approach that will re-energize my classroom this year?
- ☑ How can I get my most challenging students passionate about what I'm teaching?
- ☑ How can I enrich my students' lives so they will be inspired to learn?
- ☑ How do I ensure I don't feel burned out by February?

This book is for you if you are the type of open-minded high school teacher who looks for unconventional ideas to engage your students.

This book will provide quick, useful tips interwoven with teaching stories. I structured the book this way to provide you with non-boring, entertaining, professional development, by someone like you who knows the problems, challenges, and triumphs you go through every day.

These pages will illustrate how the stories from your life and your talents can merge to inspire your students even more than you already do.

The first moment I decided to become a teacher was when I watched Robin Williams' performance as John Keating, the teacher in *Dead Poets Society.* I walked out of the theatre as a teenager feeling I wanted to have an impact on the lives of young people like he did.

I aspired to be the kind of teacher who makes my students inspired to learn, read, create, and develop character. During a challenging Teachers' College experience in which I contemplated quitting, I attended the late Frank McCourt's book reading of his teaching memoir, *Teacher Man* at the University of Toronto's Hart House.

McCourt described his role of a teacher as "a drill sergeant, a rabbi, a shoulder to cry on, a disciplinarian, a singer, a low-level scholar, a clerk, a referee, a clown, a counsellor, a dress code enforcer, a conductor, an apologist, a philosopher, a collaborator, a tap dancer, a politician, a therapist, a fool, a traffic cop, a priest, a mother-father-brother-sister-uncle-aunt, a bookkeeper, a critic, a psychologist, the last straw."[1] I saw value in pursuing this kind of career. I modelled my own teaching style after Frank McCourt, John Keating in *Dead Poets Society,* and Jim Barry, my teaching mentor.

Teaching is the means by which I have the opportunity to impact young women's and men's lives each day. Writing about my experiences during my summers off is a way to share with other educators the lessons I've learned along my teaching journey.

THE STORY BEHIND THE STORY

I worked for Broadway Video, the production company that produces *Saturday Night Live, The Conan O'Brien Show,* the *Saturday Night Live* movies, and many more television shows and film specials. I held transient positions bouncing around from relatively insignificant jobs working for Lorne Michaels, the Executive Producer of *Saturday Night Live* and Founder of Broadway Video.

I had a unique perspective and distance as a fly-on-the-wall observer of this intriguing world. I learned valuable life lessons during my three and a half years working on the periphery of TV comedy production and I applied some of them to my teaching career. The stories in this book are as I remember them. I have changed certain names to respect the individuals involved.

The lessons I learned from my experiences working in the world of TV and film production have made me a more creative, resourceful, and fun teacher.

Read the chapters that best suit your needs. When you come across an idea that may work in your teaching environment, make a note of it for later. Reflect on your stories, travels, adventures, triumphs, and setbacks in life.

> *What is your* Saturday Night Live *experience?*
> *It doesn't have to be flashy. In your mind, it may be an incident you dismiss as trite or obvious, but to your students, it could be an epiphany. What are the stories you find yourself telling over and over to your students?*

You can go directly to the *Resources* for links, lessons and media examples that may spark ideas for an upcoming unit. You can also access at the end of each chapter actionable, summary steps.

Discover how the stories of your life can engage your students and transform your classroom from engaged to epic, as my life experiences have done for me.

Jamie Shen

DEFINING HUMOUR: A CONTEXTUAL PRELUDE

"The simplest definition of humour as it relates to teachers is the lighthearted, open and playful quality and context that permeates a curiosity-driven and creative learning environment."

— Jamie Mason Cohen

WHAT IS HUMOUR?

It's important to define 'humour' so that we are discussing the same topic within a particular framework.

How do I define humour for the purposes of this book? How did I research the topic in context to the classroom?

I was raised to believe that humour was something elusive. It was triggered by other people, often by surprise, at unexpected moments. It was a pleasant and welcome quality out of my control. I also believed humour was primarily about telling funny jokes, stand-up comedians, sitcoms, comic films and shows like *Saturday Night Live*. It was my impersonations of the way my father stumbled upstairs at night after falling asleep on the family room couch downstairs and my family's reaction, sometimes laughing until they cried.

Before I began researching this book and drawing on my decade of teaching, I used to think that you could not deliberately create a classroom environment infused with humour. If it happens that a class laughs, it's like catching lightning in a bottle. It's a magical emotion that cannot be planned out moment by moment like a Teachers' College lesson plan.

From the earliest stages of my reflections on my classroom experiences as well as the many books I referenced on the topic, I realised this is not how humour happened in my class.

It emerged as one of the best measures of positive emotional engagement and connection I have with my students. It also showed me that humour, in the framework I'm presenting here, is not purely subjective. It is a uniting force that brings young people together and builds a bond between a teacher and his/her students.

It is a means by which the majority of learners will respond favourably, regardless of their upbringing, biases and personality-type. I know the latter from first-hand experience. I've had the opportunity to teach at a high school in an economically disadvantaged community in downtown Toronto, a university preparatory college in Malaysia and a Jewish private school in Maple, Ontario. The one commonality is students are happier and more productive when they are laughing.

The research in this book shows humour has health benefits, too. It can be an emotional release with scientific data backing up that it's amongst the most beneficial stress relievers and a natural elixir. In "The Science of Humour", Hungarian writer, Laszlo Feleki said, "the greatest blessing of humour is that it relaxes tension. It is really indispensable in situations when there is nothing left but a big laugh."

It is also a coping mechanism by which we can handle the hard truth. For what's real is often funnier than fiction. The comedians of the day are amongst our current culture's most trusted social commentators. In surveys, more young people get their news from humourists than journalists on the real news channels.

"Good old-fashioned humour turns, on a surprising revelation of expectations that suddenly converges with what we know to be true. The result is disorientating simultaneity of the familiar and strange" as New York Times columnist, Lee Siegel writes in a Sunday edition piece, "Welcome to the Age of the Unfunny Joke." He goes on to say, today's comedy is about telling the "unadorned truth, its context is comedic, but its content is anything but." I'm more interested in defining the context and creating the conditions in which humour can flourish in a diverse range of classroom environments than in breaking down the content.

The simplest definition of humour as it relates to teachers is the lighthearted, open and playful quality and context that permeates a curiosity-driven and creative learning environment. The result is, "When you're laughing, you're learning" as Comedian and Speaker, Jack Milner said.

I explore the quality and conditions of amusement and good-natured, inclusive joy a teacher can deliberately create in a classroom in which meaningful humour can come to light. The results are a noticeable, tangible and transformative shift in the individual student's frame of mind and the intellectual climate of the class as a whole. It can and often will create upbeat momentum metamorphosing the energy of a class. A significant reason for this is because "all learning is state dependent" according to learning expert Jim Kwik. It leads to students' increased receptivity to the serious lesson that lies beneath the amused smile.

Humour is perspective. It is an insight into the needs of my students to find ways to lessen the burden of their day by creating spaces where wonder and big questions can flourish.

Humour integrated into teaching is putting yourself out there. It is daring to be a little uncomfortable to try something new. It is about being vulnerable and brave. As a father I can attest to Emerson's saying, "Your actions speak so loud, I can't hear what you're saying". His epigram applies to the way young men and women size up if their teachers walk their talk. If you are enjoying the process, smiling and laughing, you will be learning along with your students. It will make them feel you understand them and that making mistakes is an integral part of personal growth. If you delight in the journey, so will most of them, at some point.

The root of the word, humour as I learned from best-selling author, Mark Bowden comes from Medieval times. Humourists were the old medics who thought there were four kinds of humour: blood, phlegm, yellow bile, and black bile. These humours were necessary for the well-being of a person. The medics suggested "If one or some of the humours are out of balance, then you'd be ill essentially. So, you'd get into a humorous state to rebalance the humours." The Satirist, Feleki related the term, humour to an earlier historical period indicating it meant "fluid or moisture, showing that already the Greeks must have known both moisture and humour. Humour as a fluid probably served to dilute the hard facts of life making it possible to swallow and digest them."

What I am not referring to with this term is telling jokes to get a laugh, although some of the examples in this book such as Abraham Lincoln's use of humour often incorporated jokes. As a result, you will not find a list of jokes for which to open or close a class.

I am also not alluding to entertaining students for the sake of entertainment. The kind of humour I show may be funny but has a message or a point even when it serves temporarily to distract and refocus an audience of teenagers.

Humour as discussed in this book does not mean standing up in front of a group of high schoolers like a professional comic. Comedian, Tom Rhodes said most professional comedians are not funny by nature. He adds that some of his most moving moments on stage happen when he tells a story about his life that does not include laugh-out loud jokes. Tom's revelation surprised me but shows that it's not always appropriate to be funny.

It's also not a term I will often use to describe the act or the words that result in laughter though it may provoke different shades of mostly cheerful emotions and reactions from your students.

Humour in the context of the classroom focuses on elevating the state of mind of both the student and teacher to bring out their highest levels of effort and happiness. The struggle does not feel as daunting when sprinkled with a healthy dose of hilarity.

Why would a teacher want to improve in this area? Comedian Ron Tite answers this question in context to public speaking but it could equally apply to educators: "If you can precede a serious topic and create some softness around it with some comedy and get the audience's guard down, it makes them a little more relaxed and open to hearing the message that will come next. You're there to deliver the content. The funny just helps you deliver what you want people to walk away with. You're there to change peoples' lives, to change the decisions they make on a daily basis, and you have to use all the tools in your arsenal to do that. Humour and story are ways to do that."

A theme throughout the book is that humour is a powerful strategy to get students invested emotionally in learning before teachers can teach them. Philosopher Ludwig Wittgenstein said, "If people never did silly things, nothing intelligent would ever get done." There are chapters in this book in which I show how starting with a silly thing can unite a class and make them malleable and open to diving into deep critical thinking.

Humour is simply necessary to live a good life. Gandhi, Aung San Suu Kyi, Maya Angelou, Abraham Lincoln, Audrey Hepburn and so many leaders of all times, describe having a sense of humour as an armour for life's difficulties and essential for survival. It's in our hands to take care of ourselves for our emotional, psychological and pedagogical well-being. Our students will be the benefactors. To revise Author, Mary Pettibone Poole's words: "The teacher who laughs, lasts."

PROLOGUE

Live From New York

Jamie… Jamie!" Chris Farley nudged me. I looked up and Suri was giving me a look to hurry up and come in.

Chris said, "Good luck and say 'Hi' to Sean for me."

"I will," I said.

Suri, one of Lorne Michaels' assistants, held the door for me as I entered Lorne Michaels' *Saturday Night Live* office. The room felt like that of an Ivy League university president. It was filled with a mixture of elegant wooden shelves and walls that pictured Lorne with Paul McCartney, Mick Jagger, and even the President of the United States. And now, there Lorne and I were - alone in his office. He walked around his giant mahogany desk and shook my hand.

"Yes, yes… now I remember. You're from Toronto. Please have a seat," he said to me.

He led me over to two chairs in the middle of the room that were just the perfect distance away for a conversation between two people who were meeting for the first time.

There was no show of superiority or condescension. I felt at ease the moment he stood up to meet me. I realized at that moment he was the kind of leader who didn't feel as if he had to prove himself.

"So, how do you know Chris?" he asked.

"I just met him but we were talking about a mutual friend - Sean McCann -- one of your actors on Tommy Boy."

"Yes, I know him. You're from Toronto. Where did you grow up?"

"I grew up in the Yonge-Finch area, but my dad grew up in Forest Hill."

"How's your father?"

"He's good," I responded. Then, I added, "My father said you used to stop by his house with the other neighbourhood kids – my grandmother's house, when you were seven. Her name is Becky Cohen."

Ding.

He raised his head slightly, a little like the Dr. Evil character in the *Austin Powers* movie series. It's not hard to think Mike Myers may have based Dr. Evil's voice and certain mannerisms on Lorne. "I remember that name. Becky Cohen. I think my mother knew her. How's she doing?"

"She's great." It felt good to make a personal connection with him. *Now, what?* I thought.

"So, what brings you here?" he asked.

On the balcony of a friend's condo during my first week in New York. In the background, the World Trade Towers stand, 1998.

"I've always admired your work and how you've gotten where you are from where you were from. I've been working on a film in Toronto and developing a documentary, and I wanted to ask your advice for an aspiring film-maker."

"I love to read. I think we may have similar tastes in books."

"Is that so?" he asked.

"Yes, I heard you read Holocaust literature. Have you read the new memoir by Victor Klemperer, *I Shall Bear Witness*?"

"No, what is it about?"

"It's about a German Jewish World War I veteran and professor of French literature who kept a detailed journal of the slow, methodical limits on his freedom after the election of the National Socialists. The memoir was found nearly fifty years after it was written."

"Hmmm. Right." This was a characteristic, understated response from Lorne Michaels, as I would learn. One of my colleagues pitched his dream project to Lorne, whose sole response was, "The more you're on TV, the more you're on TV."

At that moment, there was a knock on the door. Suri came in and whispered something to Lorne.

"I'll be five more minutes," he told her. I assumed that she had been told to come in after a few minutes to keep the meeting short.

"So what film did you say you worked on?"

"I worked for one of Canada's most successful film producers, Niv Fichman, on his film called *Last Night*."

He drew a blank stare. "Who?"

I had made my first mistake. I'd tried too hard to impress him with a fact that was of no interest to him.

"I've never heard of him. What has he done?"

"He made a film called *32 Short Films About Glen Gould*."

"Oh," he said, without a slight change in his expression.

It was at this moment I was reminded of why I was here. On the surface, it was to get some advice. I knew any guidance from him would be along the lines of, "Keep trying, don't give up, do your projects, don't take no for an answer." I had read those types of statements from people in Lorne Michaels' sphere of power in the film world.

However, the thought that came into my head was this was one of those pivotal moments that if I didn't seize, I would forever regret. So, I was about to ask him if I could come to New York and work for him when suddenly he asked, "So, would you like to work for one of my companies?"

My heart leaped into my mouth. Did Lorne Michaels just offer me a job? Suri knocked for a second time, and Lorne looked towards the door and said, "Two minutes."

"Sir…" I started, but he cut me off.

"Call me Lorne."

"Okay, Lorne. I am willing to do anything, sweep the floors, buy sushi for producers, whatever it takes."

What I learned was to tell a potential mentor you are willing to do any job necessary for the company. Talk your way into an internship with the individual whose job you aspire to hold, even if it's only for two weeks just to prove you are invaluable to him or her.

"No, no, that's not necessary," he said. "When are you leaving New York?"

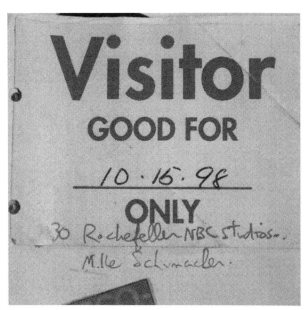

"The day after tomorrow."

"Right. Where would you like to work? *Saturday Night Live, Conan O'Brien*, Broadway Video Productions or BBN?"

I couldn't believe what I was hearing. "Anything, sir, I'd be happy to work in any of your companies."

"Right. I'll set up a meeting with the head producers of *Saturday Night Live, Conan*, Broadway Video and BBN. They will see you tomorrow. Just get along with them."

"I can do that."

"Okay. Good."

As if on cue, Suri walked in and Lorne repeated to her what he'd just told me. "Set up meetings with Jim, Michael, Jack, and Cristina tomorrow. Tell them to make time to see Jamie."

Suri wrote this down, her eyebrows arching as she tried to control a disbelieving smile. "Okay," she said. "Done."

She looked at me. I got the cue. Never overstay your welcome, especially after a moment like this one.

Lorne got out of his chair, shook my hand, and then patted me on the shoulder. "Give my best to Becky."

And that was it.

I walked out of the office and Suri treated me a little differently. "Wow. I didn't see this coming. Another first. You're in. Is there a number I can reach you at?" she asked.

I gave her the number of the family friend where I was staying.

"I'll call you tonight and tell you where to go tomorrow for the first of your meetings. I never thought I'd say this," she said. "But good for you."

"Thanks," I said.

I met with five heads of various shows and departments. Each greeted me with respect and a familiarity I hadn't earned, yet I received because I came through the boss.

I ended up working in various parts of Lorne Michaels's empire; from Broadway Video to *Saturday Night Live* Films to BBN, over the course of four years.

I didn't know it at the time, but working for this comedy TV company would help me infuse joy and humour into students' lives who felt little hope of a better future.

I remember one such instance when a Grade 10 English student in a Toronto District School Board high school came late on many days. He would arrive dishevelled and often wearing the same clothes. I wanted to help him, but didn't know how. I'd soon find out he was a child survivor of the Sudanese Genocide and had family members who were murdered by the Janjaweed.

One day during class, he arrived late. I was demonstrating a role-play by putting myself in the shoes of a character in a short story. As the student shuffled past me, I turned to him and said, "Quick, Jacob, I need a jacket."

He stopped and glared at me from the back of the class where he usually sat. "Yeah, I need *your* jacket." He reluctantly took it off and handed it to me. It was five sizes too big for me as he stood at six foot three. I looked ridiculous. The whole class laughed, including Jacob for the first time. I asked him to join me in my role-play in front of his classmates. He did.

After the class, he said it was the first time since he arrived from Sudan that a teacher had taken an interest in him. His marks slowly improved as he stayed during lunch and after school making gradual progression in his reading comprehension and writing. Along the way, my radar was up for light moments to bring a smile to Jacob and the other students, many of whom had also come from war-torn countries like Afghanistan and the Congo.

If you're laughing, you're learning. You don't have to be a professional comedian or think of yourself as a funny person to find moments of humour in a situation and be able to laugh at yourself in front of your students.

On the last day of school, Jacob said to me, "When I came into your class, I was dead inside. After your teaching, I feel alive."

I have Lorne Michaels to thank for putting me in an environment where I realized how comedy can heal and build real, emotional, powerful connections with people. I saw this first hand after 9/11. Having worked at *SNL* in New York helped me learn to create a classroom where both my students and I can't wait to get up each morning to attend.

PART 1

12 AUDACIOUS AND CREATIVE LESSONS I LEARNED FROM WORKING AT *SATURDAY NIGHT LIVE* TO CAPTIVATE YOUR STUDENTS

"As I stumble through life, help me to create more laughter than tears, disperse more happiness than gloom. Never let me become so blasé that I fail to see the wonder in the eyes of a child."

"The Clown's Prayer"

CHAPTER ONE

"These first few moments of class invite the student to the action. A teacher's enthusiasm, energy, and attitude draw kids into the learning process."

— Jamie Mason Cohen

LESSON #1: HOW TO CAPTURE STUDENTS' ATTENTION

Every Tuesday afternoon, all of the Saturday Night Live staff, writers, stars, and producers met with Lorne Michaels, the executive producer. They would sit in the writer's room, a nondescript area with white walls, gray couches, and a long table in the center. Each writer-star team would come up to pitch and perform their proposed sketch for that week. The tension was high as each group competed with each other to get their sketches on the air.

Often, the mini-pitch-performances would fall flat and an awkward silence would fill in the gaps where there was supposed to be laughter. The final judge of these pitch sessions was Lorne Michaels and the second most important voice was producer Marci Klein.

There was nothing worse for a writer-star team than glancing up to see Lorne Michaels' stoic expression. He rarely laughed out loud during these sessions, but there were variations of his response.

The pitch had to grab the audience's attention right away by being unique, different, and unexpected, but not too-far-out-of-the-box or it might turn off the viewers before they even got started. The actors had to sell their performances by believing in the words and sketch they were acting in. If the sketch artists didn't believe in the writing, it showed painfully so.

If the players gave their all but the writing was weak, it fell flat. When making a presentation to an audience, there needs to be synergy between what is said and how it is said, which includes the body language, the tone of voice, and the style. For a high school teacher, the hook is the first sixty seconds of a class, whereas on *Saturday Night Live* it is the opening monolog or scene.

These first few moments of class invite the student to the action. A teacher's enthusiasm, energy, and attitude draw kids into the learning process.

Tom Hanks, who has hosted the show eight times, figured out capturing the audience's attention right away sets the tone for the rest of the show and is ultimately what the host will be judged on.

"If you have a good, opening monolog, everybody thinks the entire show [is] great. If you have a poor one, it means you have to go and win back the favour of the people who are watching at home," Hanks said.

11 Unusual but Achievable Ways Teachers Can Capture Students' Attention in the First 60 Seconds

1. Set the class up as a SOLE (Self-Organized Learning Environment). Ask the students a big question such as: *What does it mean to be a hero in the 21st century?* Engage them by writing some of their answers on the whiteboard. Show a brief clip of a modern hero to prompt the discussion. Click here for the SOLE workbook, and here for Louis Jebb's SOLE Class.

2. Be a door stop. Greet every student by name as they walk in and leave, with a smile. Welcoming them into your class and ask them how their day is going. It sets the tone immediately. Learning each student's name is essential to build a connection with your class. Students don't care how much you know until you show them how much you care. One of the world's most

renowned learning and memory coaches, Jim Kwik suggests the following strategies to remember names:

3. Belief: Say, "I am a person who remembers every name."

    - Exercise: Stand up straight, breath fully and move. Being in a peak physical state improves the mind.

    - Motivation: Why do you want to remember the name? What's in it for you? Reason precedes results.

    - Observation: Be present. If you are distracted, it's unlikely, you will remember their name.

    - Relax: All learning is state dependent. If you are calm and cheerful, your mind will be more receptive to recalling names you've just heard.

    - Say their name: Repeat it during the interaction. Repetition is power.

    - Ask: Origin. What does it mean?

    - Visualize: Turn the name into a picture (Example: Mike = microphone)

    - As the student leaves, or you leave, say goodbye ending with their name.

Look at the student and think of a context (for example, the context would be a pair of glasses, a hair style, white shirt). Use your imagination to come up with a unique image. Reconfigure the room so the desks are pushed to the edges of the classroom. Changing them from their typical rows to a creative use of the space will change the mood of the class. Start or end a class, a unit or a student seminar with a surprise class dance component. *Saturday Night Live* incorporates music throughout the show through musical acts, sketches that incorporate songs and transitional interludes provided by a house band. Music and dance have a magical way of uniting a group of students through a fully immersive, fun, emotional activity. It brings a smile to each participants' face. I ended my *SOLE Student Leadership Seminar* with the students learning leadership through movement by way of a choreographed breakdance led by my friend, Glendale Reyes. Tactile learners think best when they get on their feet. Get kids to push past their resistance to try something new and challenge their comfort zones. View this short clip of 150 students and teachers breakdancing at the SOLE Student Leadership Seminar. Video by Glendale Reyes

4. Plan a surprise micro-field trip in the building or to a nearby location telling students upon entering the class to bring their pens and journals and to follow you. Take them outside to write nature haikus or as I did in Malaysia, into the nature garden of the school to create 15-minute 19th-century impressionistic paintings. Another example of a micro-field trip is "My Hero Next Door: Documenting the Heroic Life Journeys of Seniors". Here's a link to the lesson. I took the students to the VIVA Retirement Community residence across the street and arranged for pairs of students to interview a senior citizen about their life's journey. The interview was structured around questions inspired by Joseph Campbell's twelve stages of the hero's journey model. Students then created short documentaries on their local hero's journey, showed it to them at the retirement home and uploaded the video to a virtual reality platform.

5. Start the class with a live Skype interview/student feedback session with a fascinating expert in the subject area. I did this with musician, Nenad Bach, performing live from his studio in Irvington, New York. He then provided students with feedback on their original songs. In a world in which communication has become so electronified, it's still a gift for students to have in-person guest speakers. Find a way to have the speaker interact and engage with the students as well as just talking to them. My good friend, Jimmy Gary, actor in the Netflix series, "Orange is the New Black", had students do fun, acting exercises and take part in professional auditions in various roles of the play we were studying in class. It led to a meaningful discussion afterwards in which students stayed through their lunch period to continue the discussion.

6. Creative Attendance: Put every student's name on a playing card stuck to the outside of the door with numbers assigned to each name for group work. Each student finds their card and is told to go to the area of the class that has their group written on it.

7. Personalize tests and exams. Create a humorous first page with instructions that look legitimate until the students read

Musician, Nenad Bach live in his New York studio via Skype singing and interacting with my students in Malaysia.

them carefully. I've included an example in the Resources. One student smiles. Another student giggles and says, "What?!" It relieves tension and helps students focus in a more relaxed environment.

8. Do 10-minute Instant Productions/Plays in which students come into the class and immediately sign-up for cast and crew roles to take on for essential parts of a play. Positions can include: director, actors for specific roles, location co-ordinator, production designer, prop-master, critic, costume designers, summarizer). I write these roles on the white board and watch as students rush to take on different responsibilities in the Instant

Production. I briefly write a few key responsibilities of each role so students have a place to start.

9. If a teacher can manage it based on logistics and timing, encourage and reward students with positive specific feedback on their efforts for setting up the classroom prior to an oral presentation right at the beginning of that class. This creates social proof, healthy competition, and curiosity from their classmates as to what kind of creative space the student has set up. It also models the kind of work ethic and effort I want to bring out in all my students.

Another form of unusual feedback to get students' attention is to throw a Tea and Cookie Feedback Party during lunch or a

Guest Mentor, "Orange is the New Black" Actor, Jimmy Gary Jr. speaking with my students

study period. Students enter the room, get a snack provided by the teacher and listen to a pre-recorded audio recording of the teacher's favourite posts of students' work on a current project. I did this with my Siddhartha novel study. The technology I used was called *Xiosoft*. This recording programme is easy to use as you call a number given to you and record your voice. You save your recording, drag and drop. Attendance was 80% of the class.

The only students who did not come were absent from school or had make-up tests in other classes during this time. Click here to listen to a sample of "My Favourite Student Posts".

An additional memorable way to give feedback is to ask a student for their phone at the end of a class in which they gave their best effort or showed growth. Ask them to call their parents on the spot. Put the phone on speaker in front of the class. Tell the class to say, "Good work, Koby/Jennifer" when you give the cue. Then tell the parent why you are calling and how impressed you were with their son or daughter's effort in class today. The parent's reaction will be part shock, part joy and will put everyone in a cheerful state. Do this with every student in your class spontaneously, if possible, over the course of a year.

10. Set the space up as a 2nd grade classroom. Students take their place on the carpet. The teacher reads them a passage from a book while they sit in front on the floor. I did this to teach a class on Joseph Campbell's hero's journey applied to children's stories.

11. The Last Day Candle Class: On the first day of class, I tell students my goal is to get to know them, their strengths and their passions. I then tell them on our last day of class together eight months from now, I will share something I learned from them over the course of the year. On the final day of class, students arrive in a dark room with fake tea candles flickering on the periphery of the whiteboard ledge.

12. I push tables and desks to the walls during lunch in preparation for the class. In the middle of the room is a red cloth in the shape of a circle. I place a candle in the center of the circle. As students arrive, I ask them to sit on the red cloth circle. Every student is intrigued with the environment that has been set up. I talk to them briefly about why we're doing the Candle Class using mythological terms of coming full circle like all great stories do.

I show them what and how we learned this year by turning to the whiteboard behind us where I've written the main projects we did over the course of the year. I succinctly explain how each of these lessons helped us develop our skills and accelerated our learning through various strategies.

I then look at one student at a time and speak from the heart. Some of my memories are serious, others are humourous. I try to be as precise as possible. By the first 60 seconds of this process, there is not a stir amongst the Grade 9 students. Every teenager is either entirely focused on what I am saying about him or her or anticipating if they will be the next in line to hear my thoughts on their growth over the course of the year. When previous students walk by my classroom on the final day of school, they tell me it was one of the highlights of their high school life.

These ideas will work wonders in any classroom, but they require the teacher to do some prep.

CHAPTER ONE SUMMARY

ACTION STEPS

LESSON #1: 11 UNUSUAL BUT ACHIEVABLE WAYS TEACHERS CAN CAPTURE STUDENTS' ATTENTION IN THE FIRST 60 SECONDS

1. Design a SOLE. Start with a meaningful question and an intriguing prompt.
2. Greet students at the door by name.
3. Get students out of their comfort zone through dance and movement.
4. Take the students on a micro field trip to another space in the school or to community work within a few blocks of the school.
5. Have a live SKYPE chat with a fascinating expert beginning right when they enter the class or bring in a guest speaker to do meaningful activities with the students.
6. Do creative attendance. Students come into the classroom by finding the card with their name and join their assigned group.
7. Personalize exams by including a humorous instructions page or add inside jokes or class references embedded throughout the test.
8. Perform 10-Minute Instant Plays in which students enter, sign-up and rehearse one scene.
9. Give instant, public praise at the beginning of class to students who came in earlier to prep for a presentation.
10. Give students spontaneous praise at the end of a class by calling their parents on the spot. Once you do this form of feedback a

few times, students will be engaged from the first few moments of class in anticipation of it happening to them.

11. Set up a 2nd Grade reading circle on the floor. Sit on a chair and do story time with your students.

12. Make a Candle Class. Create a circle on the floor on the last day of class to share what you've learned from each student over the course of the year.

CHAPTER TWO

"Teachers who have lived, travelled, and experienced life deeply have the been-there-and-done-that credibility to inspire students to go out into the world, beyond the bubble of their safety zones, and discover who they are."

— *Jamie Mason Cohen*

LESSON #2: CRITICAL KEYS TO CONNECT WITH STUDENTS THROUGH YOUR STORY

When I tell students I worked for *Saturday Night Live*, some of their eyes light up, they sit forward in their seats, and say, "Wow, you're so lucky to have done that!"

They think I had a dream job. Like many things in life, appearances do not always match the reality of just how mundane, non-glamorous, and disappointing most of the jobs I was asked to do were. I was an assistant who entertained producers by analyzing their handwriting. I did a Lorne Michaels' imitation on the phone. I was an associate producer on a reality TV series about young comics on a college tour. I pitched a true-life crime movie to a VP at Broadway Video's film division, but it languished in development hell. I assisted in casting minor roles in a spin-off *SNL* movie.

The value of my experience during those four years from 1998 - 2001 was the reality of living in New York. It was meeting remarkable people who had nothing directly to do with working for *SNL*. It was all the experiences that had turned into the unusual narrative of those days when my friends called me *Almost Famous* in reference to the film by the same name. I documented many of those experiences in a scrapbook.

I never reached the destination I had set out for when I wrote my plans on paper at the age of twenty-two. My dream was to be a world-class film director. However, in those four years, I met the legendary Human Rights activist and former Amnesty International head, Jack Healey. I helped him organize an ad campaign for the Free Burma Campaign.

I collaborated on several TV and film projects with Nenad Bach, a Croatian musician living in New York. He performed with Bono and Pavarotti. I walked out of my 500-square foot condo at 104th Street and Central Park West to see the Dalai Lama tell an estimated 100,000 people, "Be kind and disciplined in your lives."

I began studying abstract painting with one of the best teachers of my life, artist Mariano Del Rosario, at the world-renowned Art Students League of New York. Abstract expressionists of the '40s and '50s such as Hans Hoffman and Jackson Pollack taught at this school. My work was even chosen to hang in the school's year-end exhibit taking first place. Just by getting the chance to live in New York, I developed character by struggling alone in such an environment and discovering a passion for painting. My fascination and curiosity for learning in new environments are traits I hope to pass on to my students.

I once asked a nightclub owner I befriended what it was like to have "everything." At the time, I was sitting with him and his glamorous Playboy centerfold wife at a table in the VIP section next to numerous celebrities: Mets catcher and future Hall of Famer Mike Piazza; six-time Chicago Bulls NBA champion, Scottie Pippen; Jon Bon Jovi; and Patrick Swayze. Many twenty-something males would probably have asked a similar question.

His response was immediate. He leaned in and shouted over the music, "You see al these people?" He gestured at the excessively stylish patrons of the club. "Most of them are living paycheque week to week. Including me. Trust me, I'm one paycheque away from the streets."

Years later, when I moved back to Toronto, I would find out this man whose life I admired then, had lost his night club, divorced his glamorous wife, and moved to New Jersey.

Teachers who have lived, travelled, and experienced life deeply have the been-there-and-done-that credibility to inspire students to go out in the world, beyond the bubble from their comfort zones, and discover who they are. My experience working for *Saturday Night Live gave* me that, and living in New York, diving into the unknown, and daring to be adventurous, away from the safety net I grew up did, too.

CHAPTER TWO SUMMARY

ACTION STEPS

LESSON #2: CRITICAL KEYS TO CONNECT WITH STUDENTS THROUGH YOUR STORY

- ☑ Share your life experience and your travel stories with students. They will remember these stories and feel more of a connection and trust with you.
- ☑ The stories do not have to be funny. Don't be afraid to disclose challenges, embarrassing moments or times when you felt like a fish out of water in your travels, no matter how mundane they seem to you.
- ☑ What's one story on your travels you find yourself repeatedly sharing with others?
- ☑ What's one lesson or connection to the material you can connect with what you're currently teaching?
- ☑ Compare your story to something in the text or contrast it if it's the opposite of what you've experienced. Either way, you are humanizing yourself and making yourself vulnerable.

CHAPTER THREE

"Where other teachers saw Tom's talkativeness as a behavioural issue, this teacher asked, "How can I encourage his passion and dream of becoming a comedian?"

In conversation with Comedian, Tom Rhodes

LESSON #3: LEARN HOW TO USE HUMOUR TO DEAL WITH CLASSROOM MANAGEMENT ISSUES

Humour in the classroom includes moments, often spontaneous and sometimes planned, that give kids permission to smile and laugh with the teacher and the rest of the class.

It gives the students a connection with their teacher and humanizes us as educators. It relieves the stress of labour-intensive units. It contributes to a classroom dynamic where students look forward to getting up in the morning to attend.

Some teachers have said to me that they are not funny. They also say it's not realistic to make humour a prerequisite for an active classroom environment because not everyone has this natural ability. My response is they may be right, but it's not necessary to be Will Ferrell to develop humour-filled activities in a classroom.

Ironically, backstage at *Saturday Night Live*, Broadway Video, and the upstart MTV-like internet TV network Lorne Michaels purchased, BBN, we did not always have an engaging, fun energy. There was a feeling akin to the night before final exams in that many staff writers, producers, and talent were trying to get their projects in on time while competing against their peers to be on the air.

What I learned from this experience is to tell short, practical stories about my life that connect with the lesson. Every teacher I've known has incredible, not-too-personal anecdotes that probably come into their head year after year as they are teaching. Rarely do they share these unique journeys for fear of showing too much of themselves. However, I think the opposite is true.

When I tell students a bit about my life, my hope is it shows them I am real, vulnerable, and don't take myself too seriously.

Show your humanity and you may reach some of your less motivated students. A story may be partially unrelated to the content, though that's not the point. Humour creates a bond with students, especially with some of the challenging ones.

Dr. James Cornelius, Curator of the Abraham Lincoln Museum in Springfield, Illinois said, "If the cabinet were just about to discuss what to do concerning the latest military loss, Lincoln wanted to tell a joke that was oftentimes completely unrelated to the situation." In other situations, President Lincoln would mimic someone, point out an absurd bit of logic, or humble himself by mocking his own appearance. In each case, Lincoln was using humour to connect and relate with his different audiences.

Bart Baggett, a best-selling author, leading handwriting expert and international keynote speaker, often uses personal stories, humourous anecdotes, and intriguing facts, as well as asking engaging questions at the beginning of a talk. He said if you just jump into teaching detailed content, you will overwhelm, bore, and lose your audience.

Two examples of personal stories I tell from my life that seem to hold the attention of the whole class are as follows:

The Steamroller Story

I tell a story about going out with a young woman when I was in my 20s. We had a nice first date, so I called her up after to set up a second date. She stood me up. I called her to ask what happened and she came up with an excuse that she was helping a friend in her condominium move. I made another date with her where I did extensive research on the right restaurant to take her to. I showed up at the restaurant early. Fifteen minutes passed. Thirty minutes passed. Forty-five minutes passed.

She never showed… again. Needless to say, I left feeling sorry for myself. When I tell students that I called her for a third time, heard her excuses, and made yet another date; they are on the edge of their seats. "Why, why, would you do that?" they ask, shaking their heads and partly laughing. I say, "I was stupid to put myself in that position."

Continuing, I made the third date and… At this point, the kids hold their heads in their hands and say, "No, it didn't happen again. Please tell us it didn't happen again!"

When I pause and nod my head, they break out into a chorus of, "Noooo!" Yes," I say. "It happened again."

I then tell them I was speaking to a Tibetan Buddhist Nun, who once was married and has two adult children, about being stood up by the same girl three times. The nun asked, "Would you run out into the street, throw yourself down on the pavement in the path of a steamroller, and let yourself get run over.

I said, "Of course, not."

The Nun said, "Okay. The next week comes around. The same steamroller is coming past your house. Would you rush out in the street again, throw yourself down on the pavement, and beg, "Please run over me again.""

"Do I even have to answer that?" I quipped. "Of course not. Where's this story going?"

The Nun then said, "Stick with me here for one more moment. You've now been run over twice, but wait, the next week comes around. Would you rush out into the street and allow yourself to get run over for a third time?"

So, I said, "No."

The Nun said, "Then why would you let this girl steamroll you three times?"

The class reacts with a collective, "Ahhh," nodding their heads.

I tell them, "Just when you forget about that person who stood you up or dumped you, they may call you back as this girl did six months later." What did I do? Well, I'd learned my lesson. I told her, "No."

Mary's Angel on 9/11 Story

The other story I tell is when I was in New York on 9/11. There is nothing funny about the events of that day; however, I don't focus on the terrorist attack. I focus on the inadvertent friendship I formed in the midst of a tragic situation.

My flight was cancelled due to circumstances that remain a mystery to this day. I didn't have enough cash to get home to Toronto and back by the next morning. So, I decided to sleep in the terminal for my new flight on September 11, 2001.

When we heard over the airport intercom that my new flight was cancelled, I was annoyed, rightly so. I wanted desperately to return home to see my grandmother, Becky, who only had a few days left to live. As I was trying to figure out how to get to Toronto, another message on the intercom was even more troubling than the first.

LaGuardia Airport, September 11, 2001, New York

No explanation was given as to why. As I speed-walked out of the airport with hundreds of others, I saw the National Guard taking positions with rifles poised on the outer perimeters of the airport.

While I was outside, Mary, a seventy-five-year old woman from Saskatoon, asked me what was happening. We were joined by a flamboyant late 30-something hairstylist named Jie who was wearing Rumpelstiltskin, pointy Prada boots.

On our way to a diner outside the airport, Mary stopped for a moment and adjusted her hat. Jie said, "Mary, you look fabulous. I love this whole thing, as he motioned with his hand sizing her up from head to toe.

Mary said, "Ah Jie, you're too kind." She then took in the moment, looked at him and me and said, "Aren't we the odd group, the three of us!"

We had lunch together at a local diner a few blocks from the airport. Mary told me she travels to one tennis tournament every few years. This year, her tournament of choice was the U.S. Open in Flushing Meadows - Queens, New York.

In the diner at around 9:30 a.m., I overheard someone on a phone say a plane had struck one of the towers of the World Trade Center, but it seemed too unbelievable to imagine. We sat, stunned, within the diner, as it was confirmed: two planes crashed into the towers. Jie headed back into the city to see if his brother was okay.

Mary and I shuffled over to a nearby hotel, where stranded passengers were put up by the airline. There were not enough individual rooms, so the airline asked all of us to find a roommate for the night.

Mary and I shared a room.

She said she trusted me.

I smiled and said, "Mary, I trust you, too."

Later, in our room, I came out of the bathroom and saw that Mary had cucumbers over her eyes and was ready to sleep.

She said, "Take ten dollars over there on the table. Go buy yourself a beer."

I don't drink, but I decided under the circumstances, I would take Mary up on it. I went downstairs to the restaurant and sat with strangers united by this terrible moment in history. Everyone was glued to CNN while talking out loud about how they were going to get home. Everyone seemed to have the same plan. Get up at 6:00 a.m. and hitch a cab to another city and another airport.

I listened, smiled, and then I went back to the room and told Mary my plan. We're going to be downstairs at 4:00 a.m. to beat the 6:00 a.m. rush.

We got up at 4:00 a.m. Mary got dressed in an immaculate outfit with a matching hat and shoes. She looked like the quintessential, stylish tennis enthusiast she was with a flare of 1950s glamour. When we arrived downstairs, two other groups of people were also waiting. There was a pair of tough-looking men, grumpy and anxious to get to a casino. There was also a doctor and his wife from Thunder Bay. I negotiated with the two groups and then with a limo driver to drop each of the groups off at their destinations, followed by our last stop – my parents' house in Toronto. Along the way, Mary and I spoke with the doctor and his wife about our lives. At one point, Mary broke out in song, singing,

"You may not be an angel, 'cause angels are so few.But until the day that one comes along, I'll string along with you." [2]

> *Mary had a soothing soprano voice that seemed to resonate from a bygone era. The song she sang was called, "I Will String Along With You." It was written by Al Dubin and Harry Warren and covered by Doris Day, Louis Armstrong, and Dean Martin in the 1950s.*

The two gamblers in the front turned their heads as if to ask, what's going on back there. Mary turned to the doctor and his wife and said, "Jamie's my angel. He saved me. I don't know what I'd do without him."

Twelve hours later, we eventually arrived in Toronto. My parents were worried sick, especially when they received calls from the New York State Police, *Saturday Night Live*, and old friends who I had long drifted away from asking about me. They gave me a relieved hug and greeted Mary like she was an old friend. We had tea that night debriefing my family on our harrowing, yet, at times moving and humorous journey. My dad booked Mary a flight on Air Canada and he and I drove her to Pearson Airport the next morning. Mary was on a flight back to Saskatoon two days after 9/11.

This story may have nothing to do with what I'm teaching at the time. Or it may. If I'm teaching *A Midsummer Night's Dream* or *Siddhartha*, I may tie it into the idea of finding flickers of humour within the tragic. As Dr. James Cornelius said, "Sometimes Lincoln used humour to lighten the mood. Lincoln said he had to laugh sometimes amidst all of this horrible tension and death of the Civil War, otherwise he would break, and he would die."

Another way to show appropriate humour is by finding examples of film, TV, or YouTube clips. Comedians have become the social and political commentators of our day. Their role as "truth tellers who give voice to what the rest of us are thinking", is nothing new, as Megan Garber explains in her article in *The Atlantic*. Comedians have now become "guides through our cultural debates," Garber writes.

Amy Schumer of the TV show, *Inside Amy Schumer,* describes her work as "comedy with a message." Comedians are taking on subjects "like racism and sexism and inequality and issues including police brutality and trigger warnings and intersectional feminism and helicopter parenting."

Teachers can embed clips from *Inside Amy Schumer* or *The Daily Show* or *Tom Rhodes TV Show* to students in connection with a theme or idea discussed in class. "Comedy has long helped us to talk about the things we need to talk about... humour has moral purpose, humour has intellectual heft, humour can change the world," Garber states.[3]

In university, a professor of a first-year course in advertising said it's not an educator's job to entertain. I put up my hand immediately and disagreed. He shot me down as being ignorant and flat-out wrong.

It's my goal as a teacher not to be boring. I must find a way to reach them before I can teach them the skills and knowledge they need.

Students often rate humour as an essential element of a real class. In a study conducted by Jerome G. Delaney at the Faculty of Education at the Memorial University of Newfoundland titled,

"How High School Students Perceive Effective Teachers," where students were interviewed on a number of criteria about their teachers, the general findings concluded the following: **If teachers are humourous, it sets a more relaxed environment and also makes the students interested in the topic. Teachers who have a sense of humour generally have a better relationship with their students.**[4]

A colleague once got a little annoyed at a professional development session when another teacher quoted a proposed policy from a school board in England of firing teachers for being boring. She said a teacher's job is not to entertain. Instead of dismissing humour as a shallow way to be popular, it can be a way to break the ice and open up channels, especially with difficult students.

Why Teachers Use Humour in the Classroom

A 2014 research finding by Academic James W. Neuliep regarding the reasons why secondary school teachers use humour in the classroom reveals that it:

a. Improves the atmosphere in the class and their relationship with their students,
b. Helps them deal with stressful situations and discipline problems,
c. Reduces the tension and pressure of teaching,
d. Draws the attention and interest of their students,
e. Promotes learning and,
f. Preserves their interest and improves their mood during teaching.

Forms of Humour in the Classroom

James W. Neuliep also shows humour recorded in classes took the form of:

a. Humour expressed by the teacher towards him or herself,
b. Humour directed at a student,

c. Innocent humour,

d. Humour from an external source (cartoon, comics, etc.),

e. Non-verbal humour.

"The humour directed at students was sometimes positive and other times negative; that is to say, it could involve teasing in a positive light-hearted mood or it could be deeply insulting and humiliating."[5] Instead of inadvertently using negative humour, here are a few alternative strategies teachers can use to deal with challenging students.

In *You Can Handle Them All*, the authors, DeBruyn and Larson, identify one of these challenging behavioural types as the "smart aleck." This student makes funny comments that actually go far beyond humour. They are often rude and disrespectful. He/she thrives on getting a reaction from teachers.

Ways to deal with the smart aleck include: never responding with a smart-aleck remark in return. If you do respond, your response is giving the student exactly what he/she wants – teacher and peer attention. Ignore some of those offhand remarks.

At other times, according to DeBruyn and Larson, a useful response is to say to the student, "I would like to continue this conversation privately after class - so I'll see you then."[6]

"Silence in response to most of his/her remarks without appearing sarcastic or vindictive may work better than any other response because it deflates the smart aleck completely."

Another strategy may be to **"challenge the smart aleck to demonstrate his/her abilities by asking, 'Why don't you try to find out just how good you are?'"**

Humour in the classroom is synonymous with a collaborative, peaceful, and healthy space for students to learn and interact.

"Humour, it seems, can enhance creativity, elevate collegiality, and improve long-term job performance. Fun meetings, apparently can be better meetings," said Cindi May, a Professor of Psychology at the College of Charleston, who cited a study which found humour boosts the effectiveness of meetings.

She "explores mechanisms for optimizing cognitive function in college students and individuals with intellectual disabilities."[7] **New research by Nale Lehmann-Willenbrook and Joseph Allen suggests there may be a way to make meetings "less onerous and more useful: a good laugh."** The article goes on to say humour helps "reduce social conflict and promotes group cohesion." Further, designer Bruce Mau says, "people visiting the studio often comment on how much we laugh. Since I've become aware of this, I use it as a barometer of how comfortably we are expressing ourselves."

These professional findings in the world of corporate meetings and offices have implications in the classroom. When I was teaching in Malaysia, I experimented extensively with group role-play in both a Grade 12 World History class and a Challenge and Change in Society class. As the videos of these classes posted in the *Resources* section show, humour unified the class and created an open, fun, and healthy learning atmosphere.

One of my principal goals is to prepare my students for evolving work environments. Why not teach students different and effective ways to learn and maximize their time in a group setting working with a diverse group of people? Humour, as the research shows, provides a solution that can be modelled in classrooms to show the benefit of laughter on creativity, collaborative skills, and efficiency. "Humour patterns in the original team meetings were positively related to team performance both immediately and over time", the Lehmann-Willenbrock and Allen study concluded.

You may also ask if incorporating humour will distract a group of students in a different way than adults in a corporate meeting framework. Yes, students may momentarily be distracted, but their level of focus and energy level upon bringing them back to the lesson, will be heightened. Lehmann-Willenbrock and Allen found that, "Within the meetings, humour patterns triggered problem-solving behaviours (e.g., what do you think of this approach?), procedural suggestions (e.g., let's talk about our next step), and goal orientation (e.g., we should target this issue)."

The researchers go on to conclude that, "Humour patterns also promoted supportive behaviours like praise and encouragement, and led to new ideas and solutions."

Humour in the class does not mean telling jokes. For one, if a joke flops, it can throw off a teacher who is not comfortable with attempting humour or it may come across as trying too hard in the students' eyes.

I once deconstructed the following joke:

*One evening a man hears a faint tapping at his front door. When he opens the door he sees no one, and then he notices a snail on the ground. He picks up the snail and heaves it as far as he can across the lawn. A year later he hears a tapping at the door again, and again when he opens the door nothing is there, except the snail, who says, "What the f*** was that all about?"*

I did my best to deconstruct why I found this joke to be amusing. To this day, all that former students remember is I used a swear word, which I regretted. So now, if I tell this joke, I replace one obvious word in the punch line that makes the joke less shocking but still funny. Jokes and magic tricks are most intriguing when the wizard stays behind the curtain.

There are places where humour is not appropriate in a class, such as when one student bullies another or makes an inappropriate comment they perceive as funny, but is demeaning. Or, when a student, who is socially awkward in some way, makes a presentation in front of the class and others laugh at them rather than with them.

These are also powerful moments to help young people distinguish the difference between appropriate times to laugh and not. These moments take time for a teacher to identify immediately and skillfully comment on in a firm, direct, yet not overreacting tone.

Jim Barry, a teacher for over forty years in the Toronto Catholic District School Board in Ontario, said, "Involve him in as much stuff as you can. Even if there's fish in the room, he feeds the fish. If anyone has to take anything to the office, he takes it. He's probably the class clown because he's got all this energy."[8]

Robert L. DeBruyn and Larson, suggest the following actions when dealing with the class clown:[9]

Don't ignore the class clown. His/her personality and needs will not allow it.

- ☑ Enjoy the humour briefly with the class. Remember, the class clown is often funny. The humour is not the major problem – knowing when to quit is always a problem. Therefore, signal by hand movement, rather than words, "enough is enough."

- ☑ In a one-on-one conference say, "Humour is a good thing. Yet, you may lose some respect if you always allow yourself to be laughed at."

- ☑ In other times, respond with silence. In a powerful way, this gets the student to settle down. When the student stops, however, don't say a word. Rather, go on with the lesson. If you say anything, the student will start up again.

- ☑ Don't attempt to handle this student with anger, rejection, or sarcasm, and don't try to outwit them. Such attempts will fail.

- ☑ Isolate the class clown from his/her audience – but don't forget this student's need for attention."

- ☑ Teachers can also establish a unique boundary for students between the importance of incorporating humour while knowing when being serious is the right approach or attitude at that moment. DeBruyn and Larson say, "After his/her next clowning episode, laugh with the class.

The second time it happens, wait until the incident is over and then explain that humour is a good thing in the classroom, at the right place and time. Follow-up with the same talk privately with the student. Emphasize maturity and respect. Explain that you don't like students laughing at him/her and it troubles you that he/she is helping them laugh."

I admit my mistakes, such as spelling errors on the whiteboard, how a professor in Teachers' College said my handwriting looked like indecipherable symbols, or when my voice cracks occasionally like a thirteen- year boy doing his bar-mitzvah reading. I am showing I can laugh at myself when I make mistakes. I try to show students that it's okay not to be perfect and healthy not to take yourself too seriously. Imperfection make you real to students. One strategy is to add a new bit to material you've taught over and over. The uncertainty of integrating that piece of content in to your presentation will make the older material come across as if you are delivering it for the first time.

> *Some teachers are afraid of not looking perfect. But looking imperfect does just the opposite of what some people may think. It shows that you know your limits; you don't know everything, and you don't try too hard.*

"If you're not prepared to be wrong, you'll never come up with anything original," Sir Ken Robinson said. From my experience, it increases the respect students have because it shows the teacher is adaptable and easy going. He/She knows and guards the line between a humourous moment and a suitable comment.

Comedians make creative connections between seemingly non-connected events and bring life to the absurdity of everyday situations. When you have a class clown or a student who sees things in an unorthodox way, like one of my students who makes a sports analogy to every subject taught in class, this uniqueness should be encouraged. Assignments can be structured or modified to support the distinct make-up of a class.

Tom Rhodes, a 30 plus year comedian, spoke to me about the impact his high school drama teacher had on him. This teacher gave Tom, a loquacious teenager, the first five minutes of every drama class to stand in front and talk about what was on his mind. Where other teachers saw Tom's talkativeness as a behavioural issue, this teacher asked, "How can I encourage his passion and dream of becoming a comedian?"[10]

The question I get asked most by school administrators, colleagues, students, parents, and the custodial staff is: "Why would you leave *Saturday Night Live* to become a teacher?" What they mean is: "Are you crazy?" The glare of Times Square eventually wears off. The four hundred and eighty square foot apartment feels more like a claustrophobic, gilded cage than a creative oasis; it was at this time I began to re-assess my yellow brick road.

Before I talk about what exists beneath the alluring siren-like lights on the corner of 49th Street and Broadway, students always want to know how I got to Lorne Michaels' office.

It was a breezy fall Thursday night in New York, October 25, 1997, in New York City. If someone told me not to set off to New York to be a TV producer, I would have resented them for trying to discourage me from going after my dreams. It's not anyone's right to tell a young person that he/she cannot at least attempt to become a director, a CEO of an App start-up, or a TV producer.

Thoreau said, "Most men lead lives of quiet desperation."[11] A life that transcends this state begins when a young person embarks down a path that is of their heart's will and answers to that inner voice. Often, that voice is full of criticism and self-doubt in one moment, quixotic and lacking in practical wisdom in the next. I travelled down a path that felt right at that stage in my life. I can relate to a young man's or woman's need to see where a road may lead, even if the initial vision takes them to a shallow and hollow place.

I was compelled to see what was behind the curtain, like Dorothy did in *The Wizard of Oz*. When my hot-air balloon of expectations never took off in the way I imagined, it led me a decade later to the real life waiting for me in the place I belong – as a teacher, husband, father, speaker, and author.

The encouragement I received on my path in New York, from a few generous adults whom I looked up to, was transferred to all my dreams and goals in different directions, two decades out.

In one particular job interview at a small advertising firm, I was asked "Where do you see yourself in five years?" Nobody knows the answer to this question including the interviewer. It also doesn't tell you anything substantial about the candidate, especially if they're young. What are they going to say: "In five years, I want your job."

I answered, "I want to direct a film."

In response to this, the couple interviewing me snickered at my reply and wrote notes to each other in the moment. I noticed this and became self-conscious.

Her response was, "Good luck with that."

The woman who was writing notes and passing them to her partner reminded me of two mischievous eighth-grade students at the back of the room. Their actions seemed to suggest I had no business dreaming big. Needless to say, I didn't get the job. It also burned into my mind a lesson so crucial to dreaming big dreams and realizing them.

Bob Dylan spoke about it, when he said, "It's a feeling that you know something about yourself that nobody else does. The picture you have in your mind about yourself will come true. It's a kind of thing you gotta keep to your own self because it's a fragile feeling and if you put it out there, someone will kill it. It's best to keep all that inside."[12]

I don't know if I'd go this far because you need to surround yourself with one or two angels of optimism who see the light within you before you see it in yourself. Learning to keep the key points of your dreams to yourself, is a hard-earned lesson.

Fortunately, I ran into some people who encouraged me to pursue those wild dreams of youth. At a Thornhill bagel restaurant, I was with my late charismatic grandmother, Becky Cohen, having breakfast, sitting next to Marky Michaels, the late brother of Lorne Michaels. He had heard I had been pursuing a job with his famous brother's company.

The friend he was eating with, who happened to be my mother's first boyfriend named Harold urged me to go for it because, "There's nothing in Toronto for you." His words were an act of kindness. I still remember his graciousness sixteen years later.

How Did I Get There?

The first thing I did when I wanted to work in TV in New York was brainstorm a list of the most successful Canadian TV and film professionals I could think of. The two who immediately came to mind were: Norman Jewison and Lorne Michaels.

I've struggled for years with the statement: "It's who you know." I've tried to erase it with the belief that it is the excuse used by those who never felt successful. I didn't have a direct connection, but I heard my dad once mention that Lorne Michaels grew up around the corner from him. Michaels hung out with local neighbourhood kids on adjoining Forest Hill streets.

A black and white photograph with "1955, Ridge Hill" scrawled on the back with smudged, black ink exists in a dusty, cardboard box in my parents' basement. The photograph depicts my Uncle Stan talking to another boy who is a seven-year-old Lorne Michaels (formerly, Lorne Lipowitz, then just a shy boy, several generations removed from the legendary Svengali of network comedy.)

With this photographic evidence of an inadvertent photo bomb taken over forty decades earlier, I worked up the nerve to call New York's 411. This resource was the best way I knew how to find someone's number in the days before Google. I asked the operator for the contact information for NBC Studios and was patched through to the offices of *Saturday Night Live*. The operator provided me with a 212 area code. I took a deep breath and dialed, not having a plan of what I was going to say. I phoned from my parents' basement where I was living after graduating from the University of Western Ontario the previous year.

The voice that answered said, "*Saturday Night Live*, how may I direct your call?"

I gulped and asked to speak with Lorne Michaels.

Pause.

The woman's voice on the other line asked, "Who may I ask is calling?"

I mustered up my most confident and overcompensated deeper voice and said, "Um… Jamie Cohen from Toronto."

Right away, I second-guessed whether I should have added… "Toronto". It sounded like someone inexperienced and insecure trying too hard to impress, which was exactly what I was.

The woman paused and then asked, "And what is this regarding?"

I said, "I'm an aspiring film director and producer from Toronto."

The woman said, "I'm sorry, Mr. Michaels is not available. What did you say your name was?"

"Uh… Jamie Cohen from…" I repeated.

She cut in…"From Toronto, yes I remember. "I'll pass on the message," she said.

This same conversation went on twenty-six times over three and a half months. On the twenty-seventh call, the woman on the other end of the phone whom I now knew from bits of small talk accumulated over ninety days of nudging, was one of Lorne Michaels's assistants, named Suri.

Before I could say my name or where I was from or what this was regarding, Suri asked, "Jamie, what would it take for you to stop calling?"

I knew this question was a good sign, representing the tiniest of openings into the waiting area of an exclusive members-only club.

I also knew from multiple viewings of one of my favourite films of the 80s, *The Secret of My Success*, starring fellow Canadian, Michael J. Fox, this is what was supposed to happen. After countless calls, the gatekeeper, the assistant or the secretary would relent to my persistent and annoying charms, for just one, brief glimmering moment for me to get to the next stage of my hero's journey. I must have projected this fictional tale onto my mission to speak in person with Lorne Michaels because of what happened next.

To her question, I said, "Please just give Mr. Michaels a letter I'm going to send, and I promise, I'll never call again."

Suri said, "Is that so? So, what you're saying is that if I put your letter at the top of the huge pile of mail he receives every day from people like you, you will never, ever, call this number, again?"

"Yes," I responded, and then realized how I backed my word into a corner, which had nowhere to go. "Yes, I promise I will not bother you again if you give him the letter I'm signing as we speak."

"Deal," she said. "When I get it, I'll put it on the top of the pile. I can't promise he'll read it, but I will put it in front of him."

After I hung up the phone, I looked at my bulldog, Wendel and asked him what he thought should be in the letter.

He snorted, rubbed his bottom on the floor, and climbed the stairs, never looking back.

The site of Henry David Thoreau's cabin. Thoreau wrote my favourite book, Walden here. Walden Pond, Concord, Massachusetts.

I sat on my parents' basement floor and started writing the letter that would change the course of the next four years of my life.

Two hours later, I mailed it and waited. I waited for one week… two weeks… a month…two months. Nothing. I worked as a part-time tour guide for foreign-exchange students by day and then rushed to my parents' home to see if a message was waiting on their answering machine from Lorne Michaels.

During these two months, I told anyone who would listen about my improbable plans of working for *Saturday Night Live* — without knowing that first I'd have to be offered a job. Next, I'd need to hire a lawyer to obtain a visa. This scenario was a long shot considering I had only one volunteer experience working on an independent Canadian film crew for twenty-three straight days. I would also have to save the money to live in one of the most expensive cities in the world that I had never even visited.

The next step in the pursuit of the dream was visualizing a goal I had become obsessed over. I had little else to go on other than a voice at the other end of a phone, who owed me nothing and whom I had annoyed for twenty-seven previous attempts. The woman would not be able to identify me in a police line-up of two individuals.

Lorne's assistant said she would put a piece of paper at the top of a daily pile of paper for one of the busiest TV production executives in show business.

I talked about my plan to friends, impersonating Lorne Michaels based on seeing him in interviews over and over. I told my bulldog, Wendel, about meeting Lorne Michaels. I announced it to my extended family at the twice-yearly gatherings. I said it to whoever would listen so that it became a part of my identity even without any rational proof that such a thing could happen based on where I was in my life at the moment.

It was three months since I'd mailed the letter. I poured myself a dish of corn cereal and pondered on the futility of the whole experience. I fell asleep on the beige basement carpet with Wendel sleeping on me, tongue sticking out of the side of his mouth, front fangs adorably menacing, pushing up against his spotted jowls. Then, a minor miracle woke me up.

"Hon… honey… telephone…", my mom yelled down as my family had the habit of doing when the phone rang on a different floor.

"What?" I asked.

"Telephone," she yelled again.

I answered the phone.

"Hello." There was a pause at the other end of the call and then.

"Hello, is this James Cohen?" a deep, indifferent voice on the other end asked.

"Uh, yes it is," I said.

"This is Lorne Michaels… how can I help you?"

My initial knee-jerk reaction was I thought it was my friend, Jeremy, playing a prank on me like he had done before.

Ha… nice one, Jer…" I said.

Another pregnant pause on the other end of the line ensued which seemed to fill the space with an embarrassed tension from my side. I forgot to breathe for a moment.

"Hello… oh, Mr. Michaels, uh… thank… thank you for returning my call. Uh… I'm an aspiring director and producer from Toronto; my dad grew up in the Forest Hill area. I look up to you - what you've accomplished since you left Toronto. Is it possible I could meet with you for just fifteen minutes to ask your advice on how to break into TV and film?"

Another pause at the other end seemed to fill an eternity.

"Okay. Set something up with Suri. I'm on my way to Los Angeles. I'll see you in New York when I return."

"Thank-you sir, thank-you."

My adored pet bulldog, Wendel, on the morning I got the return call from Lorne Michaels, 1997.

Click.

Two years earlier, I wanted to meet the Right Honourable Prime Minister Pierre Elliot Trudeau, for a documentary film idea I had attempted to put together in Cape Town, South Africa. I engineered a fifteen-minute meeting with the out-of-the-spotlight, former PM. He was now a figurehead at the Montreal-based law firm, Heenan Blaikie.

I asked a rising lawyer in his firm, Steven Lewis, if he could try and arrange a meeting with Trudeau. Lewis said he had seen something in me when I pitched him my idea for this South African project. Lewis agreed and approached Trudeau at the Heenan Blaikie annual picnic and surprisingly, Trudeau said, "Yes, I'll give the fellow fifteen minutes."

Mr. Trudeau said at the end of the meeting he saw a "promising road ahead" for me. This meeting taught me the value of developing strong speaking skills so when a once in a lifetime chance arises, I will be ready to seize the moment.

What I also learned from that experience was if you ask a future mentor, public figure, or celebrity for fifteen minutes, make sure to request their advice on a cause you know they have a passion for which they rarely get asked about.

It works much better than asking them for a job or money or a connection. If your approach is sincere, without being pushy, and you can find a way to add value to their lives somehow, then you have a chance to get in the door.

Just before my heart felt like it was going to leap into my throat, I realized… I hadn't asked Mr. Michaels what the next step would be. Should I call his assistant, Suri, or was she going to call me? I wrestled with this dilemma for twenty-four hours until I got the sweetest call a wannabee twenty-two-year-old film producer could receive.

It was Suri, Lorne Michaels' assistant. "I don't know what you said or how you pulled this off, but you've got yourself a meeting with Lorne Michaels," she said.

So, it did actually happen. I didn't imagine it. He did say what I thought he'd said.

"Do you realize, Jamie, that he turns down one hundred requests like this a week from people who actually have good reasons to see him? This kind of thing rarely happens."

I asked her when the meeting would be.

She said, "Three months from now."

That meant on Friday, October 24, 1997, on the 17th floor of Rockefeller Centre at 7:00 p.m.

"Okay. Got it. I'll be there! Thank-you!" I said.

"I'm sure you will," she said.

"I'm looking forward to finally meeting you, Suri".

"In a strange way, I'm looking forward to it, too," she said.

During the next three months, I worked as an intern on an independent Canadian feature film, *Last Night* starring Sandra Oh (before she was a well-known name) and directed by Don McKeller. On this film, I called supermarket chain head offices for permission to show their logo for two seconds in the background of apocalyptic scenes. I also camped out on a High-Park rooftop for twelve straight hours to measure the amount of sunlight for a thirty-second panoramic 360-degree shot. The roof was covered with white rocks as the sun hit it every thirty minutes.

Between coffee runs, I would rehearse what I was going to say to Lorne Michaels. What would the great producer ask? What would every minute of the fifteen I had with the Canadian producing legend look like three months from now?

I finished the last day on the set of *Last Night*. Three days later, I was in New York looking out over Central Park from the condominium of a family friend. I couldn't sleep that night. I had a chorus of butterflies in the pit of my stomach. It felt like the night before a big baseball game playing for the Leaside Lancers during my teen years. I would go over and over in my head what I would do when I got to the plate the next day.

Finally, the day came. It was the 24th of October, Friday night. 1997. I dressed in what I perceived to be appropriate attire for an entertainment company - blue jeans with a black, button-down shirt and a leather jacket over top.

One of the keys to a first impression is to dress the part. Don't be overdressed for that particular culture because it makes you stand out as amateurish or trying too hard. However, if you under dress, it can come across as disrespectful, untrustworthy, unlikable, and out-of-touch with the surroundings.

I waited outside the cordoned-off elevator of 50 Rockefeller Plaza. An NBC security guard called up to the SNL offices as I tried not to look out of place. The security guard nodded and pointed for me to cross into the cordoned-off area and enter the elevator. A tower of a man followed behind me, smiled, and said, "Hello." I did a double take and realized it was NBA basketball icon, Bill Walton.

I arrived at the 17th floor. My heart was pounding furiously. It felt like I was crossing the first threshold of the hero's journey. The gatekeeper who greeted me was a university student sitting behind a desk.

I said, "I'm here to meet with Lorne Michaels."

She gave me the once-over and said, "Hold on a minute, please."

She picked up the phone, spoke briefly, and then motioned for me to sit in one of the chairs in the lobby.

Over a five-minute period that seemed to last an hour, the woman behind the voice, the one who had to answer my twenty-seven calls over several months was finally in front of me, face-to-face.

"Hi, Jamie. I'm Suri. How was your flight?"

Before I could answer, she walked with a brisk pace as if to motion with her body language for me to keep up. I pivoted and moved in step trying to look in-place and relaxed which probably had the opposite effect.

"The flight was good. Thanks."

We walked past framed photos of former guests over the show's 25 years. There was Eddie Murphy smiling with Joe Piscopo and Steve Martin doing the *2 Wild and Crazy Guys!* sketch with Dan Aykroyd. The musical guests for the night, The Mighty Mighty Bosstones, nodded at us as they walked past.

We arrived at a room with a non-descript door. Suri said, "Can I get you something?"

"Water would be great," I said.

She walked over to a fridge in the corner, picked up a bottle of water, and handed it to me. She then disappeared.

I sat there for a few awkward moments. Suddenly, a lumbering force of nature came barrelling through the door with an equally hefty assistant trailing him. It was none other than Chris Farley. Nobody knew then that this would be his final appearance on the show.

On this particular episode, an eerie foreshadowing of things to come occurred in the opening sketch in which Farley asks Lorne Michaels's permission to host the show. Farley said he'd been sober for six weeks with Chevy Chase as his AA sponsor. Sadly, the awe-inspiring Chris Farley would pass away less than two months later from a drug overdose at the age of thirty-three.

Out of the corner of my eye, I saw people who worked for the show slightly cringe and keep their distance. Chris nodded at me and made a direct line to the fridge where he double-fisted two tequilas and started pounding one back after another. I sat there, adjusting my posture. **I tried to play it cool as if Chris Farley running around the room was no big deal. What came to mind was Dorothy in *The Wizard of Oz*, when she said, "I'm not in Kansas, anymore."** [13]

Just as I searched my brain for how to fit into such a moment, I heard a clank, and there he was sitting directly across from me - Chris Farley. He continued drinking and banging the bottle on the table as his out-of-breath assistant tried unsuccessfully to dislodge one of the bottles from his clutch.

"Who are you here to see?" Chris Farley asked.

"Uh… Mr. Michaels," I said.

"You're here to see the boss? What are you, an actor?"

"No, I'm just a guy from Toronto who---"

He cut me off. "Toronto… I was just in Toronto. I love Toronto!"

"I was at Sean McCann's house just a few minutes after you left," I said.

"Sean McCann! You know Sean?" he asked. As his voice rose, his face got red and he slammed one of the bottles down again.

"Yes, he's a family friend," I said. "He coached me in Little League, and I'm friends with his son."

Chris kept at me. "I love that guy!"

There was nowhere for me to hide at this point. I started getting looks from people coming in and out of the office, including Suri, who had just returned. Her look said to me, *I leave you here a few minutes, and you're consorting with the talent.*

I glanced back at her with a shrug of the shoulders as if to say, *Sorry, I didn't mean to.*

"What's your name again?" Farley asked.

"Jamie… Jamie Co---"

As I was answering Chris Farley, Adam Sandler quietly entered the room and I stopped talking. I only noticed him after he opened the fridge, got a bottle of water, and sat down on a chair in the corner.

Adam Sandler nodded at me. Chris jumped out of his seat and gave Adam a bear hug. Lorne Michaels arrived ninety minutes after our scheduled interview appointment. Silence filled the air. In came the man I had dreamed about meeting for years. Michaels was five-foot–six and dressed impeccably in a gray Armani suit and polished shoes. His nails and hands were flawlessly manicured.

He glanced at Chris Farley.

Chris bellowed, "Hey, Chief."

Lorne said, "Hello Chris."

Adam, wearing a baseball cap and a faded sweatshirt, nodded with his boyish grin. "Hey, Lorne."

"Hello, Adam." He then glanced at me for an iota of a second. He clearly had no idea who I was.

I broke the silence as young people tend to do when they are trying too hard to impress an authority figure. "Hi, I'm the guy from Toronto… I'm here to meet you."

He gazed at me, expressionless. Then, he said, "Right."

He continued to his office with the door closing behind him. At that moment, it occurred to me that one of the key moments in *my* life thus far was not even a blip on Lorne Michaels' radar. I didn't need to be humbled by the moment, but it relaxed me a bit. It made me realize I had nothing to lose. No matter what I said in this brief meeting was of minor consequence to this man. I could be bold without fear of something embarrassing happening to me. I could be myself without having the fear of losing anything. I could say what I had planned in my head dozens of times a day since I talked my way into this office three months earlier.

> *I let students know when you are just starting out and you meet someone of higher status who you want to work with, act the way you would if you were already confident and bold. Be present and listen.*

Teaching Life Lessons Outside of the Classroom

Usually, I would say not to ask for anything before you add value to them first. However, in this situation, I did the opposite. Asking for an internship is not adding value to them because it's a favour to you. They still have to train you. You get to hang around them or their staff and learn their secrets. Some things you could do to add value to them include: write a thoughtful, well-crafted summary of their book and send it to them. You could write a detailed, positive review of their product on Kindle. You could promote one of their items on your list of subscribers and show them.

You could hire them to coach you, even for an hour at $1,000, which seems like a lot, and it is, but it buys you the opportunity to show them what you're made of. You could promote a paid evening or event and offer them part of the profit, if not all of it, to be the keynote speaker taking no money for any products they sell from the stage.

You could offer a testimonial in a unique and effective way I learned at Jonathan Sprinkles' excellent Presentation Power Speaking Training Workshop, Jonathan also spoke of the power of innovative thank-you notes to people in positions of power. The more engaging, creative, thoughtful, and timely the thank-you is, the more memorable it will be. Send the thank you within five days of the encounter. [14]

You could also dig deeper and do more research to find out their passion. If you find out they love fly fishing, like I found out through research before attempting to meet with actor Michael Keaton for a role I wanted him to play in a film, you could go to a related website and find the perfect antique accessory that only a devoted fly fisher would love. Then, send it to him with a note.

If you want to meet with the CEO of a company who is impossible to connect with and you find out he runs in certain kinds of marathons, you could ask his secretary, what his shoe size is and what his favourite pair of running shoes are. Then, buy him a one-of-a-kind pair of sneakers and send them to him with a note.

These are the kinds of bold moves young people may consider making in a crowded and competition space where everyone is taking, but so few are adding value.

You could also study the person's website for issues you could resolve with your own skill set. Then, send them the solution.

So, never ask the question to a mentor, "Is there anything I can do for you?" That's what amateurs do. The bottom line is, focus on adding value over and over again without expecting anything in return for years, if necessary, before your generosity and hard work may bear some karmic returns. Take their course, be in their mastermind groups, and be an action taker who stands out for his or her application of the mentor's lessons.

Some ways to start a conversation online with a mentor may be to ask for their advice on a resource or a book. Make it something easy and quick for them to access. Add merit in some of the ways above followed by minor requests. One of these eventual requests could be to interview them for your podcast once it reaches a certain level. This is an excellent way to get to know future mentors, promote their products to your audience, and demonstrate your knowledge to them about their work.

How to become a Teacherpreneur

Educators can use their valuable skill set to develop multiple income streams as well as instructing in the classroom.

In today's current job market for teachers, educators may consider thinking like entrepreneurs. There are fewer full-time positions available for teachers coming out of Teachers' College.

The strategies presented in this book on how to incorporate humour into story-telling and lightening a learning environment can be applied to a teacher's entrepreneurial projects. Teacherpreneurs are teachers who want to continue teaching to help colleagues or write curriculum or create beyond the system.

Some ideas may include: making lesson plans with a humour framework for the site, *www.TeacherspayTeachers.com* or integrating humour into your personal stories in a webinar. Some of the practical information in this book is meant to help you in getting students laughing while they are learning in your role as a teacherpreneur.

Brian Setser wrote in an article titled, "The Teacherpreneur Opportunity" that some ideas for teacherpreneurs include:

- Teach for a virtual or blended school

- Teach your passions and strengths: provide content design or assessment services in your field. Resource: *Edsurge*

One of my teaching colleagues is a triathlete and plant-powered food advocate. He uses his teaching skills to host a podcast, hold webinars, nutrition consulting and workshops with his wife who is also a teacher. They guide mothers on how to provide healthy plant-based foods for their family. Resource: *www.planttrainers.com*

- Teach for Start-ups: non-public school markets like character schools hire teachers to help in their planning stages. Resource: *nextgenlearning.org*

- Teach in a SMOOC (Synchronous Massive Open Online Courses) Resource: *straightenline.com*

- Teach and Travel Overseas: see Chapter 19 on my specific tips to consider before accepting a teaching job overseas.

CHAPTER THREE SUMMARY

ACTION STEPS

LESSON #3: LEARN HOW TO USE HUMOUR TO DEAL WITH CLASSROOM MANAGEMENT ISSUES

Be present and open to unexpected moments of spontaneous humour.

You may not think of yourself as funny. You may believe it's not realistic to make humour a prerequisite for a successful class. Don't focus on being funny because that won't work. Instead, construct a light, fun, warm environment by starting with a story before you dive into content.

Tell short, practical stories in which you don't take yourself too seriously. Tell students a mistake you made in your life and what you learned from it. Students open up only after you share and show yourself to be vulnerable.

A recent survey showed secondary school teachers use humour because it:

- ☑ Improves the atmosphere in the class and their relationship with students
- ☑ Helps them deal with stressful situations and discipline problems
- ☑ Reduces the tension and pressure of teaching
- ☑ Draws attention and interest of their students
- ☑ Promotes learning
- ☑ Preserves their interest and improves their mood during teaching

In the book, *You Can Handle Them All,* the authors suggest the following in dealing with the smart aleck student:

- ☑ Never respond with a smart-aleck remark in return.
- ☑ Ignore some of the minor offhand comments.
- ☑ Say to the student, "I would like to continue this conversation privately after class – so I'll see you then."
- ☑ "Challenge the student to demonstrate his/her ability by asking, "Why don't you try to find out just how good you are?"
- ☑ "Silence in response to his/her remarks without appearing sarcastic may deflate the smart aleck completely."
- ☑ Deal with a student, who uses inappropriate humour by involving him as much as you can by giving him responsibilities as they come in class.

Manage the class clown in the following ways:

- ☑ Enjoy the humour the first time.
- ☑ The second time gives him/her a look that signals, "enough is enough."
- ☑ Say to the class clown in a one-to-one conference, "Humour is a good thing. If you regularly put yourself in a position for others to laugh at you, you may lose some respect."
- ☑ Isolate the student from his audience but don't ignore him/her.

CHAPTER FOUR

"Production itself is pleasurable because of its collaborative nature; being part of a team, sharing work with your peers, having a laugh." [16]

— David Buckingham, Education researcher

LESSON #4: LEARNER-CENTERED TECHNOLOGY YOUR STUDENTS WILL LOVE

In university, I studied Film Theory, which was essentially three years of watching classic black-and-white Russian and American auteur films like, Eisenstein's *Battleship Potemkin* and Altman's*Nashville*. My education in New York working for Lorne Michaels' companies taught me the politics and business of making media. However, I learned the most by going through the process of writing, producing, and directing my own short films.

When I worked in New York, I pitched a mini-series taken from a true story called *Mr. B* about a Canadian carnival owner who killed his childhood friend over an unpaid debt. I learned the importance of focusing the story on its most commercial elements. I also gained the knowledge that making a film is a collaborative effort, right from the idea stage until production, if you're lucky enough to get there.

When I left *SNL*, I took the knowledge of getting the story in shape through revising the treatment or outline. This experience helped me get my story idea down to one clear sentence. Failing to pitch an idea for a film or TV series successfully helped me build self-reliance and resilience. I sought out young film-makers to ally with on three short films, a national TV commercial, and a national TV segment I directed, wrote, and produced upon leaving New York.

During my first teaching experience at a school in an economically disadvantaged community in Toronto, I put my SNL education to the test in a room full of under-motivated Grade 10 students I was working with part-time as a teaching assistant. Their empathetic and wise English teacher, Brooke Hodgins, agreed to use part of her English class for project-based film production. I led the creation of a class docudrama inspired by situations in their lives filled with peer pressure to sell drugs, low-level crime, going to jail, and being in a gang. It also covered the respect and esteem these students had for a teacher, like Brooke, who truly cared for them. The students showed increasing joy as the production process went on.

They stayed afterschool, came in on weekends and asked if they could be more involved. Their grades were positively impacted, too. The Head of the department at the time said that in her career she had never seen students in the Special Ed Department respond so enthusiastically to a class in her career. My students in Malaysia responded with similar passion and energy several years later when I asked them to make films about Malaysian teen culture.

The short docudrama, School'd, that my students created showed genuine moments of friendship amongst the daily difficulties many of them faced. Some students used language and included humour that the adults in authority considered unacceptable. These moments were ripe for critical debate as to what was suitable to include in a school-based production. One of my challenges was to "encourage self-expression without rejecting or judging their creative output during the process." Professor David Buckingham, one of the leading researchers in media education further suggests, "Students must be able to work with what they have and who they are, rather than in terms of what teachers might like them to be."

Students need to feel what it is like to be successful. It gives me inexplicable satisfaction when this happens. I saw it in one of the stars of the film, a Grade 10 student with a history of gang violence. He glanced over at his mother as she viewed the docudrama. With that feeling comes a spark of belief in a teenager that can motivate an inner shift in his/her self-esteem. A week after this student got his final grades, I received a letter from him with the enclosed report card showing an "A" average, up from a "C" average from the previous semester. I knew at that instant how Jackie Robinson's epitaph, "A life is not important except in the impact it has on other lives", can apply to teaching.

School'd, a short docudrama,(dir. Jamie Mason Cohen), 2004

Following my recent presentation at the RAVSAK educational conference in L.A., there seemed to be a real openness of the educators in attendance to integrate new digital tools to enhance students' learning experiences of texts. I demonstrated how I went from being a sage on the stage who reached many, but not all, to a guide on the side, who tapped into the passion and potential of all of my Grade 9 students by combining three new technologies. The results exceeded my highest expectations: 100% engagement based on a survey of the students' experience and learning outcomes that surpassed the achievement levels on any unit I have taught in ten years.

After realizing my teacher-centered approach to teaching the play, *Pygmalion* reached the analytical, auditory learners but was not wholly successful in reaching some visual and tactile learners, especially those with learning challenges, I decided to make a shift. I recalled what my former Vice Principal and school mentor, Ray Buchowski said to me once: **"A teacher's effectiveness is in direct proportion to the impact he/she has on his/her most vulnerable students."**

For the next unit I would teach, a novel study of Herman Hesse's, *Siddhartha*, I experimented with two educational technologies and a new way to create a learner-driven learning environment. The results have transformed my approach to teaching novels, plays, short stories, poetry, and articles.

During our school's next PD Day, we were given the option of deepening our knowledge in an area of education of our choosing. I chose educational technology. I woke up early with good intentions and ample enthusiasm but by the end of the day, I was more overwhelmed than when I had started. There are over 20, 000 educational apps and programs from which to choose. Where do you start? Who has time to start from scratch? How do you apply a new technology to the curriculum? I stayed the course, persisted, and something extraordinary happened. **I discovered using a** combination of three educational technologies and strategies, resulted in 100% engagement in both classes, inspiring both students with learning challenges and gifted learners to do their best work of the year.

Students making a Hero's Journey documentary on the life of Professor Don, VIVA Residence, Maple, Ontario.

3 learner-centered educational technologies you can use in your class to get 100% engagement are:

1. **Genius** – Students are asked to access a digital version of the novel on Genius, an annotation site that allows students to analyze, annotate, and discuss. Project Gutenberg is a site teachers can use to access a free electronic copy of a text published prior to 1923.

- Genius.com
- Gutenberg.org
- Overview and Guidelines Mr. Cohen
- Hermann Hesse's "Chapter 1: The Brahmin's Son"

2. **Inverse Teaching Videos** - Students posed questions on each chapter or sent them directly to me. I would then go to the tech room at the end of the day and answer their questions in front of a screen, with a river or an Indian landmark in the background. I would post the video that night and embed it into the online chapter. See an example in this link: Siddhartha: Chapter 4 Questions and Answers

3. **Self-Organized Learning Environments** – In the second half of the novel study, students got into groups and investigated significant questions to, as one student said, "make connections between a story and real-life." I posed questions to students to spark their curiosity including, "What does it mean to reach enlightenment or the ultimate state of wisdom?" "What is a true friend?" "What is a mentor?" Students then presented their findings through annotations on quotations in the text. They could submit their results in writing, audio or visual recordings.

4. Below is the basic outline and structure of a self-organized learning environment: School in the Cloud

I wanted my students to be "fully engaged, talking to one another, grappling with interesting questions, and exploring any and all resources to find answers, and more importantly, questions." This description is how U.S. Professor of the Year, Michael Wesch articulated what he considers to be an ideal learning environment. The combination of these three learner-centered technologies created a space "more conducive to producing the types of questions that create lifelong learners rather than savvy-test-takers" as the article, *Anti-Teaching: Confronting the Crisis of Significance* describes.

The outcome of this unit resulted in students calling it "addictive," "fun", "interactive", "cool", "different", "helpful", and "spectacular". One student wrote in an online survey, "What I learned from this experience will stick with me way longer than if I were to learn it by writing notes followed by a test."

Grace and Tobin - Claim not to be celebrating the children's transgressions of classroom norms,

they do not explain how teachers might intervene in this kind of activity,

beyond using their intuition and judgement to block projects that might prove unduly offensive.

CHAPTER FOUR SUMMARY

ACTION STEPS

LESSON #4: LEARNER-CENTERED TECH. YOUR STUDENTS WILL LOVE

- ☑ The Future of 21st Century Learning with Educational Tech.
- ☑ Combine the following educational technologies and strategies to engage your class in fun, challenging, student-centered learning.
- ☑ Genius annotation site - Annotate, analyze and discuss a text online
- ☑ Inverse teaching videos – Record yourself answering fact-based questions. Show your fun side as I did by introducing the unit by standing on my head.
- ☑ How to Make Flipped Videos in the Classroom: Siddhartha Intro. by Jamie Cohen
- ☑ Investigate a significant question raised during the first half of the unit.
- ☑ **Inspire Curiosity and Wonder:** The Simple and Practical High School Teacher's Guide to Create Self Organized Learning Environments (SOLES) A Free E-book

CHAPTER FIVE

"When you are young, everyone tells you to follow your dreams and when you get older people get offended if you even try."

- Ethan Hawke in The Hottest State

LESSON #5: INCORPORATING RESILIENCE INTO YOUR CLASSROOM

As my journal from 1997 reveals, I had big hopes and dreams of making it in New York as a world-renowned TV producer like Lorne Michaels. I did what all of the experts suggested. I wrote down my goals first by hand and then revised them in type. I glued them in a scrapbook that I would look at right after waking up in the morning and before going to bed. I did as Brian Tracey suggested and wrote out the aspiration in the present tense at least once a day on a single sheet of paper. [17] I tried what Wayne Dyer suggested. I visualized my goals and said them aloud seventeen times in a row with as strong optimistic emotion that I could muster.[18] I cut out photographs in magazines and created a vision board of my dreams and goals. Nietzsche said, "He/she who has a 'why' can bear with almost any 'how.'" [19] I took this advice to heart and wrote out a page full of reasons why I wanted this particular goal.

I repeated mantras such as: "I intend to become a world-class film producer or director" director, and over, while I meditated in my barren, cramped apartment or spoke affirmations aloud when I was the only one in the Equinox workout facility sauna. There was no method I would not have tried to get closer to my goals, and yet they never happened — not even close. After four years of working and feeling like Sisyphus, I felt dejected. It was the start of one of the key lessons I learned first-hand - how to deal with temporary setbacks, failures, or disappointments.

Years later, a wise mentor said to me that the door of working in TV production and the door of education would ultimately lead to the same place. I didn't quite understand what he meant at the time but now I do. Teaching and the chance to share my message with teachers would prove to be more fulfilling than the world of entertainment. Being a guide on the side gives me the opportunity each day to pour my creativity into inspiring young women and men to learn, discover their strengths and encourage their passions.

In his study of how to get the most out of receiving feedback from a respected source, journalist Shane Snow writes, "Crucially, experts tended to be able to turn off the part of their egos that took legitimate feedback, personally, when it came to their craft, and they were confident enough to parse helpful feedback from incorrect feedback. But when we do that, feedback becomes much more powerful."

Learning how to take feedback objectively is relevant for teachers because we find ourselves constantly being judged and evaluated by administrators, government officials, parents, students and colleagues. I feel that as a teacher, the more skilled I become at honestly reflecting on my mistakes without dwelling on them, the more impact I will have as a teacher and role model for my students.

Snow provides an example in his book, *Shortcuts,* from the world of comedy, of how to extricate the lessons from negative feedback without being defensive or interpreting the statements about one's performance as offensive. "The Second City improv group where many *Saturday Night Live* stars such as Tina Fey, Dan Aykroyd and Seth Meyers received their training, teaches its students to take [failures] in stride, to become scientists who see audience reaction as commentary on the joke, not the jokester. To turn off the part of their brains that says 'I fail' when they get negative feedback."

The legendary improv group re-frames failure, defined as a fixed, unalterable result, in to feedback or information useful to help a person grow. This process is repeated "hundreds of times a week." The actors learn how to, "fail fast" and how to re-frame the uncomfortable feedback as input – "without taking it personally," Snow observes.

In summarizing the ideas of psychiatrist and brain researcher Daniel Amen, on the subject of seeing failure as an opportunity to get better, author Brian Johnson writes:

"Daniel Amen talks about a similar idea in his new book Change Your Brain, Change Your Life where he says: 'Do you learn from your failures or ignore them? New brain-imaging research suggests that when some people fail, their motivation centers become more active, making it more likely they will be able to learn from their experience. When others fail, the brain's pain centers become more active—it literally hurts—making it more likely they will do whatever they can to avoid thinking about the episode, which means they are more likely to repeat the mistake. Learn from your mistakes and use them as stepping stones to success.' Dr. Amen tells us we need to get CURIOUS not furious." From a humourous perspective, it may also be a reminder to take what we do as educators seriously, but not ourselves.

Impactful Ways to Incorporate Resilience into your classroom

"We need to put ourselves out there, give it our all, and reap the lesson, win or lose. The fact of the matter is that there will be nothing learned from any challenge in which we don't try our hardest. Growth comes at the point of resistance. We learn by pushing ourselves and finding what really lies at the outer reaches of our abilities."
(Josh Waitzkin, author of The Art of Learning)
http://theartoflearningproject.org/resources/

For the past two years, I've collaborated with Josh Waitzkin's JW Foundation, a nonprofit organization, devoted to, "maximizing each student's unique potential through an enriched educational process" on integrating real-world skills into my lessons and SOLE Student Leadership seminars. The concepts from the book that I've implemented include challenging students to be willing to make mistakes and to learn to develop empathy through investigating, seeing, hearing and feeling the world from different perspectives.

In an upcoming unit, The Hero's Journey, I plan to incorporate ideas from their new manual called, *The Teacher's Guide to The Art of Learning: Resilience* Developed by Katy Wells and the JWF Team. This guide poses questions to help teachers become aware of their own process of building resilience in their students. It offers suggestions to help educators reflect on the way they evaluate their success and their students' growth.

I think that real-world skills are most effectively learned by students when integrated within the context of a classroom project as opposed to being taught on their own. The most efficient way I know to try something new in my classroom mid-year is to take an existing unit plan and look for ways to connect the new material. This approach is what I am doing with the Resilience Guide in my upcoming Hero's Journey Unit that I've done for the past two years. I can introduce the unit with resilience as my thematic frame and discuss it as it applies to Dorothy's persistence in the face of adversity in The Wizard of Oz (which I'm recording as a flipped class similar to a director's commentary on DVDs) to model the stages. Students will answer questions after watching each stage of my analysis so that they understand what the stage is, why it's significant and reflect on their own journeys.

At each stage of the movie, I will have students reflect on one of The Art of Learning's resilience questions or prompts in working towards building a daily habit. Once we work through this process, students will then make a short documentary or digital book on the heroic lives of senior citizens at a local seniors' residence. I will then team up with my good friend, Louis Jebb, the CEO of a virtual reality platform called, "Immersivly", to upload the short documentaries so that my students can share, learn from and appreciate the epic lives of seniors and experience their incredible journeys in 3-D.

http://theartoflearningproject.org/wp-content/uploads/2014/12/Resilience_Teacher_Guide.pdf

Here are the results.

http://theartoflearningproject.org/wp-content/uploads/2014/11/Inspiration-Board-SOLE.pdf http://theartoflearningproject.org/wp-content/uploads/2015/08/The-Curious-Empathy-Board-assignment.pdf

The Art of Learning Guide is filled with practical, actionable questions, habit-building ideas, and strategies. I've highlighted four strategies to build resilience, that I'm excited about implementing, in current and upcoming units.

1). "After an assessment, have students go over their own ungraded work and identify the areas in which they need more practice and assistance. Score the evaluation based on their ability to determine their areas of need, rather than their correct answers." I just included this approach in grading a literary essay. It's often a challenge to get students to see the value in the process or rough drafts. On top of asking students to do a peer and self-essay checklist before handing in their final drafts, I've asked them to answer the question: What areas of essay writing do you need more practice on and assistance with? Be specific. Point form is okay. Use the Feedback Checklist as a guide. Your score out of five will be based on your ability to identify your areas of need.

"Daily Habits: 1) Give process-orientated feedback to at least three students every day. For example:
   a. I see you're working really hard on this…
   b. It doesn't seem like you're putting a lot of effort into this. Let's think about how I can help you stretch yourself a little further…
   c. It's exciting to see/hear about how you're approaching this problem. I can see you're putting a lot of thought into it…"

2). I've heard teachers dismiss the idea of using canned lines or certain operative words to speak with students as a substantive way to foster good learning habits and improved behavior. I disagree based on my experiences with seeing radical, positive transformation in students over the course of a year. I think a teacher's words and the tone a teacher uses to communicate with students can significantly increase a teenager's sense of self-worth and confidence or crush it. One student told me that he felt like giving up in a class because the teacher picked apart his work and never acknowledged any positive aspects in it. He said it ruined his desire to learn or come in for extra help anymore.

3). Daily Habit: Choose an activity in which you will stretch yourself just outside of your comfort zone every day. Share your experience with your students each day with a quick discussion of a moment that was challenging for you and how you think you'll change your approach next time. After modelling this for several weeks have the students begin to do the same. This strategy would work well for content in teacher's stories to open a class. It's more powerful and meaningful for a teacher to give practical examples of what it means in their daily life to be resilient than to provide distant, theoretical examples only. The activity I will share with my students as a way to model daily resilience is to commit to practice hot yoga several times a week and to share the challenges I face in re-integrating this practice into my life.

4). "Begin your day with a focused breathing routine. Commit to practicing this routine for 10 minutes a day for ten days with the help of a guided meditation app such as Headspace."

https://www.headspace.com

Josh Waitzkin, who is one of the world's top chess experts and a national Tai Chi champion, writes about the importance of meditation and breath work in the process of achieving success in two diverse disciplines. I have meditated intermittently over the past decade and am always looking for a way to help make it easy to build a consistent meditation practice. The Headspace meditation app makes sitting for ten minutes a day through a variety of guided meditations an easy to monitor daily progress. Why would meditation help a teacher in managing their day-to-day life at school? Why is meditation a tool that teachers could use to dramatically impact the lives of their students? The next example of a resilience-building tool will show you why and how mindfulness meditation can transform your students' experience in the classroom.

The Interconnectedness of Mental Health with Academic Success

"Academic learning is completely inter-related with social and emotional skills." Educator Patricia C. Broderick, Ph.D, educator, mindfulness instructor.

It helps to have a sense of humour in cultivating a balanced, cheerful attitude through challenging times. Humour is a, "release from the emotional tension of the miserable moment, inviting you to see yourself and your life as an amusing play," states authors Douglas Stone and Sheila Heen in their book, *Thanks for the feedback*. The authors go on to add that if you can view the lighter side of each situation, you develop perspective; or as Elsa sings in the movie Frozen, that I've now seen twelve times with my two-year-old daughter, "It's funny how some distance/Makes everything seem small." Stone and Heen state that the, "ability to laugh at yourself is...an indicator that you are ready to take feedback." "When you think something is funny, you are helping to disrupt the panic and anxiety that are taking hold, and to calm down those upsetting signals." The reason is, Stone and Heen suggest, that humour puts you into a different emotional frame of mind, literally. Your thoughts shift to the "prefrontal cortex on the left side of your brain, where amusement lives."

I've noticed that individuals who I admire display resilience in working towards long term goals. They have the ability to endure or ignore demeaning feedback and learn from constructive criticism. I can attest to this in my own teaching career. On the day I was ready to walk away from Teachers' College because a teacher I was asked to shadow, demanded that I give up my, "out of the box" teaching methods, my bird, Fred, flew out of the house. All of my attention at that moment was taken off my troubles in Teachers' College and focused on getting my adored green and yellow budgie back inside. "Fred, it's me," I pleaded. After a few minutes of negotiation, he slowly side-stepped onto my wrist off of the outer ledge of an upstairs window. The incident made me break down in laughter with my parents after he was safely back in the house. It was at this moment that my mindset shifted back to a relaxed, calm place. I didn't quit that day because I thought back to my original inspiration for going into teaching, the movie, *Dead Poets Society.* I realized that the opportunity to impact young peoples' lives far outweighed the short term setbacks I faced. I finished Teachers' College and was in a more optimistic state of mind from that day forward. I decided that in the future I would pick my battles.

The importance of seeing the difficult moments of your teaching life with an amused lens to increase overall peace of mind is backed by a growing number of leading doctors and researchers. *In Anatomy of an Illness as Perceived by the Patient*, author, Norman Cousins, "detailed his successful efforts to overcome a degenerative collagen disease using, among other things, large doses of self-prescribed laughter therapy. Laughter appears to be a profoundly healthful state of momentary body-mind integration and harmony. In Cousin's view, cultivating strong positive emotional states through humour and not taking oneself so seriously, even in the face of life-threatening circumstances, are of major therapeutic value in the healing process." This example was cited in what is essentially the ultimate mindfulness guide for western audiences, *Full Catastrophe Living* by Jon Kabat-Zinn. Recently, my wife Karen and I decided to take a mindfulness-based stress reduction course inspired and grounded in the work of Dr. Zinn.

Karen is the kind of teacher who has earned the trust of her high school students over the past fifteen years to such a meaningful level that they regularly confide in her about their most pressing, difficult life challenges. In our regular discussions about our teaching days, we have both expressed a desire to manage and balance the demands of our professional lives with our personal lives as parents of two young children. It was at this point we decided to take an 8-week mindfulness workshop called the MBSR program (The mindfulness-based stress reduction program developed and used in medical centers worldwide by Dr. Jon Kabat-Zinn). He and his wife, Myla Kabat-Zinn, are, "engaged in supporting initiatives to further mindfulness in K-12 education and to promote mindful parenting." It was taught locally by a wise and humble man named Roy Hintsa, a former successful businessman in his 70's who volunteered his time to teaching the course after training directly with Dr. Jon Kabat-Zinn.

There were other teachers in this workshop, aside from my wife and I, which showed us that there is a need for strategies to help teachers cope with the day-to-day stress and challenges that occur in an educator's life. We learned how to self-regulate our emotions through body scans, sitting meditation, walking meditation and activities meant to experience fully and accept our emotions, without judgment. The experiential activities were supported by the scientific theory and case studies from Zinn's book, *Full Catastrophe Living*, which we consistently discussed during the course. I wanted to make sure I have the tools to manage my own emotions in a healthy manner before teaching students how to deal with their state of mind. As Emerson said, your actions speak so loud, I can't hear what you're saying.

Wang, Haertel, and Walberg (1997) reported that among 11 factors that are most important for classroom learning, social and emotional factors accounted for 8. When feelings are not well managed, thinking can be impaired. Recent scientific advances have shown how the interrelated development of emotion and cognition relies on the emergence, maturation and interconnectedness of complex neural circuits in multiple areas of the brain. In *Growing Success: Assessment, Evaluation, and Reporting in Ontario Schools* (2010) one of the critical learning skills and work habits that teachers are asked to teach and assess is "self-regulation". The student, "perseveres and makes an effort when responding to challenges."

Patricia C. Broderick, Ph.D., found that in her research that mindfulness training for students:

- "cultivates present-moment attention
- supports emotional regulation and emotional balance
- fosters positive self-development
- improves stress reduction
- supports academic success."

Mindfulness is a uniquely powerful tool to aid teachers in coaching young men and women to overcome their resistance in the face of academic and social challenges and to thrive in the face of adversity. In addition to the MBSR course, I highly recommend teachers consider another programme, grounded in the principles of Dr. Zinn, which adapts the ideas and strategies of the MBSR to the classroom and is run by Patricia C. Broderick, Ph.D. Information can be found at http://learning2breathe.org/.

"*A Me to We Trip* is just the beginning of a journey of sustainable change that will leave a positive impact on your students, yourself and the place you visit long after you return home."

http://www.metowe.com/school-trips/

https://www.youtube.com/watch?v=0KoE1Tf9Uf8

https://www.youtube.com/watch?v=8HFXA4i99CM

(Every day, I created a brief video to share with my kids, Koby and Maya, my trip to the Amazon to help build a health clinic in the Amazon with educators from across Canada.)

At the end of last June 2015's school year, I attended an Educators' scouting trip with *Me to We* and *Free the Children* in the Amazon in Ecuador. *Me to We* runs service-based overseas educational trips for middle school and high school students. I came back renewed, with laughter and joy, cheerful, lighter, more positive and resilient. There are times in a school year when it seems both teachers and students are tired, irritable and a bit too serious. I was surprised that a trip with this meaningful, powerful intent was so much fun and brought out my sense of humour! They provide the opportunity for educators to first experience what their students would, which includes: helping build a local health clinic, experiencing the life of a worker on a local coffee plantation, and learning first-hand about the surrounding ecosystem through local guides. At the end of an enervating school year, I went on this trip and returned reinvigorated, re-energized and committed to organizing this trip for my students. The first two resources are about building resilience through mindfulness and practical, in-depth self-reflection. A trip like this would provide students, as it did the group of teenagers I observed working and struggling and bonding together as they carried bricks up a hill with local labourers, the opportunity to step out of their comfort zone and stretch towards a common goal.

The trip helps students see how the pillars of a local community work together: education, clean water, health care and sanitation, alternative income and food security. When you are laying and moving one brick at a time in the service of building a valuable community project in scorching heat, side by side with locals, resilience goes from an abstract term to an empowering feeling of overcoming adversity in the pursuit of a goal greater than oneself. This kind of experiential education shows students that they can pull themselves out of any emotional turmoil or difficulty through hands-on, all encompassing, practical and meaningful service to others. The *Me to We* team has set up a module with an interactive pedagogical framework of debriefing and re-integrating students upon coming home from a life experience like this, which is essential for sticking with something beyond the initial emotions of the activity.

When students just jump right in and immerse themselves in an experiential learning adventure, the lessons have a more emotional and lasting impact than book learnings. It also makes it easier to be comfortable with discomfort because of the self confidence developed by overcoming difficulties individually and collaborating within a group. True resilience was modelled through the real life case studies. The case studies in this case were not part of an outdated text book. We learned about the inception, daily struggles and mechanics of the Vargos family farm from Mr. Vargos himself. Nothing shifts perspective more powerfully than seeing how others live and find gratitude and acceptance in their enormous life challenges. *Me to We* leadership emphasizes, "gratitude over guilt" and "the way out of guild is through gratitude and service".

The significance in this message in connection to creating a resilient mindset is that negative or destructive emotions often destroy the will to carry on in the midst of life's temporary setbacks. It's hard to be sad, pensive and burdened with guilt about past actions when you are completely present, and drenched in sweat in the service of strangers half a world away. Carol Dweck's seminal work in exploring the power of a growth-mindset vs. a fixed mindset transitions from a powerful theory to practice in this kind of learning environment. A growth mindset is essential for helping teenagers cope, endure and thrive in the midst of emotional waves.

The daily curriculum was structured so that each day we learned new things, and were encouraged to adapt to our own edges of discomfort, being open and nonjudgmental to whoever we came in contact with, unselfconscious and not needing others' acknowledgement for helping others, whether that be someone from our school community or the locals. A trip like this will surprise teenagers by showing them that they are emotionally and physically stronger than they thought or felt just a few days earlier in their familiar home environment. In giving to others in this way, I was impacting myself and returning my best self for my wife Karen, our kids, Koby and Maya, my family, friends and students. The trip had the dual effect of allowing gratitude to flow into my life for what and who I am, offering myself some kindness and ultimately for the great fortune for my life. True learning is in immersing yourself, speaking with the people who live it, and stepping into their shoes, even for an hour. Service-based education builds resilience and empathy through authentic experiential activities that reverberate long after the school day or year is done, living in the bones, memories and hopefully a student's mindset, and informs her or his students for a lifetime.

CHAPTER SIX

"If a story means something to you, you will re-tell it with emotion and honesty and any class will feel it. "

— Jamie Mason Cohen

LESSON #6: MASTER THE ART OF HUMOUROUS STORYTELLING

I used to get annoyed when a student asked why I left New York to become a teacher. Other commonly asked questions were how I got the job working for Saturday Night Live and what was it like working in the presence of famous people. Most times, when students asked, I'd tell stories. There's something about sharing a sui generis, personal anecdote. So, I embraced my life's adventures and made a practice of tweaking the telling of it and its delivery each time. Fifteen years later, I'm still asked.

Once again, it is the experiences on the journey itself, not the destination of working in the dream job that is intriguing to the listener because I relive it each time. Steve Job's famous 2005 Stanford Commencement Speech consists of three reflections on different life lessons. Jobs breaks his speech into three parts: How to connect the dots in life ("You can't connect the dots looking forward, you can only connect them looking backwards"), doing what you love ("you have to follow your heart even when it leads you off the well-worn path and that will make all the difference") and loss and death ("Sometimes life hits you in the head with a brick, [but] do not lose faith.")[20] People respond to real accounts. So, if you're not sure what to say during a presentation or at a gathering of any kind, ask yourself this question: *What stories from my life, or my interactions with another person, mean something to me?*

I believe that if your story means something to you, you will re-tell it with emotion and honesty and any audience will feel it. If you have no experiences that match the moment, research one that does and tell it.

In the book, Tell It Slant: Writing and Shaping Creative Non-Fiction, *Brenda Miller and Suzanne Paola suggest a few ways to tell a story with humour: incongruity, the twist, life's irritations, exaggeration and understatement and self-deprecation. Incongruity refers to the "juxtaposition of odd or unexpected things".*

The authors reference humourist David Sedaris' essay, "The Drama Bug" in which he falls in love with the theatre and tries on a Shakespearean speech that "becomes hilarious in contrast to the ordinary events happening in his teenage years." Over a chicken dinner with his family, he says, "Methinks, kind sir, most gentle lady, fellow siblings all, that this barnyard fowl be most tasty and succulent."

The twist refers to a surprise, usually at the end of a story. Miller and Paola give the example of writer, Patrick McManus who describes in an essay how he fell in love with writing. "I bore down on my next essay with a diligence and concentration previously unknown to me in any academic subject. The effort paid off. A D-minus!" The D-minus comes as a funny surprise considering the author went on to become a professional writer.

Patrick McManus is written about for a second time in "Tell It Slant" when he provides the advice to "write humour out of your bad experiences, not your good ones."

A literacy device I teach my English students is hyperbole. Hyperbole is the usage of exaggerated descriptions of a situation for comic effect. One such example of the application of hyperbole by the author, Annie Lamott who described her state of mind: "I had jet lag, the self-esteem of a prawn, and to top it off, I had stopped breathing. I sounded just like the English Patient."

A tool a teacher could use to tell humourous stories is self-deprecation. It is having the confidence to laugh at yourself. In the previous example Anne Lamott says that she had the "self-esteem of a prawn". David Sedaris did the same thing when he looked back at his "fake Shakespearean diction encouraging us to laugh at them, and in the process, at the whole human condition."

One place a teacher may consider starting is by asking yourself: "What experience in your own life led to the most unexpected conclusion? Can you find a way to tie this story to a theme or idea in your upcoming units?

Storytelling is a tool a teacher can use to show students who you are and make them interested in what they are learning. There has to be a journey. The goal is to achieve the result you want by telling the story. Top public speaking coach Michael Port says, "You are not obliged to be funny. Humour sometimes presents itself out of conflict. Trying to be funny is generally not funny. It's not about you, it's about the message. Turn your presentation into a playful experience."

Author Tynan offers a fun, creative exercise to help trigger your memory for stories from your life. "If you don't' feel you have a lot of interesting stories, a good exercise is to take a sheet of paper and write the letters of the alphabet down the left side. Then come up with a short description of a story that begins with each letter."

Once you have a story that you think has a connection to the subject matter you are teaching, you may experiment with this outline.

The 3 Act Structure Outline by Aristotle (2-minute story)

Here is an example of how I share my story of how I went from working at Saturday Night Live to teaching.

The Situation: Keep it short. Provide context, time, l0cation and emotional theme.

I thought I was successful.

I was working behind the scenes for Saturday Night Live in New York. My father called me one day and said my grandmother was sick in Toronto so I booked a flight home.

The day was September 11, 2001.

The Conflict or The Build-Up: The body of the story. Author

Tynan writes, "The buildup tells the facts of the story, in such a way as to build the tension and keep the listener engaged. Make it so that the listener will try to guess what happens next, but constantly be hit with surprises."

The next morning I hitched a ride back to Toronto.

I mourned my grandmother's loss after spending her last hours with her. I returned to the office floor where I worked.

People were packing staplers and pens.

I walked up to my desk and there was a pink slip.

A pink slip means you're fired. The company was cutting back.

I asked myself, 'What am I going to do with my life?'

'What's next?' I didn't realize it at the time but what it taught me was, sometimes you have to let go of the life you think you want for the life that's waiting for you.

The Resolution: What's the revelation of your story? "Release the tension created by the buildup, or to sidestep in such a way that all of the tension was unnecessary," Tynan suggests.

That point hit home when I became a teacher.

A few years later I was teaching in the Toronto District School Board.

Most of my students were refugees from war-torn countries like Afghanistan, Congo and Sudan. On the last day of my grade 10 class, we shared a beautiful, homemade potpourri of food from around the world. Many of the students wrote me handwritten notes of thanks. One student in particular had a hard time with some of the content in class.

We stayed after school for months until he got it.

This student, Jacob, approached me on the last day of school.

He said, "Sir, can I give you a note?"

I read the note and it said,

"Before your class, I felt dead inside, after your class I feel alive."

And at that moment, I felt successful.

http://www.rogerstv.com/page.aspx?lid=237&rid=16&sid=6550&gid=241867

The link above is my delivery of this story on a local TV interview show.

Storytelling is a tool a teacher can use to show students who you are and make them interested in what they are learning. There has to be a journey. The goal is to achieve the result you want by telling the story. What is the purpose of the anecdote and how is it connected to a theme or idea in the curriculum? Top speaking coach Michael Port says, "you are not obliged to be funny. Humour sometimes presents itself out of conflict. Trying to be funny is generally not funny. It's not about you, it's about the message. Turn your presentation into a playful experience."

Author Tynan offers a fun, creative exercise to help trigger your memory for stories from your life to use in class. "If you don't' feel you have a lot of interesting stories, a good exercise is to take a sheet of paper and write the letters of the alphabet down the left side. Then come up with a short description of a story that begins with each letter."

Once you have a story that you think has a connection to the subject matter you are currently teaching, you may experiment with this outline.

The 3 Act Structure Outline by Aristotle (2-minute story)

Here is an example of how I share my story from working at *Saturday Night Live* to teaching.

The Situation: Keep it short. Provide context, time, l0cation and emotional theme.

I *thought* I was successful.

I was working behind the scenes for *Saturday Night Live* in New York. My father called me one day and said my grandmother was sick in Toronto so I booked a flight home.

The day was September 11, 2001.

The Conflict or The Build-Up: The body of the story. Author Tynan writes, "The buildup tells the facts of the story, in such a way as to build the tension and keep the listener engaged. Make it so that the listener will try to guess what happens next, but constantly be hit with surprises."

The next morning I hitched a ride back to Toronto.

I mourned my grandmother's loss after spending her last hours with her. I returned to the office floor where I worked. People were packing staplers and pens. I walked up to my desk and there was a pink slip. A pink slip means you're fired. The company was cutting back.

I asked myself, '**What am I going to do with my life?'**

'What's next?' I didn't realize it at the time but what it taught me was, **sometimes you have to let go of the life you think you want for the life that's waiting for you.**

The Resolution: What's the revelation of your story? "Release the tension created by the buildup, or to sidestep in such a way that all of the tension was unnecessary," Tynan suggests.

That point hit home **when I became a teacher.**

A few years later I was teaching in the Toronto District School Board. Most of my students were refugees from war-torn countries like Afghanistan, Congo and Sudan. On the last day of my grade 10 class, we shared a beautiful, homemade potpourri of food from around the world. Many of the students wrote me handwritten notes of thanks. One student in particular had a hard time with some of the content in class.

We stayed after school for months until he got it.

This student, Jacob, approached me on the last day of school.

He said, "Sir, can I give you a note?"

I *read the note and it said,*

"Before your class, I felt dead inside, after your class I feel alive."

And at that moment, *I felt successful.*

CHAPTER SEVEN

"One learns by doing. Experience is the best teacher."

— *Jamie Mason Cohen*

LESSON #7: A CANADIAN PERSPECTIVE

I spent four years plotting, visualizing, setting goals, and interviewing people who held a professional creative position I aspired to. I also created a scrapbook journal of what I wanted to be which was a successful TV or film director, writer, and/or producer. I never got close to the dream during that time, but it made me reflect on why I wanted it in the first place. I had seen famous people up in some of the trendy nightclubs of New York where I'd gained access through acquaintances I had made with the doormen, bouncers, and promoters of these clubs.

One well-known nightclub doorman, Mike D., who became a friend, once said to me that he felt let down when he realized he was doing the same things world-famous rock stars were doing in the same clubs, drinking the same champagne, wearing the same clothes, and he thought: *That's it?* Mike was a native Australian who looked like a chiselled gladiator with a goatee and a Pharrell-style hat on his head. His dream was to become a rock star and we bonded by being ex-patriot outsiders who aspired to artistic success in New York.

We'd support each other by making introductions to people we'd meet who might be able to pull some strings or help us get nearer to our goals. I gained access to parties, most of which were superficial gatherings. None of it seemed real, nor the reason I wanted to make a film. Suddenly, I had access to behind-the-scenes at *SNL*. I was a regular in the VIP area in a few trendy nightclubs.

What Makes Canadians Funny?

The Canadian Consulate General's wife welcomed me at a diplomatic party at the Canadian Consul's Residence in 2000, even though the invite was meant for Lorne Michaels. I found myself sitting in a group of young Canadian diplomats who had been stationed in places like Algiers, Algeria and Accra, Ghana. The young man posted in Algiers said he had to take an armoured car flanked by security guards back and forth to work each morning only a mile away.

At one point, the Canadian Consulate's wife asked me, **"Why are so many Canadians funny like Jim Carrey, Michael J. Fox and Lorne Michaels?"** I thought it was odd that she asked me this question when Mark McKinney of *The Kids in the Hall* and *SNL* fame was in the room.

I gulped and attempted to answer the question. "Well, there are three reasons why Canadians are funny." If in doubt, stall by repeating back the question asked. "The first reason is that we have grown up with U.S. television and movies, yet there is just enough geographical and cultural distance from Americans to see the irony in their culture."

At this moment, I took a breath and noticed something that slightly terrified me. I was no longer speaking to one or two young diplomats. Now, it seemed the whole UN was listening to my explanation of what made Canadians funny. I continued.

"The second reason," I said, "is we're the perennial underdog, little brother, quiet unassuming, unthreatening neighbour to the north of the most powerful country in the history of the world. We're in a position literally to poke fun at our friendly giant next door."

I told them I briefly discussed this with Prime Minister Trudeau when I met with him a few years ago. I asked him about his famous line, "Living next to you is, in some ways, like sleeping with an elephant. No matter how friendly and even-tempered is the beast, if I can call it that, one is affected by every twitch and grunt". [21]

The Canadian intelligentsia and political set's mouths collectively gasped. Even some of the comedians who were qualified to answer this question were looking at each other as if to ask, "Who is this guy and why is *he* answering this question?"

However, the political crowd was curious now. Did I just say I'd met with Trudeau? This was the right crowd to drop a line like this as the Liberal Party's Jean Chretien was Prime Minister at this moment in 1999. Chretien was Trudeau's protégé serving under him as Minister of Finance and many other posts during Trudeau's time in office. Thank goodness I had researched seven books on Trudeau before getting a lucky meeting with him. That was one of those instances when you never know how book knowledge on one area would come in handy at different times in your life.

I then asked, "Would you like to hear the third reason I think Canadians are funny?"

"Yes," said the ever-growing group.

I said, "I think Canadians are funny because of the underlying British influence and cultural roots over many generations. Mike Myers clearly based Austin Powers on 1960s British television shows and the music scene of the time. Lorne Michaels has said Monty Python's was an influence for early *Saturday Night Live*. The British love self-deprecating humour, parody, and satire. Canadian humour is self-effacing, in which I make fun of myself before you do."

I stopped while I was ahead. I was invited back to the Consulate's Quarters, this time on my own accord.

When I was a guest at an invite-only Roots Store Opening, I started believing I had made it, whatever that meant. I played the role convincingly as an up-and-coming producer for *SNL*, although I felt the self-conscious sting of the imposter syndrome. I didn't correct the nightclub owners, doormen, or new friends who told me they thought of me as a rising star. I read that a colleague of the editor of*Vanity Fair* said he lived the adage, "Fake it until you make it." I wasn't proud of existing with this mindset. There was something self-deceptive about it all. The only way these people would accept me was to act a few steps ahead of where I was.

When my Visa expired and I moved back to Toronto, I was depressed and empty for six months. I didn't even have that false identity for friends and family in Toronto as an up-and-coming New York director or producer anymore. This crisis turned out to be an opportunity. I was forced to start becoming what I wanted to be in New York. I wanted badly to make a film, but spent four years waiting and searching for mentors to give me that specific chance which never came.

Within one year of returning to Toronto, I made a short dramatic film about a young compulsive gambler called, *Know Chance*. From the moment we lost all our equipment three days before production to the -30-degree weather shooting outdoor scenes, it was a challenging, yet intensely rewarding, journey. I'd finally taken a step in the direction of my dreams.

Know Chance, a short, dramatic film (dir. Jamie Mason Cohen, starring Emil Beheshti, co-starring Jimmy Gary Jr.) 2002

The lesson was that travelling and working in exotic places, even in what we first think is a dream job, sometimes disappoints. Yet, it forced me to look at myself and my dreams and question why I was holding on to this particular thought and trying to force it into existence when it clearly was not my path. Would it not have been better to skip the New York experience and just make the film four years earlier?

No, because:

I needed to go through the experience to realize what I had to do to take a step forward.

1. I made lifelong friends like Jack Healey, Executive Director, Human Rights Action Center, Nenad Bach, international human rights activist and musician, Jimmy Gary, Jr., Actor and former NFL football player, Nick DeNinno, producer and former VP, National Lampoons, Mariano Del Rosario, artist and art teacher, Barry Strugatz, Co-Writer, *Married to the Mob*, Emil Beheshti, Comic Actor, Tom Rhodes, Comedian and Cristina McGinniss, Mentor at Broadway Video. I got the chance to spend my Saturdays walking from 104th and Central Park West to used book stores and art galleries on the lower east side. I re-discovered abstract art and studied where Jackson Pollack and Hans Hoffman once taught. I assembled a series of scrapbooks of my experience that are amongst my most cherished possessions documenting my years in Manhattan.

2. It also forced me to grow up and live out of my comfort zone. Every young person should set sail into unknown waters or to mysterious lands in their 20s. As Author, Michael Crichton said in his travel memoir, *Travels*:

"Often I feel I go to some distant region of the world to be reminded of who I really am. There is no mystery about why this should be so. Stripped of your ordinary surroundings, your friends, your daily routines, your refrigerator full of your food, your closet full of your clothes -- with all this taken away, you are forced into direct experience. Such direct experience inevitably makes you aware of who it is that is having the experience. That's not always comfortable, but it is always invigorating." [22]

CHAPTER EIGHT

"Steve Jobs looked at the catalogue of Apple products in development. He took his pen and crossed out over 80% of them. He questioned the executives as to why they were spreading their company so thin. "

–Walter Isaacson on Steve Jobs

LESSON #8: WHEN IS THE RIGHT TIME TO QUIT A PROJECT?

I recently listened to Seth Godin, a best-selling author, entrepreneur and marketing expert in which he said successful people know when to quit a project and that it's not worth spreading your time and energy amongst too many projects at once, especially those that don't seem to be working out and sap your energy and enjoyment in the creation process. [23]

In Walter Isaacson's biography on Steve Jobs, he recounts Steve Jobs' return to Apple. Jobs looked at the catalogue of Apple products in development and production. He took his pen and crossed out over 80% of them. He questioned the engineers and executives as to why they were spreading their company so thin. [24]

Jobs believed in focusing his company on a few projects. The question I asked myself and still do is: *When is the right time to quit a project?* I grew up thinking quitting was a personality fault or a sign of a weak character and that persistence was one of the necessary qualities of creatively successful people.

I, along with several of my colleagues in the *SNL* family, were fired just after 9/11. The company was making significant cuts in certain departments. I had already cleared out my desk two weeks prior to getting an actual pink slip. Months before this day, I felt like a hamster on a treadmill running as fast as I could but going nowhere.

I would have loved to create and sell abstract art and continue living in NY, but that wasn't a financial option. I hung around for a few more weeks. The magnanimous head of Human Resources, Fred, made sure I got a severance check only days after I was let go, instead of waiting the usual two months. I walked the streets of New York. I felt like James Dean, without the coolness quotient, in the classic black-and-white photo of him ambling through Times Square. I felt lost amongst the noise. If every step on your quest for success is feels relentlessly and stressful, intuition is telling you it's time to move on.

CHAPTER NINE

"During my years in New York, the goals I planned didn't turn out as I expected, but the failures led me to become a bit bolder."

- Jamie Mason Cohen

LESSON #9: CHUTZPAH

Getting the Aung Sun Sui Kyi Shirt to U2

I met Jack Healey, the Executive Director of Human Rights Action Center and former Director of Amnesty International after his letter to Lorne Michaels ended up in a pile of mail on my desk.

I e-mailed Jack telling him where I worked and that I would be willing to use my position over the next few years to help his causes. I then told him my call-to-action was that I'd like to volunteer for his organization. He got back to me within two days. He was completely down-to-earth, thanked me for the e-mail, and listed several causes his organization was behind.

One human rights campaign, in particular, caught my attention: the Free Burma Campaign. The mission was to support Nobel Laureate Aung San Suu Kyi's fight for democracy for her people against the military junta that had taken power by force, despite her earned victory in 1989. Jack and I met up outside the United States Holocaust Memorial Museum in Washington D.C.

We bonded instantly. Over the next few years, while living in New York, I would work with Jack to co-ordinate a national magazine print ad campaign for the Free Burma Coalition. We would also travel to Sydney, Australia, during the Olympics with a pair of nightclub owners to attempt to organize a human rights concert.

Jack called me at 10:00 p.m. on a Thursday night with an urgent request. U2, the most famous band in the world at that time in 2000, was set to perform on the stage at *Saturday Night Live*. Jack had helped introduce U2 to North American audiences during the whirlwind 1986 *Freedom Now Amnesty International Tour*. The U2 quartet was known more as a post-punk, up-and-coming Irish band with a small audience of teenagers in Europe. Bono was most grateful to Jack and for some time after the Amnesty Tour, he called Jack Healey his "Irish brother."

Jack and Paul McGuinness, the manager of U2, had a falling out and McGuinness cut off all professional correspondence between Jack and the band. He wanted Bono and The Edge to wear Aung San Suu Kyi T-shirts during their coming North American tour.

Jack, who was not a phone person, called me in his distinctive voice that musician, Sting had said, "Had a tear in every word he spoke." Jack asked me if I could find a way to get the T-shirts to the band. I told him security was tight around them and I could get fired if I tried. This excuse was only part of the reason.

I was feeling like my time was running out at *SNL* and I didn't want to go out like a crazed stalker-activist who would be carried out by security for attempting to give a few T-shirts to U2. However, I didn't want to let Jack down. He was and still is one of the most inspiring mentors in my life. I would have even snuck into Burma and risked my life if he had asked me to do so. I had planned to enter Burma in 1999 by smuggling a video camera in my shoe and secretly record an interview with Aung San Suu Kyi, who was under house arrest. However, my mother found out about this when a friend slipped and asked my mother how she felt about me sneaking into the most repressive and dangerous country in the world.

I said, no to Jack a few times, but I eventually gave in. On the day of U2's appearance on the show, a Fed-Ex package with four shirts arrived. I folded them up as tightly as I could and stuck them in the two oversized pockets of my leather jacket. With security tight backstage, I wondered if they would think I had a weapon in my bulky pocket. I took the subway the usual fifty-five blocks to Rockefeller Centre.

I bypassed the already long line of minor VIPs waiting to get in. I walked backstage into the writers' room and had the gut feeling of how different this night would be. There was twice the amount of entertainment-type people, as usual, milling around, acting like teenage groupies at a boy band concert. I took a deep breath, patted my pockets every minute or so to remind myself of my mission, and then decided to go into the heart of the lion's den, immediately.

Target: Paul McGuinness, the irascible manager of U2. Jack told me to avoid him, but he also said he was the only one who could get the band to do something like this on such short notice. I asked Scott, Lorne's assistant, where U2's managers would be and told him what my plan was. He said he'd help in the cause. Scott was one of the few people who worked on the show who thought it would be an intriguing mini-mission to make this happen.

We walked through the A- to C + celebrities, industry-types and their sycophants who were lining the halls. There was Kirstie Alley and her niece demanding more tickets, a few actors from the NBC show, *Third Watch*, one of the castaways from *Survivor*, and a soap opera star.

"That's him, I think," Scott said in a restrained voice. "Do you want to approach him?"

"Yeah, I'm just not sure what I'm going to…"

He was there in front of us. He nodded at Scott, who was omnipresent back stage on the show and handled a million little tasks on behalf of Lorne Michaels.

Scott introduced me to Paul McGuinness.

"I work for Lorne," I said. "Jack Healey says 'Hi.'"

He raised his eyebrow and then ever so slightly snickered.

"Quick question, Paul." I showed him the Aung San Suu Kyi T-shirt.

"What's that?" he asked.

"Your band wrote a song for Suu Kyi and the people of Burma. Why don't you all put this on and dedicate the song to her tonight?" I suggested. I knew I had his attention.

He paused for a moment and said, "Not the right time."

I said, "Seven million people in this country who have never heard of Aung San Suu Kyi will know her name if Bono wears the shirt."

"Not the right place or time. It's the anniversary of John Lennon's death," Paul McGuinness said.

He was about to walk away when I said, "That's even more of a reason. Lennon stood for peace. So does Aung San Suu Kyi."

He did a double take. Walking away, he smirked at me and said to one of his team, "Who is this guy?"

Scott started laughing. He said, "I can't believe you just did that. Wow."

A tall, striking man wearing a gaucho Argentinian hat with custom-made Croatian flair and a black body length coat approached me. His look seemed to suggest he had some admiration for me for having the chutzpah to stand up to the sardonic manager of the most famous band in the world.

"You want to get to U2?", he asked in a calm and melodic voice.

"Yes," I said.

"I played with Bono a few years ago. I'll help you. My name's Nenad Bach."

I shook his hand. "I'm Jamie Cohen. I work for Lorne Michaels."

Little did I know this meeting would be the beginning of a deep friendship and collaborations on several film, TV, educational projects, and mastermind groups that continue to this day. Nenad is a musician who has reached omnipresent status in his country of Croatia and sold over one million albums around the world. He had also played on the same stage with Bono. Meeting Nenad showed me that the journey is the destination. It's the people and experiences I met along the way in New York that became more impactful in my life than the original goal.

Now, I had my friend and co-worker, Scott enrolled in my mission to get the shirts to the band.

U2 was set to perform in about ten minutes. All three of us headed to the most exclusive, security-laden backstage spot of SNL. It is the place just outside the doors where the performer gets make-up done and then waits for the director's cue to perform live. Usually, there are only a handful of special guests of the hosts, cast, or network executives, who are allowed in this area.

This time, I had to re-focus my eyes. We joined a group in the small space that consisted of Michael Stipe, the diminutive and diffident lead singer of R.E.M., who seemed to be hiding behind the orange scarf of his boyfriend. Val Kilmer appeared. Also present were Joey Ramone - less than two years before his death, Adam Sandler, Jay Mohr, Tom Cruise, and Nicole Kidman, one year before their break-up. I took my spot in between Michael Stipe and Val Kilmer. Nenad was my new best ally as he knew many of the musicians present. Nenad was looking around figuring out who to approach, next, with T-shirts.

I turned to Michael Stipe and his boyfriend. I told them how Jack Healey and I were talking about how we admired Michael for his human rights campaigning on behalf of Tibet.

Michael asked me, "What did you say your name was?"

I told him and then talked to him about my interest in Tibetan, as well as Burmese causes.

Michael's boyfriend was looking at the T-shirts I had in both hands. "What are those?" he asked.

So I told him. He turned to Michael and said, "Can't we help in some way?"

Michael shrugged, his eyebrows lifted slightly as if mildly curious. I was right. As I started filling in Michael's boyfriend on the details of my plan and the cause behind it, Michael went from an indifferent stare to a more open and inquisitive expression. He seemed to be disarmed and amused a bit by the novelty and sincere intention behind this unusual request, in the context of this situation.

Val Kilmer had been listening in on the conversation between us and asked me to see the shirt. I showed it to him. Michael Stipe smiled. His boyfriend said, "Let's help."

The dynamics of social proof was in effect. Nenad and I nodded at each other. At that moment, all eyes turned toward the staircase behind us. A tall, pale woman with a stunning white full-length coat showed up. It was Nicole Kidman. Tom Cruise seemed to draw all the energy in the hall to him the moment he appeared. He had the kind of boundless energy and presence you'd expect from his roles in films like, *Top Gun* and *Jerry Maguire*. He looked like you would imagine him to look, just smaller. He couldn't have been more than 5'7", but his aura almost knocked me off my feet.

What impressed me was he greeted everyone in the room, regardless of their status with the same magnetic, genuine smile. He looked me in the eye. In a two second span, in the narrow, cramped fluorescent hallway, it felt as if I was the only person in the room to whom he was speaking. Michael Stipe and Val Kilmer suddenly disappeared along with Tom Cruise, Nicole Kidman, and Joey Ramone to the VIP area. I could see in to the barely opened dressing room door on the other side of the walkway that they were saying hello to the band. Val and Michael were talking with Bono. U2 walked through the hall to the stage.

Gigantic security guards shadowed them on either side. U2's collective charisma, led by Bono, radiated a star power. They were making their way in our direction. As they strode directly past us and through the doors to perform their first song, "Beautiful Day," I couldn't get in to a strategic position to make my pitch to Bono. We watched them perform on stage from just inside the hallway doors. There was no mention of Burma or Suu Kyi and no sign of T-shirts on national television. I expected this for the first song because performers usually sing their biggest hit on their newest albums during this time slot.

I knew that immediately after singing the song, U2 would directly pass us again in the hallway. If previous shows were any indication, sometimes the performers were more willing to stop and talk after they had finished the performance. I also knew they had one more song to sing during the second half.

There was still a chance. The first thing I thought of was if Bono does walk by me, what could I say in one sentence or even a few words that would make him consider my request? I had been in pitch sessions for television projects which prepared me for this moment.

As I was scoping out possible places to wait for the band and get noticed amongst the sea of celebrities around me, Nenad tapped me on the shoulder. "Jamie, I'd like to introduce you to Morleigh."

The woman he introduced me to was an attractive, modest woman in her thirties.

"Tell her your plan," Nenad said.

"I'm trying to get Bono or The Edge to wear this shirt to bring awareness to Aung San Suu Kyi's cause in Burma."

She listened and nodded. "Let me see what I can do," she said. "Stay right here."

I didn't know who or how this woman was connected to U2, but a lot of people were greeting her. It turned out Morleigh was U2 band member, The Edge's partner and soon-to-be wife.

Then, the moment happened. The massive backstage performance doors flung open and Bono led his band like an emperor walking through ancient Rome. You can tell a lot about a man by his walk. Bono strode through the gauntlet of stars like, "a tiger in its prime moves slowly but heedfully through the jungle… he likes his body and his bounciness and sense of rhythm, he is relaxed…his movements are like waves." [25] Tibetan Buddhist Master, Chogyam Trungpa's analogy of a warrior's confidence applied to Bono.

Bono was a rock star the moment he entered the room. He stopped and said hello to each person in the line that formed, bowing ever so slightly each time he greeted someone.

"Hello, Michael. Val, Nice to see you."

Tom whispered something to him and they laughed.

He shook Nenad's hand and touched his own heart.

Then, there was me. Bono looked at me as if to ask, "Who are you?"

Here was the moment for which I had prepared.

"Bono, Jack Healey sends his love. Sing one for Suu Kyi."

Bono slowly peeled off his iconic wrap-around black sunglasses, held both of my shoulders, which was a good thing because I felt like I was going to collapse. He said, "Thank-you for that."

He continued down the line, and I could see his manager, the ever present Paul McGuinness shaking his head, this time with a little, grudging respect for my annoying persistence. I got another tap on my shoulder. "Jamie," said Morleigh, whom I met moments earlier. "This is my husband, The Edge." I turned. Morleigh was the key.

"So you want us to wear the shirts, huh?" asked The Edge.

"Yes. Jack Healey asked if you could wear the shirt when you sing your next song on live TV."

The Edge looked the shirt over. "I'll see what I can do." He took the shirt and walked off backstage.

Val Kilmer nodded at me and smiled. The band passed us once again about twenty minutes later for their second and final song. I couldn't see through the wall of security guards if they were wearing the shirts. U2 went on stage and I fought my way through the crowd situated just inside the performance doors. Bono approached the microphone. The band members approached their instruments. 5, 4, 3, 2, 1… The red "Live" neon sign flashed.

Bono said, "We'd like to dedicate this next song to one of our heroes…" I held my breath. "…Someone who devoted his life to world peace…John Lennon." I felt deflated as I listened to a breathtaking version of, The Beatles, "All You Need Is Love" performed by U2.

I looked over at stage left where Paul McGuinness stood with the shirts in his hand.

During my years in New York, the goals I planned didn't turn out as I expected, but the failures led me to become a bit bolder.

CHAPTER TEN

"I learned to trust people's actions more than flattering words."

— Jamie Mason Cohen

LESSON #10: RELATIONSHIPS

Have you ever asked yourself: *How did he or she get to where they are?*

I spent my adult lifetime fascinated and sometimes frustrated with my findings when trying to answer this question. I struggled with the belief that who you know determines your success in a company and life. Everyone needs a first break, including Lorne Michaels. I had heard Lorne got his initial break through his first wife's father, a famous Canadian comedian.

It was Lorne's father-in-law, it's been said, who made the call to New York to get him in the door at NBC, so Lorne could pitch his idea of a live show featuring comedians and music performers. Most of the SNL writers came through Harvard University's comedy magazine or the comedy improv groups such as The Groundlings or Second City. Even my mentor at *Saturday Night Live*, Lorne Michaels' long-time right-hand woman, Cristina McGinniss, once said to me after I had asked her how you get ahead in this business, "Honey, it's who you know." This revelation was difficult to swallow.

I couldn't believe that hard work, playing the game within a company, persisting and having some talent wouldn't result in moving ahead. Well, in my case, it didn't. Another one of Lorne's assistants said she thought I was one of the up-and-comers in the company.

I told Lorne with all the chutzpah I could muster, "I can be a star in your company if given the chance."

Lorne's response was, "What do you mean?"

I said, "I know I have a lot to offer this company if I'm given the chance to really contribute."

I provided references from senior producers at Broadway Video and *Saturday Night Live* Films who would vouch for me based on my efforts over the past year and a half. As I spoke to Lorne, I couldn't get the image out of my head of Michael J. Fox in the film, *The Secret of My Success*, as his character, Brantley Foster, tries to move up the corporate ladder.

I did jump from department to department within Lorne Michaels's comedy empire. I thought these moves I had requested were a hopeful sign. There just wasn't any opportunity to earn my way up the chain which appeared to have a bottom rung and a top rung — no real middle. I was told another time by Erin Fraser, a co-producer on SNL film, *Superstar*, "You know more than 95% of the people in the organization."

I learned to trust people's actions more than flattering words. This compliment kept me going for weeks, but didn't translate into any real chance to prove myself creatively or in any substantial way. **If you do the best you can, contribute as a team player, put in longer hours, show up earlier without signs of professional advancement, then it may be best to walk away and take a first step in a new direction.** The alternative – temporary uncertainty - is almost always a better option than working and living in quiet desperation.

CHAPTER ELEVEN

"Most people overestimate what they can do in one year and underestimate what they can do in ten years."

— *Bill Gates*

LESSON #11: MENTORS

Seek and be open to the right mentor. Work for them in exchange for their guidance if needed. Do other jobs to keep afloat while you do. In some Buddhist traditions, there is a minimum five-year period where mentee monks are instructed to devote their lives to their guru/mentor/teachers in order to absorb and learn the ways of becoming an enlightened being.

Jiro Dreams of Sushi is a documentary about one of the top sushi chefs in the world and his son. His son, who trained under his father for thirty years, said it takes ten years of working under a sushi master to become proficient in the skill and craft. He also mentioned that an aspiring sushi chef needs talent. [26]

I would have spent ten years devoting my life in pursuing the mastery of film or TV producing and directing under Lorne Michaels, but the company was not set up to foster such learning. There was no mentoring program in place regardless of how much I asked or showed commitment to the enterprise. One of the most important pieces of guidance I can give any young person starting out in the world is to find your mentor and convince him/her that you are worthy of being his mentee. The flip side of this is to make sure you have a Plan B. I spent a lot of energy searching for mentors when I could have spent some of it in developing my skills. There needs to be a balance between making the right connections, building relationships with mentors and spending thousands of hours in developing your craft.

Don't quit even when it seems impossible. Bill Gates said, "Most people overestimate what they can do in one year and underestimate what they can do in ten years." [27] Give yourself a ten-year time frame. This length of time sounds like an eternity, but here I am writing about my journey in New York, which happened fifteen years ago. It's a lifetime, and yet it goes by in a flash.

If necessary, get a second job to help pay the bills. I thought Lorne Michaels would be my Jiro and I spent a decade looking for mentors. More than looking for a job, young people should consider seeking out the individuals upon whom they want to model their professional careers. Find a way to intern for them and prove you are indispensable.

CHAPTER TWELVE

"I took a deep breath, feeling that even getting to this moment was improbable enough from where I was, in my parents' basement less than one year ago, so I dove in."

— Jamie Mason Cohen

LESSON #12: LEARN HOW TO USE YOUR HOBBY AS A FUN ICE BREAKER

I have a passion for examining people's writing and have become a certified handwriting analyst and TEDx Speaker on the topic. It started twenty-five years ago when I became intrigued by this hobby after watching my mother, a Certified Handwriting expert, analyze doctors, lawyers, and professional hockey players' handwriting. It led me to ask her how she did this and what else one could tell from a person's hand-written letters. The height of t-bars represents how high or low their goals are. The length of a t-bar and its thickness represents the persistence and enthusiasm of a person in the attainment of those goals.

Here is my TEDx Talk, "How to Spot a Leader in Their Handwriting".

When a person underlines their signature, it means he or she is self-reliant. When a person dots the "i" close to the stem, it means a person pays attention to detail and is loyal to friends. Forgetting the dot altogether means forgetfulness and lack of attention to details. I studied writing samples like John F. Kennedy, who was a supremely logical decision-maker in stressful situations and Steve Jobs, who was a visionary with high goals. Through the science of handwriting analysis, I discovered a skill that fascinated just about every person I met. People love to hear about their favourite subject: themselves.

Upon my arrival in New York, I inspired some curiosity from young staffers at *SNL*. Just after I arrived, there was a Christmas party. In the days leading up to it, a memo went around the office that anyone with a hidden talent would be welcome to show it off then.

There were talented singers, jugglers, and magicians amongst the twenty-something workers on my floor. As a way to deflect the daily barrage of questions I was getting and in an attempt to ingratiate myself, I quietly offered one of the organizers to put my name down to do handwriting analysis. I didn't expect anything would come of this.

On the day of the party set for the evening, new colleagues introduced themselves to me. I didn't know what to make of this until a Broadway Video Producer said, "For those of you who don't know, Jamie Cohen, who just joined us two weeks ago from Toronto, Canada, is an expert handwriting analyst."

Before I could jump in and correct her, she continued, "...and he volunteered to do readings for all of us tonight."

There were over fifty people at this gathering. I thought nobody would care. It's hard to impress skeptical New Yorkers - but they started gathering around me, not one or two people, but about forty. The remaining ten new colleagues were standing at the back of the scrum to see what would happen. I went from the mysterious Canadian to the quirky dancing monkey at the Christmas party.

I said to the producer who introduced me, "I thought people were going to show their 'hidden' talents tonight?"

"Yeah, well, no one signed up... except for you," she said.

Great, I thought. Instead of trying to slip under the radar or maybe make a few connections with staff, a sense of panic set in, in that all eyes would be glued on me, waiting for me to fail. What happens if I give a wrong reading on a trait? What happens if I give an inaccurate description of a personality trait? How do I frame an on-the-spot analysis in such a way as to not publicly humiliate the person and make an enemy within my first few weeks in my dream job?

These were some of the questions that went through my head as I set myself up for a near impossible situation. Usually at that time, it would take me an hour to sit quietly with a piece of handwriting and analyze a trait before making evaluations based on the complex and paradoxical combinations of qualities that exist in a person. A person's writing is a reflection of their individuality, as diverse as snowflakes. I didn't have one hour to sit with each piece of handwriting. I had thirty seconds for each analysis which I had never attempted before.

I took a deep breath, feeling that even getting to this moment was improbable enough from where I was, in my parents' basement less than one year ago, so I dove in.

One after the other, barely looking up, I stared down at a signature plus a sentence and told the person two positive things about themselves and one thing they probably would like to improve. I carefully chose adjectives to describe how they respond emotionally to a given situation. I pondered whether or not they liked spicy foods. I told them if they were passionate about collecting something. I revealed if they live in the moment or have long-term plans. I showed whether they had a few trusted friends or many acquaintances they keep in touch with over a lifetime.

As I went through each one, many people said, "Wow, that's so true." As is usually the case, a few cynics shot down whatever I said as being too general, palm-reading kind-of-stuff.

I told one skeptic that he'd been working very hard in the past month to develop an exercise habit. I was right. The criticisms became quieter as the night went on. Handwriting experts are not supposed to give people time frames like that because it's a science, not a psychic predictor, so it's a risk. However, there's a time to be bold to see how good your skills are and I took the chance.

About two hours later, I looked up. Most of the staff were staring at me with a sense of respect and intrigue. Some people in the room were clapping. Others waited around to ask me to elaborate even further on my initial insights into their writing.

A decade later, I would use this skill when I did the same on-the-spot analysis of colleagues at TanenbaumCHAT, the private high school where I teach. After two hours of analysis, a group of rabbis sought me out to expand on my comments about how philosophy and spiritual ideas show up in handwriting. It has led to me doing handwriting analysis talks for high school teachers, performing for a synagogue congregation, in front of a packed crowd at a media executive's home, and doing a relationship seminar for couples through their writing.

Humour in Handwriting

There are a few surprising and unexpected traits teachers may have in common with comedians. These traits can be seen in handwriting analysis. However, the traits represented here are a mere handful of similarities that may exist between the professions.

Some teachers and comics demonstrate fluidity of thought. This trait is a sign of intelligence, and the ability to seamlessly move from topic to topic in speech or in writing or conversation. "There is an efficiency of thinking" as comic master, Greg Wilson said in an interview with one of the world's leading handwriting experts, Bart Baggett. It is the skill of weaving together words. It can be seen in the figure 8 formation primarily in the letters "s" "j" or "g". "There are smooth-flowing unbroken strokes which connect words or letters," according to the Handwriting University Trait Dictionary.

Other characteristics educators and comedians I've known share are: persistence and analytical thinking. Persistence is the "quality of not giving up when confronted with temporary setbacks. She will persist until completing a task. It can be seen in tied strokes within the writing. It shows up in the downstroke which turns to the right, crosses itself, then repeats into the future or comes forward, crossing back into the action.

It takes years of practice and stick-with-it-ness to master the myriad of skills a teacher possesses to create lessons and manage a class. Thousands of hours of deliberate effort is also needed for a stand-up comedian to create, tweak and deliver material. Both professions have to fend off rejection and hecklers and endure long days.

"Analytical thinking is the sound judgment and a knack for problem solving. This trait is demonstrated in the natural v's at the baseline or bottom of letters.

Additionally, a silly sense of humour is "shown by a wavy t-bar and/or flourishing wavy beginning strokes in word patterns. This person has a silly sense of humour and can become witty if the stroke ends with a sharp point at the end of the small t-bar (sarcastic) or angle (analytical)."

For more information and examples of handwriting samples of comedians and what your handwriting says about your personality, you can go to: handwritinguniversity.com

Silly sense of humour = swiggly lines on the t-bar and the "w"

Analytical mind shown in the "v" wedge of the "i" and "n"

Fluidity of thought in the "S"

Strokes that double back over the letter and end toward the right. Usually located in the t and f. This person has the quality of not giving up when confronted with temporary setbacks. He will persist until he completes the task.

persistence

A figure eight shape anywhere in the writing. Most commonly found in the lower loop of the g or in the capital letters of a signature. Signifies the ability to follow and change thoughts smoothly. Often a good conversationalist, speaker, writer, or radio host.

fluidity of thought

Examples of handwriting traits - Humour, Persistence and Fluidity of Thought from the Graphodeck by www.handwritinguniversity.com

PART 2

"WHEN YOU'RE LAUGHING, YOU'RE LEARNING."

- JACK MILNER

CHAPTER THIRTEEN

"Teachers need to engage inspire, and enthuse students by creating the conditions in which students will want to learn."

Education Reformer and TED Speaker, Sir Ken Robinson

HOW TO USE HUMOUR IN YOUR CLASSROOM LIKE FAMOUS COMEDIANS, TED SPEAKERS, MAGICIANS, BODY LANGUAGE EXPERTS, IMPROV ARTISTS, COMEDY WRITERS AND SITCOM ACTORS

Students sometimes ask, "How do you know such interesting people? Where did you meet them?" Over the past decade and a half, I've been lucky to get to know some truly *sui generis* and creative people.

I interviewed some of my friends – a comedian, comic actor, leader of a comic troupe, keynote speaker on body language, professional speaker and magician to explore what high school teachers can learn from professional comedians and speakers about how to integrate humour into a class.

Tom Rhodes is an American Comedian, Actor, Host, and Travel Writer. He was the star of NBC's *Mr. Rhodes*, in which he played a teacher at a preparatory school. His podcast *Tom Rhodes Radio* often features other comedians or people he meets while traveling. He writes for *The Huffington Post* and has released three comedy albums, two DVDs, and a comedy special on Netflix called, *Light, Sweet, Crude.* You can see this modern comedic renaissance man of the world's projects at Tom Rhodes' Website.

I met Tom during my first year in New York working for Broadway Video and *Saturday Night Live*. What struck me when I first met him in 2000, when I helped organize a college comedy tour Tom co-headlined, was how open, humble, and generous he was with the younger crew members. He remembers me as the guy on the bus who analyzed his handwriting.

We were all on this comedy tour bus together, travelling from one college to the next in the cities of Boston, Baltimore and Washington D.C.. Tom pulled out a black notebook intermittently adding insights and tweaking material from the previous performances. I asked him about it and he shared with me his creative process.

Mark Bowden is a Keynote Speaker and Bestselling Author. He is an expert in human behaviour and body language and the resident body language authority on CTV's daily talk show, *The Social.* He has trained business people, teams, and politicians, presidents, and CEOs of Fortune 50 companies and current Prime Ministers of G8 powers from around the world. He is the creator of TRUTHPLANE®, a communication training company and unique methodology for anyone who has to communicate with impact. He also happens to be the best-selling author of three books including, *Winning Body Language*, and *Tame the Primitive Brain*.

I saw Mark's TED Talk at TEDxToronto. Mark Bowden's TEDx Talk: The Importance Of Being Inauthentic. I was in awe of his masterful command of the stage as a professional speaker, expert on the subject of body language, and the ease in which he interspersed wit, and techniques to engage the audience. His talk inspired me so much that I wrote him a letter inviting him to be the keynote speaker at my yearly SOLE Student Leadership Seminar for high schoolers.

He accepted the invitation and mesmerized the 125 students in attendance with actionable, practical, and fun body language techniques they used to help them the next day during a charity event pitch to administrators. One year later, when I was asked to give a TEDx talk in Luxembourg; I contacted Mark to ask for some guidance.

Dan Trommater is is a Keynote Speaker and Professional Magician. He spent a year studying the art of magic at the Magic Castle in Hollywood - the world's most prestigious magic performance venue - where he's a repeat performer. He is also a speaker and trainer for such world class organizations as The Rotman School of Management, Queens University, TD Financial Group, and The Marshall School of Business at the University of Southern California. He uses the intriguing tool of magic to challenge assumptions and inspire new ways of thinking.

I was introduced to Dan through Mark Bowden. Right after we met, I watched Dan's TEDx Talk. Dan Trommater's TEDxTalk, Perspective – A Magician's View of Subjective Reality. What moved me was his ability to weave magic, humour, and lessons together in a way I haven't seen before. One moment I was near tears; the next, I was laughing. In the end, I got up and I started clapping.

My wife came into the room and said, "What was that? Are you talking to someone?"

I said, "No, I just watched Dan's talk. You remember the guy who came to speak at my seminar?"

She said, "Really? Okay, I've got to see this."

Emil Beheshti is an Actor and Producer, known for *Big Momma's House 2, Puppy Love,* **and the upcoming remake of** *The Magnificent* **Seven.** We became immediate friends after I was stuck in a random part of Koreatown in L.A., after getting lost trying to find a place to stay during a visit. I called one of my friends at *Saturday Night Live,* Hilla Narov, who was friends with Emil for years. She asked him to track me down and pick me up. We've been friends ever since. Emil was instantly likeable, open, personable, and passionate about acting. A few years after meeting him, I was putting together a cast and crew for my first short film, *Know Chance.* I called Emil and asked him to star in it. He flew to Toronto from L.A. and was totally committed to a demanding role that mixed comic and tragic elements. On top of the intense shooting days, he was the unofficial leader on set. He was a bridge builder, the social coordinator, and kept things light. You can check out the latest film he's co-starred in here. All For The Card, short film (dir., Bru Miller, co-starring, Emil Beheshiti)

Jim Annan is a Professional Actor, Writer, and member of a sketch comedy troupe. As an alumnus of The Second City Toronto, Jim wrote and performed in four revues. He is one-third of the

Canadian Comedy Award-winning sketch troupe Falcon Powder. Jim has appeared in various television and film projects including *Murdoch Mysteries, The Stanley Dynamic, Coconut Hero, Odd Squad, Rookie Blue, The Ron James Show,* and *Unlucky.* You can see a list of Jim's television and film work here.

I met Jim through my sister, Carly, prior to working for *Saturday Night Live.* I admired that Jim had made the decision, while still in university, that he had one path that was to become a professional actor. He has stayed true to this path, fifteen years later, quietly building one of the most successful comedy careers in Canada as a Second City performer, writer, omnipresent actor in commercials, TV, and film.

Why attempt to add humour into a classroom if a teacher doesn't think of himself or herself as "funny?" How do you integrate humour into a classroom of teenagers? These were two of the questions I explored with these performers.

The interviews with the comedians, speakers, performers, magicians, and actors will provide some non-obvious theories and easy-to-implement practices of using humour to improve the environment in your class.

Humour is Balance

Bestselling author on body language and TED speaker, Mark Bowden, spoke about the medieval idea of humour. Humourists were the old medics of the medieval time who thought there were four kinds of humour: blood, phlegm, yellow bile, and black bile. These humours were necessary for the well being of a person. The old medics suggested if "one or some of the humour are out of balance, then you'd be ill essentially. So, you'd get in a humorous state in order to rebalance the humours."

The connection to the classroom is that there is an implied or real imbalance of status. He spoke about the relationship in status between a teacher and a student. "If I'm a teacher and you're a student, doesn't it imply that I know, and you don't know?" [28]

Keith Johnstone, legendary theatre teacher and author of the classic book on improv called, *Impro*, discusses how he deals with status on the first day of class. He says, "The first thing I do when I meet a group of new students is (probably) to sit on the floor. I play low status, and I'll explain if the students fail, they're to blame me. Then, they laugh, relax, and I explain that really it's obvious they should blame me, since I'm supposed to be the expert." [28]

Johnstone continues, "I play low status physically, but my actual status is going up, since only a very confident and experienced person would put the blame for failure on himself." He goes on to say that changing his status has other positive effects mainly that failure suddenly does not become so frightening to them. If a student fails, he will apologize to them and ask them to be "patient with me, and explain I'm not perfect." He says this method works and most students succeed because they're not trying to win anymore.

"You need to get knowledge from me, and I'm either going to allow you to have that knowledge and you'll either get it or you won't." Bowden acknowledges that this may not be essentially true, and an extreme representation of a decent classroom, but to the student, there may seem like there is a "huge imbalance of power."

This imbalance of power or perceived disproportion may also extend to the status relationship between the "teacher and their management" or the disparity between the "parent and the teacher." Often, the parent may feel like they've got more power. Mark's suggestion is to look at what is perceived to be the power that is going on.

Humour is a highly subjective term that has a thousand different meanings to a thousand different teachers. **I've learned not to focus on being "funny" or in forcing humour into my classes.** When I mispronounce a word or come up with something on the spot like, "If I go on too long on this subject, do as my three-year old son, Koby does and say, "Stooooooop!!!!" (palm of hand extended towards the students with a straight arm). The kids usually laugh. The line about my son telling me to stop rambling reminds them to let me know when we can move on to another question if I ramble on.

Humour is Creating an Easy-going Learning Environment

It's not about telling jokes; it's about the environment. Rich learning and increased student engagement often emerge from a warm, light, open environment in which students feel safe in taking risks, making mistakes and enjoying the learning process.

Create a SOLE (Self-Organized Learning Environment). See lesson examples at the back of the book or download the free SOLE Toolkit. A SOLE class is divided into a three-part structure: [31]

1. **Question:** The teacher comes up with a big and meaningful question relevant to your learning outcomes such as: What does it mean be a hero in today's world? Can music change the world? How do you know when you've reached enlightenment?

2. **Investigate:** In groups of four, students investigate this question using online sources. I find this is an apt time to have students explore library resources and collaborate with our school librarian.

3. **Presentation:** The last part of the class is the presentation component, in which each group presents their findings in an auditory, visual or tactile way. Please see a brief, highlight reel of the SOLE auditory and tactile presentations my students created in a self-organized learning environment called, "Can music change the world?"

Mark Bowden spoke about the importance of creating an environment that is "accepting." What students really want is "a safe, social environment." A teenaged student wants to know, "Am I socially safe here? Will I get accepted?" If a teenager has a humorous teacher, it is setting the stage for an inclusive space for a healthy learning environment.

How to Use Humour to Balance Power in a Class

Mark suggests giving away some of your power as a teacher. "It's that little moment where suddenly everybody in the room has a moment when some power disappears from you, and they laugh."

What humour is not is an environment in which students feel like they have to walk on eggshells around their teacher. It's not an environment in which the power is solely focused on a sage on the stage or a benevolent dictator commanding the front of perfectly aligned rows. And, it's not about the teacher discouraging or shooting down any signs of disagreement with the ideas they present in class.

My teaching mentor, Jim Barry, welcomed students disagreeing with him because it showed they were thinking aloud. **Humour empowers students to share their opinions, make mistakes, and push themselves without fear of being embarrassed or feeling self-conscious.**

Keynote speaker, Mark Bowden engaging with our students on the power of body language during presentations. SOLE Student Leadership Seminar, 2014.

Revealed: Why Use Humour to Engage Students

Keynote Speaker and Professional Magician, Dan Trommater, says humour "taps into something deep within us. If it's done right, it's like magic. Humour can be an emotional experience. **By definition, laughter is sort of an outward physical manifestation of an inward emotion.**"

"In terms of being engaging, who doesn't like to laugh? If you can put in a moment of humour, even to get a little chuckle, you've started down the path to a connection with an audience, whether that audience is a classroom situation or a boardroom situation, it doesn't really matter."

Professional speaker and master Magician, Dan Trommater entertaining and educating my students during my annual, SOLE Student Leadership Seminar, 2014.

How to Create an Open Class Environment Using Body Language

Bowden says it's simply about "open body language." He suggests teachers "Think of all the things that would be closed body language and go, 'Well, how could I do more of the open things than the closed things?'"

Specifically, Mark says teachers could reflect on the current environment in their classroom with questions such as:

- ☑ Do I have to sit behind a table as a teacher?
- ☑ Do I have to sit behind my desk?
- ☑ How can I be more open to the student when I'm talking to him or her?
- ☑ Is there a position I can take around the student that is more open to them?
- ☑ Where can they see more of my body rather than being hidden by the implements of the classroom?
- ☑ When I'm demonstrating a strategy or when I'm talking about an aspect of the subject, how can I keep my body language open?
- ☑ "Open palm gestures are a place to start as it's showing you've got nothing dangerous in your hands," Bowden explains. Mark says it seems odd saying, "Openness in your body by showing you have no weapons in your hands, but the primitive brain is asking those kinds of questions. The primitive brain doesn't know it is school. It's just looking out for its own safety."

Humour is Feeling Safe in Class

Questions Bowden brings up about how body language can contribute to setting the tone for an open and safe environment facilitated by the teacher include:

- ☑ Can we see you?
- ☑ Are you open?
- ☑ Are you hiding anything from us?

- ☑ What's your proximity like? If you're too close, you might be overbearing.
- ☑ He says, "If you're too far away, I'm not socially linked to you, so how can you move around the classroom in order to get more proximate with students so you're not in just a public place with them a lot of the time. You're in a social space or even personal space with them, which is within six feet of them. Within six feet of somebody, that's when the bond really starts to develop."

Humour Builds a Bond and Trust with Students

Jack Milner, a stand-up comedian who does presentation training for corporations, says, "When they're laughing, they're learning." [33]

The way Bowden interprets Jack Milner's statement is, **"If we laugh at something, it means we've recognized something together. We've got a link. We've got a bond. Laughing as a group is social. It means we recognize something as being true or accurate and it releases some tension together."**

Dan Trommater thinks, "If you use humour in a respectful and a light-hearted way, then it can build trust. I know if I use a joke or a line or a comment and it gets a laugh where everybody wins, then that can't help but to win trust."

Mark Bowden says humour can build trust because it "rebalances the power and helps me trust that the humourist is going to treat me well, that I'm safe, that there's not an overabundance of power on one side because that could be damaging to me."

An Unconventional Way to Build Trust

One unorthodox way I immediately build trust with a group of new students is how I deal with the first swear word I hear from them. When I overhear a pupil use a swear word, not directed at anyone in particular, I turn and ask, "What did you just say?" with a serious, no-nonsense tone and stern look. The young man or woman and the surrounding teenagers freeze. Before he or she can respond I say, "Do not *EVER* say the word 'the' in this class again? Is that understood?"

It never fails to get a laugh of relief. It also builds trust because it shows that I have a sense of humour while stating the boundaries in a fun way. I'm willing to forgive minor transgressions, yet make it clear I am aware of everything going on in my class. I rarely, if ever, hear a swear word in my classes after I give this initial response.

HUMOUR IN THE CLASSROOM MYTHS

Myth #1: A Teacher Has to Be Naturally Funny to Use Humour

Some teachers think they're not funny. As a result of this belief, they feel uncomfortable or resistant to incorporating humour into their lessons.

Comedian, Tom Rhodes responded that [he] knows "thousands of comedians who are not funny. They're not funny naturally as people, but they work on it really hard; they look for their jokes." [34]

Comedy actor, Emil Beheshti, said he actually finds himself rather "boring as an individual, but enjoys taking on those characteristics of people [he] finds amusing." [35]

"It's not necessarily about laughter," Bowden says. "Some moments of humour are "very internal, they're just light, and they lighten the mood. They produce a laugh. However, humour doesn't have to produce a laugh. Some people laugh when anxiety has built up around a subject. The body is tense with that energy."

The moment of humour releases tension that results in laughter. Some humour can also create crying. Bowden describes this kind of release of energy as "anxious energy around the power structure." My experience in the classroom matches the way Mark Bowden describes humour in this context. **Teenagers sometimes giggle uncomfortably when a topic comes up that's tragic, relatable, or during awkward silences.**

Students laugh for different reasons, which aren't necessarily responses to humorous moments. The way to respond to this may be to acknowledge why students sometimes laugh in different circumstances so that others don't become offended if they perceive someone is laughing at them during a sensitive moment.

Comedian, Actor, Host and Travel Writer, Tom Rhodes

Improv actor, Jim Annan, says **if teachers don't find themselves funny "then that's great. Anyone who's trying to be funny is usually annoying."**

Dan Trommater suggests learning a magic trick to elicit humour if a teacher doesn't know where to start. "Don't be afraid of learning one trick you love. Do it for friends and family before you get in front of a classroom audience so you're confident you can do it, and don't worry about trying to integrate it into a specific message. Do it as a trick. I guarantee you it will get laughs, even if you're not funny. A moment of magic for some reason just automatically elicits laughter."

Dan goes on to say, "When we see something we don't understand, quite often, laughter is a natural outcome, even if it's not funny. I don't know whether it's a nervous reaction, but it's pretty common. I'll do something that is a great trick with no humour, and it still gets laughs."

Myth #2: Humour is ONLY About Telling Jokes

Emil Beheshti talks about what a good friend and fellow actor said when they were doing a scene together: "You always want to bring a little drama to your comedy and a little bit of comedy to your drama, because that's just life."

Emil elaborates on the point that tragic comedy is one of the things I've been intrigued with because I had a significant loss at a very young age with my mother passing away. I think maybe I was given some liberty as I grew up and got a bit older to have fun with some things that might have been sacred, things you talked about quietly or kept to yourself.

Jim Annan says he's "not really a jokey improviser." He likes to listen and forward the scene to keep it going. "It's not going to be a laugh a minute."

Myth #3: If the Audience is NOT Laughing, You Failed

Jim Annan says in the back of his mind, sometimes, he thinks, "Oh, the audience hasn't laughed in a while. Am I doing tragedy up here? You've got to trust that maybe your partner is going to say something funny or someone is going to come in and take us somewhere else, but you just stay with it."

Don't always judge an audience's reaction by their expression. Tom Rhodes speaks of such a misjudgement. "About ten years ago, I was in Dallas; it's sold out and I'm destroying the place. There was a young couple, late 20s, and they were not laughing at anything. After the show, I saw them and asked, 'Hi, how are you? Did you enjoy the show?' That was my own insecurity, wanting to know why they didn't enjoy the show. They were from Spain; their English wasn't that good. I'm sitting there thinking they didn't enjoy the show. They simply didn't understand it. "

In Dan Trommater's TEDx Talk, he recounts a story of playing a set in a bar. A man named Dave was sitting first-row center. Dan calls the person sitting in this seat the "emotional keystone" of the audience. As this audience member's emotions go, so do those around him. This guy, from Dan's vantage point on stage, was not having a good time.

He wasn't getting into Dan's act, no matter what magic he performed. Dan never reached him. Dave's energy affected Dan and the whole show. Dan was packing up his stuff at the end and beating himself up for not reaching him. He felt like a failure. Dan then felt a tap on his shoulder. It was Dave, who looked him in the eye and said, "You're looking at a broken man. I'm right at the end of a year-long divorce and thanks to you I had the best night I've had in over a year."

Dan said, "Wow! It blew my mind because I thought I knew what he was thinking, but the opposite was true. Just because I thought I knew what was going on in his mind by his outer actions doesn't mean it's true."

Next time you feel like you've failed in reaching your "emotional keystone" student sitting front-row center, remember Dan's story. You don't know what's going on in this student's mind. **You don't know what challenges they are experiencing in their life at home, socially at school, or within themselves, regardless of what they display to you on the outside. In other words, take nothing personally.**

How to Use Humour in Dramatic Situations to Lighten the Moment

Emil Beheshti says, "Sometimes the way we get through difficult times in our life is through a very roundabout, unsuspecting, unplanned way that could come off to someone as comedic. When you look at a situation, it's funny to observe how we might resolve something because it's not normal all the time."

This is not meant to imply that we sit back in judgment and laugh at another person. Emil's statement is a way to laugh together, relating to others' vulnerabilities and human follies. As Emil puts it, "What's the human thing to do through this? What if this really happened to me? What would I really do, though? He goes on to say, "we're all just little kids inside and some of us have it a little more together than others."

How to Discover the Humour in Boring Material

Humour can make a boring subject interesting. Emil says, **"The key is to find something about it that is real to you, even if it's not common or if it's not something you've been through before."**

"Make it personal based on observations of life around you, your family, your friends, your neighbours, strangers, people you've worked with in the past."

If the material you're asked to work with seems boring to you, then "Sometimes you have to go absurd with it just to make it interesting. You have to make a really strong choice because there's nothing else that can be done with it," Emil points out. He concludes by saying the key is, "to find the truth in it and show the audience themselves. That's what we all want to see. We all want to be seen, like the message from *Avatar*. I want you to see me. I want to be seen. I think that's what life is."

When I've been asked to teach boring material, I look for words, sentences, topics, ideas or themes that stick out to me and zero in on that. In Teachers' College, I was asked to teach a Grade 8 Geography Unit. In a lesson demonstrating the distribution channels of Ontario food, I brought in an egg and proceeded to roll it along the whiteboard ledge.

Every few rolls of the egg, I stopped to explain what stage of the journey the egg was now at along its route to the local grocery store. When I reached the end of the distribution link, I asked, "What would happen if one of these distribution channels were eliminated?" I then crushed the egg under my foot like a glass under the groom's foot at a Jewish wedding. The students laughed in disbelief why I did that with the egg (though the custodians were not too happy with me.) An engaging discussion ensued in response to the question.

Self-Deprecating Humour Makes You Relatable

Jim Annan says, "What people find affable in someone is usually a character trait they find funny, or just someone's cadence or how they deliver the material or self-deprecation."

Jim, who also teaches Beginner's Level Improv at Second City, says, **"The teachers who are self-deprecating get you on their side. Not necessarily to be their friend." The teachers he loved let their human side show.**

This idea of deliberately knocking yourself down a peg seems to be a common suggestion brought up by those I interviewed. If a teacher can find ways to balance power showing they don't know everything or are superior or perfect, it can lead to a more open learning environment.

I look for small, unforced moments to make fun of myself. This doesn't always come easy for me. Thank students for correcting you.

Students appreciate humility in their teachers. **Self-deprecating humour. Humility lowers people's defenses.**

How Comedians' Favourite High School Teacher Inspired Them

Tom Rhodes's high school drama teacher, Mr. Martin, encouraged him to pursue his passion of wanting to be a comedian. He says, "Mr. Martin did the most brilliant thing. In the drama and speech class, there was a small stage in the center of the room. He gave me the first five minutes of every class to do a comedy routine. Every day, I would be thinking of jokes and I loved writing speeches for his class."

Tom says, "Some teachers were rubbed the wrong way by that. There were a couple of them who made me sit in the desk right in front of theirs so they could control me. I tried to wreak as much havoc on those teachers as possible, especially because they punished me before I did anything wrong. They were just going by my reputation."

Emil Beheshti has studied with some of the finest acting teachers in L.A. and New York and is developing an online acting class for fellow actors. He says he wants a teacher "to be very real. I don't want them to be better than me. I want them to nurture me, and I want them to show me things I haven't seen before."

Dan Trommater said of his favourite teacher, Neal Marshall, "I imagine he would've had a year or two of student teacher experience before we got him, but he was young and certainly passionate. **I don't recall any specific use of humour, though the entire attitude in the classroom was pretty light-hearted.**"

Dan recalls this teacher would prepare games for his class. "I remember pretty often we would play Jeopardy and he would've spent all this time coming up with questions and answers for whatever the topic was. It was all science. He spent enough time creating all these questions and answers on slips of paper that he would tape up on the board, and we would spend the class playing Jeopardy, the entire class."

"I think that really gets to the heart of it. **You don't necessarily have to worry about being funny, provided you can have an atmosphere of productive fun.** You want your audience to want to be there, to look forward to being there. If you can create an environment where at least some of the time, it's fun, it's going to be a lot easier."

What's Similar Between Great Teachers and Great Comedians

Tom Rhodes spoke about the *Great Courses* audio series where professors from around the world lecture on various topics from philosophy to history. "The Great Courses are really great, but there have been two of them that I stopped listening to because the teacher was not good. The teacher was monotone, boring, didn't have passion in what he was talking about."

> *"I'm not sure he had jokes, but by playing a game where people were allowed to have right answers and wrong answers, laughter would have been a part of it. Humour would have been a natural outcome of it. Whether it was funny or not, it was certainly fun."*

Tom paints a different picture of the teaching style of the Great Course he loved. "The guy who did the Voltaire course... had so much passion when he tells this story. I never get tired of it. **The passion with which this teacher is telling the story, I wish it was a movie, because the teacher is grabbing you by the heart and by your brain and making you care about this person."** [36]

Emil Beheshti thinks, "Good comedy directors allow actors freedom to try their interpretations of things, give them rehearsal, give them time to work things out, and let them find their voice. They know how to nurture their actors." He adds that comedy directors, "trust their actors, are their biggest fan, try it their way and listen to them. The director obviously has a vision, but there are a lot of humourous ways to present something. I think it's about affording someone the space to try it different ways."

Actor and Producer, Emil Beheshti in a scene from the film, Know Chance, 2002.

Successful comedic directors are, "very giving and very generous," Emil continues. They say things like, "Go ahead and try that. Try and keep building on that. Just tweak things here and there, reign things in, so it doesn't become the absurd unless you're going for the absurd. It's knowing when to rein them in a little bit and to keep it grounded in truth."

Dan Trommater infuses humour into his keynote presentations. As a former college teacher, he has a unique perspective on what attributes various types of performers have in common with teachers. He says, "Good magicians and teachers share, more than anything, passion. They both have to actually possess a love and a fascination for their subject matter. With that passion, it becomes apparent to the audience, whether it's a class or an audience, that there's something within the subject matter worthy of one's attention. Maybe I don't get it on the first day of class or the sixth week of class, but I can see in this person in front of me that there's something that's driven them to dedicate their life to this."

Dan builds on this point. "Beyond that, **I think good teachers and good magicians have a dedication to the preparation**. I want it to seem like when I step on stage, this is the first time I've said these things. I want it to feel fresh; I want it to feel authentic and exciting."

"I've spent countless hours labouring over magic, not only the script, but the coordination of that script with the physical actions and then the coordination of both of those things into interaction with the audience. Whether it's interacting with an audience from their seats or bringing somebody up on stage to take part in the magic. While hopefully [those moments] feel very spontaneous, they're prepared."

"Now, there may be deviations from script, but in my experience, if I have a script, it creates a safety net. If something unexpected comes up, then I have the freedom to deviate away from that script, and react to the moment."

"If there's a question that comes out of the blue, I can deviate away and deal with that question or concern or comment and then swing right back into that script pretty seamlessly. Without that preparation, there's just so much more left to chance, and I want to leave as little to chance as I can."

How to Tell a Story with Humour

"Humour is a great way to tell a memorable story," award-winning copywriter, Alex Brownstein says. [37] Integrating humour into the class is about storytelling, not about telling jokes. Filmmaker Jon Favreau says in an interview, "The laughter doesn't last if there is no story. Story is king. You think it's about the laughs, but really, it's about investing in the story and being drawn in." [38]

Telling an appropriate, passionate, story is not a risk; it's a revelation to teenagers. I've rarely regretted telling a story in class, even if it failed to get the response I hoped for. The response is only part of the point. The bigger picture is in showing another dimension of your humanity to your students. It keeps your students on their toes. One of my kids said, "I love coming into your class because I never know what to expect next."

Tom Rhodes is a storyteller. His comedy is rooted in his life experiences travelling the world. Tom spoke about real life stories being more valuable than well-written jokes for a comedian. The rise of narrative programs like *National Public Radio*, which produces the critically acclaimed, podcast, *This American Life*, is an example.

Mythology teaches us throughout human history, across every culture, people learn through metaphors. They learn through the power of archetypal characters, symbols, and story structures. Stories have the power to elicit a goose bump-inducing emotional response that the most impressive facts and figures cannot touch.

Students look forward to when I tell stories. It may be a welcome momentary redirection from the lesson of the day. Certain students feel more connected to the material and to the class when the teacher shares a brief anecdote. Some of my favourite teachers told vivid, hilarious tales that still resonate with me today.

Some of the accounts I share with students are in this book such as how I got the job working at *Saturday Night Live* or when I got Bono the Aung Sun Sui Kyi T-shirt on the night U2 performed on*SNL*. We can try out stories in multiple classes to see if they work or not as a comedian does. We can revise parts of a story to improve pacing, tone, body language, and style and decide what details we include and exclude.

Tom reveals something I found surprising and refreshing to hear from a performer who spends his life on stage making people laugh. He says the real stories he tells in his show now may not be the funniest thing he says in it, "but they seem to be what grab people the most. When I talk to people after the show, that's what they want to talk about, and that's the thing they remember the most."

Some teachers may think storytelling takes away from the lesson or makes it too hard to get students back on track. Both of these situations occur. It's worth the risk of doing because it creates another layer of connection to enhance the learning experience.

Personalizing the course material by infusing relevant anecdotes into the curriculum makes the content come to life for students.

When students whisper or look at each other after I tell a story, I give them a few extra moments to absorb it. There is power in the pause. Each teenager will relate to a story based on their life experiences, values they were taught growing up, biases, a mood, negative or positive social interactions that day or their level of emotional intelligence.

Rhodes says "It could be a great joke that got the biggest laugh of a show, but that isn't what people want to talk about. They go, 'Oh, the story you told about the hotel you stayed at in Hong Kong and the mishap you had with the goldfish… that was so funny and I had a similar story.'"

What if You're Not a Good Storyteller?

I believe it's a skill any teacher can develop. It's no different than developing presentation skills. **The number one point Tom suggests teachers can do to improve their storytelling is to "get to the point."** He says it comes with practice in "developing night after night and learning how to cut the fat off your piece of meat."

Teachers are in an ideal environment to practice what to leave in and what to leave out of their stories. I find the tale I tell in the morning often changes and improves by the afternoon. Musician, author, and TED speaker, Amanda Palmer, says she spent months honing the stories she included in her moving TED Talk, "The Art of Asking."

One story about a family of immigrants who provided her a bed to sleep on during her early journeys started out as a five-minute re-telling. She practised it over and over until she reduced it to ninety seconds without sacrificing the heart and emotion of the meaning. The final result is an emotional real-life incident told in a few masterful strokes born out of finding the time and putting in the effort of giving her audience a profoundly moving experience. [39]
Your students are your best feedback system.

Get to the Point and Eliminate Unnecessary Details

Tom recounts a story he was preparing to tell on stage. It was about when he lived in Amsterdam and he had a bicycle wreck. He landed on his face on the street and had to be on television the next day. He practiced telling the story to his wife. After Tom had told his wife the story many times, she said, "Why do you have to say the name of the department store? Nobody cares what the biggest one in Amsterdam is" I'm thinking, Dutch people who hear this story will know De Bijenkorf department store. She goes, 'Yeah, yeah, yeah, it's irrelevant. It's funny you went to a department store and not the hospital.'

Be Present and Listen

One strategy Rhodes suggests to integrate humour into a class is to encourage a funny comment a student makes. It will help them remember "that knowledge nugget for the rest of their life. Just stop and acknowledge that something is funny to them or the class."

Discourage Students From Coming Late with Magic and Humour

Dan Trommater says, "Before I became a magician, I taught photography. The magic I was learning and performing in the classroom was fairly beginner. I was a relatively new teacher, as well."

Dan says, "My first experience doing magic for something other than entertainment was in the classroom. **Every day before the first two minutes of class, I would do a trick. If they were there, they got to see the trick, and if not, I wouldn't do that trick for the rest of the semester. The students' tardiness rates plummeted. People wanted to see that trick!"**

Dan says he didn't use it as powerfully as it could've been used in terms of illustrating ideas or communicating concepts, but just simply getting people to show up on time and engage. He continues, "You don't need to be a magician to use magic. You can go to your local magic shop or to a virtual magic shop. A good place to start is watching magic tricks. You will find a huge range of quality. Most of the stuff you find on YouTube is going to be pretty terrible, but you'll be exposed to different magic that may tickle your fancy."

"Surprisingly," Dan said, "A great number of really good magic tricks are pretty simple to learn and execute. Also, a local public library is going to have any number of basic magic texts, magic for beginners type of books, that will have tricks which are simple to execute and more importantly, have the ability to have a message applied to them."

Humour is Play

In Daniel Pink's book, *A Whole New Mind*, he references a study by Researchers Shammi and Stuss that maintains that humour represents one of the highest forms of intelligence. It concludes that humour "embodies the ability to place situations in context, to glimpse the big picture, and to combine differing perspectives into new alignments." [40]

A "playfully light attitude is characteristic of creative individuals," author, Mihalyi Csikszentmihalyi tells us.[41] **Developing a sense of humour, Fabio Sala, of the Harvard Business Review, states, "reduces hostility, deflects criticism, relieves tension, improves morale, and helps communicate difficult messages."** [42]

Laughter is Healthy

Laughter is good for you, according to the studies in the book, *Laughter: A Scientific Investigation*. It has "aerobic benefits, activates the cardiovascular system, increases the heart rate, and pumps more blood to internal organs." Laugh researcher, William Fry found that it "took ten minutes of rowing on his home exercise machine to reach the heart rate produced by one minute of hearty laughter." [44]

Laughter can also decrease stress hormones and boost the immune system according to Lee Berk of the Center for Neuroimmunology at the Loma Linda School of Medicine. [45]

The greatest blessing of humour is that it relaxes tension. It is really indispensable in situations when there is nothing left but a big laugh". This was writer, Maria Popova's summary of Hungarian writer, Laszlo Feleki's essay, "Keeping Up with Science".

Jim Annan says improv is, "our natural way to learn and play and interact. That's why it's called playing. I guess it must be in the junior age, where it gets taken out of us from the lecture style of learning." [43]

Do a Yoga Laughing Break

As odd as this may sound, my students really like yoga in class. At the halfway point of most lessons, I stop what we are doing and ask the students to stand up. I lead them through yoga stretches or tai chi or breathing exercises. Recently I've combined yoga breathing with laughter to make laughter yoga, inspired by Dr. Kataria, who wrote an article entitled, "Laughter: The Best Medicine" and founded the Laughter Club in India. [46] At first, some students resist participating. They are self-conscious and think it's a little weird. By the second month of school, they ask for the yoga break if I forget to do it. Sometimes, it's the students who are most resistant on Day 1, that remind me to do it three months later.

This simple social activity can alter the mood of your class and re-focus students' attention. Tactile learners need to move when they learn with a social element attached. When a few students giggle, it's contagious. It turns out that people who have, "regular, satisfying connections to other people are healthier and happier," Neuroscientist, Robert Provine states in his book *Laughter: A Scientific Investigation*.

Yoga satisfies students' restlessness and their social needs within a class. **Studies have shown that attention dips by up to twenty percent in the last ten minutes of class.** This is especially true with classes that do not allow for breaks. By having a yoga-laughter break, teachers can help students rejuvenate themselves and thus, increase their focus in the last third of the class, especially the kinesthetic learners. Doing yoga in the class produces a light atmosphere. It gives the teacher a moment to model stepping out of her or his comfort zone and not taking herself or himself too seriously. It also balances the power for a moment between teacher and student. Everyone does the exercise together.

3 Resources to Encourage Humour Through Play and Exercise

1. **Start a Lunchtime Laughter Club**

2. Resource: Laughteryoga.org
    Take a Humour Test [48]

    "The test asks whether you use humour to cope and whether your friends consider you humorous. Thorson's research has found, "Those who score high on a multidimensional sense of humour scale have lower levels of depression and higher levels of purpose than those who score low in humour."

    Resource: Tinyurl.com

    Invent [49]

    The belief is that the best inventors are playful. The Smithsonian Institution's travelling, "Invention at Play" exhibit, "focuses on the similarities between the children and adults play and the creative processes used by innovators in science and technology and examines the various habits of mind that underlie invention."

    Resource: Inventionatplay.org

Humour is Respecting Your Audience

Dan Trommater says, **"There has to be a level of respect from the person on the stage to the audience. If there's not that respect, then there won't be the engagement."**

Dan continues, "I think it's particularly important in magic and in comedy. I never understood how comedians or magicians can get away with being disrespectful to an audience. It immediately puts up a barrier. I've walked out of shows based on disrespect for the audience."

How to Deal with Indifferent Reactions from an Audience

Tom Rhodes says, "You don't know what's going on with anybody's home life. In recent years, I'll look at them and now I feel sorry for that person. It used to be I would be on stage and think, "This is really a strong joke; this one will get him for sure." Then, you look back and that person still isn't laughing."

Joel Osteen says,

"25% of people will not like you.

25% of people won't like you, but could be persuaded.

25% of people will like you a bit, but could be persuaded not to.

25% of people will like you and stand by you no matter what."

Pastor Osteen's division of how people respond to us is applicable to the make-up of the classes I've taught over my teaching career. Osteen concludes with the belief that, "Some people will not like you no matter what you do, so don't waste your time and energy trying to win them over."

Respect for a class is fundamental to a healthy classroom environment. There are classroom situations when a rude student needs to be put in their place when they attempt to embarrass a fellow student or show up a teacher in front of the class. What's the best way to respond? Ignore minor slights. Refuse to fight most battles.

Students watch what teachers do more than what they say.

My teacher mentor, Jim Barry, suggests some of the following strategies in dealing with various negative behaviours of students:

What Do You Do if a Student Tells You to F*** off

"It's happened, not a lot. I haven't always been as polite as I should have been there. I'd probably walk down the aisle and say, 'What!' It happened a couple of times. Well, I wouldn't react very politely. I'd get through the idea that that's not appropriate talk. I think I ejected one kid that I can remember immediately."

Learn How to Address a Student Who Says Something Derogatory About a Group of People

Jim Barry says, "You call it. It sometimes can be a learning experience. That's all I can tell you. I think you'll know what to do. I remember teaching, *Merchant of Venice*, I wasn't even sure I knew this. Someone asked if shylock meant money-grubber. Someone else said, "all Jews are money-grubbers." I said, 'No, you don't make generalizations, like that.' I tried to treat it academically. I said, 'Shakespeare's time was anti-Semitic and he may have been anti-Semitic, but look at where this play is going. He seems to feel pity for Shylock.

He has Shylock saying, 'Hath not a Jew's eyes...' I think Shakespeare was honestly trying to do something about it. You do your best but that's when you truly earn your stars when you handle that right." [50]

Dan Trommater adds, "If there is that respect and kindness and sort of a sense that we're all in this together, then you can get away with a lot. My technique is good, but if I make a mistake, I can get away with a lot if the audience is on my side."

Master teacher and author, Jim Barry and I

Humour Happens When You Let Go of Some Control

Tom Rhodes talks about a science teacher whose class he loved walking into each day. He said his science teacher, "treated science like it was the greatest television show in the world. He let other people be funny. He let other people find ways of what was so great about science. He would say, "Chuck, in the back, you've got a silly observation about it, let's hear it."

Tom says, **"You can't be a dictator who has to have everything your own way because you can't control a classroom 100% any more than I can control a nightclub full of drunk people."**

It's liberating and refreshing to give students the power to figure out problems and provide solutions for themselves with the teacher as facilitator.

What to Tell Yourself After Failing to Reach Students

Tom says he always has to "be his own best corner man." He said, "You've got to be inside your own head as you're making mistakes, as you're losing the crowd. The voice in the back of your head has to be telling you, 'Get off the ropes, champ, keep jabbing, keep sticking, okay, give him this, give him that. You can't give up.'"

I've always struggled with this. Now, I look at it from a growth mindset. Did I learn something from this class? What would I do differently next time? **I give myself some credit for trying new ideas because the only way I can grow as a teacher is if I experiment and continue to learn new teaching strategies, and apply them in class.**

It's a really bad habit you have to break yourself of. Rhodes continues, "It's a bad mistake every performer makes to look at the person who's not enjoying the show. Even if you do that, which everybody does, certain people are unreachable, and that's their family, education or economic situation. That's their problem, not mine. Now when I see that person is not laughing, I feel bad for [them], it's their own issue."

Author and renowned speaker, John Gray says, "It's not up to me to convince anyone of anything", when he's giving a talk.[51] The late great, Wayne Dyer summed it up in a similar way in his book, *Erroneous Zones,* **"If there are a hundred people in the room watching me, that's a hundred different perceptions, opinions and biases about my performance, about me."** He follows this up with the mantra, "Nothing will get to me today, not an insensitive slight or a dirty look!" Nothing! [52]

Humour in Body Language

Mark Bowden suggests teachers can immediately shift how they move, gesture, and use their hands to build confidence. He also says teachers can teach these tips to students prior to their class talks. When guiding teenagers to deliver parts of a talk infused with humour, Mark offers these tips: "Open palms at belly height, allow them to gesture as much as they like. All of that will provoke good eye contact. So, rather than starting with the eyes, I would be starting with the hands."

Mark says to, "Allow students to gesture and speak with their hands, but try and get those hands up at belly height, which is the truth plane or even chest height, which is the passion plane. They'll come across as sincere and genuine if they're at that belly height. They'll come across as energized and passionate if they're at that chest height.

Humour Builds Confidence

He also discusses how a teacher can lead a student to move in front of a class to increase their confidence in a light-hearted talk. "Have them practise walking in front of the class and deciding where to stand and staying there. Help students make a decision about where to stand. If you can settle the simplest thing, what you get is a cascade of others working naturally."

Bowden also talks about where to stand in a classroom during a presentation. "Can I get you to practice walking and standing and taking space? Not standing near furniture or the table or the desk or not standing close to things, really standing in a way where you're taking up a lot of space, because if you were a confident person you'd be taking up space. Can you help them perform like a confident person, even though they may not psychologically be confident?"

Mark goes on to say, **"Rather than try and teach them a mindset and say, 'Hey, you should be more confident about this, your work is great, be confident,' you go, 'Yeah, your work is great, but I can totally understand why you'd be very, very nervous and a little bit self-conscious about this.** Here's what we'll do, let's practise performing like a confident person. You get them to perform like a confident person and believe me; they're going to start feeling confident really, really quick."

Make Eye Contact with an Audience like a Comedian

Every speaker I interviewed said eye contact is essential for connection with your audience. Tom Rhodes describes why it's so crucial for a teacher. **"When I'm on stage, I look everyone in the eye. At one point during the performance, I will look each person in the eye. It's just like real life. When you look people in the eye when you're speaking, the words come out of your mouth more naturally.** There's a certain sincerity that comes out of what you're trying to convey just by the simple gesture."

Author, John Gray said when he first started teaching, he would find himself "making eye contact with the two people in the room who didn't like what he had to say. **After many years, [he] realized those two people were mirroring back to him his inner critic." Once he became more at peace with himself, he started focusing on the eighteen people in the room who liked what he had to say.**

I can relate to Gray's early mindset in front of students. Sometimes, I still focus on the two students in the room who may not be responding to what or how I'm teaching. They are students who have their arms crossed or head on their desks or look up at the clock every three minutes. Tom Rhodes said, "This is something every comedian is guilty of. **You can be on stage killing it, everyone in the place is loving you, and there's one person not laughing, and you will keep looking back at that person. Did that joke get them? I still try and combat that."**

Encouraging Words for a Student Who Doesn't Fit in

The comedians and professional speakers I spoke to did not fit in to the educational system. Sometimes they misbehaved and were considered class clowns, overly talkative and troublemakers.

Tom Rhodes says, "It's the rebels who don't fit in that are the ones who eventually change the world, or whatever chosen field that they get in to. I didn't fit in. **The fact that a few specific teachers liked me and believed in me and showed faith in me, kind of helped me more than going to university.** I love biographies. Voltaire didn't fit in to the Jesuit school. He was into aesthetic beauty and learning beyond what curriculum was being forced on him. It's the rebels who make all the important, memorable art in the world."

Emil Beheshti says he would tell a student who doesn't feel like he or she belongs to, "Invest in yourself because no one else will, and believe. If you believe it, others will believe it, too, and that'll be infectious."

Jim Annan reflects on the encouraging words he may offer a student who doesn't feel that he or she fits in. "Follow what you want to do. Don't settle. Some people just want the stability, and that's what they crave and that could be what their passion is. You never know where your passion is going to lead you. It may not be a logical conclusion or where you thought you were going to be, but it most likely will lead you to where you should be."

Dan Trommater's advice to a student who may feel different or out-of-place is to "Do it. The world is full of normal, by definition. The world needs more people who are not normal. More than what the world needs, what you need is paramount. I spent the first two years of my university education studying science. It was something I was good at; I enjoyed it… but I certainly wasn't passionate about it. It wasn't until I discovered photography, which coming from a very small town, certainly wasn't seen as a normal way to make a living. It wasn't until I found [magic] that I found a passion, something I was excited about."

Dan adds, "If you find something that is exciting, whether that be juggling or magic, speaking or accounting if you're excited by it— that's where to put your energy. Not because you think it will lead to a good job or not because it will lead to stability or predictability. I've seen far too many people go through four years of university for a subject that they weren't passionate about, only to spend three years in the workforce, peter out, and go back to school for what they actually care about. There's no sense wasting that time. If you have something that you're passionate about, follow that passion; the money will follow."

Mr. Martin, Tom Rhodes' favourite high school teacher, gave the comedian the first five minutes of each class to tell his jokes to "get it out of his system." Tom said he would sit there and have "complete loyalty to this guy for the remaining of the class. **I was the most well-mannered child imaginable because this guy believed in me. He let me have my little moment."**

In dealing with students with special personalities, "find out what their dream is and encourage them to follow that path."

CHAPTER THIRTEEN SUMMARY

ACTION STEPS

HOW TO USE HUMOUR IN YOUR CLASSROOM LIKE FAMOUS COMEDIANS, TED SPEAKERS, MAGICIANS, BODY LANGUAGE EXPERTS, IMPROV ARTISTS, COMEDY WRITERS AND SITCOM ACTORS

On Balancing the Power in the Classroom

☑ On Day 1, sit in a group on the floor with your students. Tell the students if they fail, they are to blame the teacher since he's the expert. Then they laugh and relax. This approach lowers the teacher's status physically but raises his/her actual status since only a very confident and experienced person would put the blame on him/herself.

☑ If a student fails, a teacher could say to him/her privately, "Be patient with me. I'll explain I'm not perfect" and continue to try new ways to reach them.

☑ Make fun of yourself for mispronouncing words or small mistakes you make in class.

☑ Use the improv game, "Yes and…" to open a lesson.

☑ Create Tea and Cookie Feedback Sessions through "My Favourite Podcasts" or videos.

☑ I invite students during their study period to come into class and hear which of their posts on the annotation unit is my favourite. Attendance is high during these sessions.

- ☑ Take the class to an outdoor space to act out a scene
- ☑ Experience and demonstration over instruction: Paint impressionist paintings in the school's garden in a lesson about European Impressionists in a History class
- ☑ Guest speakers via Skype
- ☑ Ask yourself: Have I created a learning space that's socially safe?
- ☑ Tell students you welcome them disagreeing with you as it shows they are thinking. This models for them how to respectfully disagree. The first student who tests you on this, walk your talk. Smile, pause for a moment and listen to their disagreement.
- ☑ Ask students a question and patiently clarify your point. If they make a good point, tell them so, even revising your initial statement. This moment will be observed closely by the whole class and immediately neutralize some of the know-it-alls in the class.
- ☑ Use open body language like open palm gestures at belly height.
- ☑ Ask yourself the following questions to do this:
- ☑ Do I have to sit behind a desk?
- ☑ How can I be more open to a student when I'm talking to him/ her?
- ☑ When I'm demonstrating something or when I'm talking in front of the class, how can I keep my body language open?
- ☑ What's your proximity like? If you're too close, you might be overbearing. If you're too far away from them, you're not socially linked to them.
- ☑ Try reacting to the first student who swears like this: Say, "What did you say?" Break the tense silence by saying, "Don't ever say the word 'the' in this class again? Or comment on any other harmless word other than the swear word. The student and the surrounding teens will break out in laughter. This kind of response shows students you have a sense of humour while pointing out inappropriate language.

- ☑ Teenagers sometimes giggle when they feel uncomfortable by what they have heard or the situation in which they find themselves. React compassionately, not reactively to these giggles.
- ☑ Elicit humour by learning a basic magic trick on Youtube as a class opener.
- ☑ Don't always judge a student's reaction by his/her stoic expression. You don't know what challenges a student is facing in his/ her life at home, socially, at school or within themselves. In other words, take nothing personally.
- ☑ Make a dull subject interesting but find something about it that is interesting to you.
- ☑ For example, look for a particular sentence, topic, idea or theme that sticks out to you and zero in on that.
- ☑ Try giving the class clown, the first few minutes of class to put on a show one day a week. This approach turned Mr. Martin into Tom Rhodes' favourite teacher and lifelong mentor.
- ☑ The performers interviewed said their favourite teacher did the following:
- ☑ Found creative and appropriate class outlets for the class clown
- ☑ Acted real and didn't show they were better than him
- ☑ Nurtured him
- ☑ Showed him things he hadn't seen before
- ☑ Designed a pretty light-hearted environment in the class
- ☑ Modeled a self-deprecating attitude
- ☑ Proposed productive fun assignments
- ☑ Exhibited passion for their subject matter
- ☑ Expressed an aliveness, rather than a monotonous tone of voice
- ☑ Personalized the course material by infusing relevant anecdotes into the opening part of the unit.

How to Tell a Story with Humour:

1. Get to the point

2. Eliminate unnecessary details
   - ☑ When a student makes a harmless or witty remark, be present and acknowledge it. This moment will surely help them and the class remember and connect to the topic at hand.
   - ☑ Discourage students from coming late by learning a few simple magic tricks and performing them right at the beginning of class. If students were there, they got to see the trick. If they were late, they missed it. Students wanted to see the tricks, so tardiness rates plummeted.
   - ☑ In recent scientific studies, laughter has been shown to have aerobic benefits, activate the cardiovascular system, increase the heart rate and pump more blood to internal organs.
   - ☑ It takes ten minutes of rowing on a home exercise machine to reach the heart rate produced by one minute of hearty laughter.
   - ☑ Laughter can decrease stress hormones and boost the immune system.
   - ☑ Do a yoga laughing break or just yoga during the mid-point of each class.
   - ☑ Start a laughter club. www.laughteryoga.org
   - ☑ Take a Humour Test
   - ☑ Invent
   - ☑ Avoid publicly putting down students with sarcastic remarks or condescending tones.
   - ☑ Model appropriate adult responses to inappropriate behavior in class.
   - ☑ If a student swears at you, walk down the aisle and say, "What!" Then eject the student from the class immediately.
   - ☑ If a student makes an inappropriate comment about a group of people, call out the statement immediately by saying, "No, you don't make generalizations like that." You do your

best. That's when you truly earn your stars when you handle that right.

☑ Let the students find ways to make the subject meaningful. Let students find the humour in the subject matter at hand, encouraging them to share their observations, both serious and silly.

☑ Give yourself some credit for trying something new in class because the only way you grow as a teacher is if you experiment and continue to learn and apply new teaching strategies.

☑ If you have 20 students in your class, you will have 20 different perceptions, opinions and biases about you.

☑ When you're telling a story with humour, do your best to make eye contact with as many students as possible. Don't focus on the one or two students who are not enjoying your story. Make more eye contact with the students who are engaged.

☑ Most of the comedians and professional speakers I interviewed did not fit into the educational system.

☑ In dealing with students with special personalities, find out what their dream is and encourage them to follow that path.

CHAPTER FOURTEEN

"It felt kind of like final exams every week, because the time from coming up with a skit to performing seemed like it happened so quick."

Martin Short on performing on Saturday Night Live

GUIDE ON THE SIDE

Here's a Quick Way to Create Learning Environments Like SNL and Pixar

At SNL and its sister companies, I felt like Charlie Chaplin's character, The Tramp. He always seemed to have one foot in the cinematic frame, always on the periphery, never quite a part of any one particular group. This gave me a unique perspective as I got the chance to observe colleagues at different levels of the company interact and work with each other.

In my three and a half years in Manhattan, I worked in seven different departments for five bosses in Broadway Video, Burly Bear Network, Saturday Night Live Films, and *Saturday Night Live.* Being perpetually the new kid in the class heightened my sense of group dynamics much quicker than if I had one secure, complacent position working for just one section.

One advantage was I met some generous mentors, who had been with *Saturday Night Live* and its companies for many years. I asked questions like: what was the environment like in the early days amongst the players who would become comedy legends? I've put together what I've learned both directly and indirectly about what has made *Saturday Night Live's* collaborative environment produce a show that has persevered for four decades. Also, I've outlined what teachers can make note of and apply to their classrooms from my experiences. What I learned shifted me from the sage on the stage to the curiosity-cultivating guide on the side.

The structure of the workweek at *Saturday Night Live* has stayed the same since 1974. It has deadlines that keep all members of the cast and crew on their toes. Every member of the team has responsibilities they focus on. The writers are the foundation of the show. They submit their sketches to the actors who move between penning sketches for themselves and forming strategic partnerships with writers who have the power to choose to write for them or another actor.

The costume designers jump into the action once the first round of sketches are cleared for air. The producers do everything from finding the show's host and musical guests to managing the internal conflicts that exist within the cast and crew. Finally, there is the Executive Producer, Lorne Michaels, who oversees all aspects of the show. Some of his responsibilities include the read-through of proposed sketches to what ultimately goes on live on Saturday night.

I explain to my students that every week at *Saturday Night Live* is like studying for a final exam. I've included a weekly schedule of the creative process of *Saturday Night Live*. I sometimes reference it when I ask students to do collaborative work within challenging deadlines.

THE STRUCTURE OF THE WEEKLY COLLABORATIVE PROCESS AT SNL[57]

MONDAY

On Monday, the research department provides everyone with a bio on the week's host. Writers assemble in Lorne Michaels' office along with the host to pitch sketch ideas for the upcoming week.

This is the beginning of the collaborative process. It brings the whole team together to hear what the target of this week's show is. The objective is to write for the host of this week's episode.

On Sunday, prior to the Monday meeting, individual writers and performers begin to formulate ideas for sketches they will bring to the Monday meeting. Brainstorming is not nearly as efficient if it starts at the group stage for a few reasons as summarized by Mikael Cho: fear of judgment from people in positions of power and extroverts take center stage. Groups prefer safe, practical ideas over novel concepts. [58] **According to a study conducted in the *Journal of Personality and Social Psychology* by Michael Diehl and Wolfgang Stoebe, there is a measurable productivity loss in brainstorming groups. It must first begin with individuals coming up with their own ideas they then bring to the group.** [59]

Everyone on staff needs to learn who the host is to be on the same page in terms of expectations. When the cast and the writers hear each other's ideas, it may trigger competition and motivate members of the team to push themselves.

This relates to the classroom, in that it's crucial for the teacher to define clearly the learning goal or objective. What is the target of the lesson? What do we want the students to learn by the end of this unit? What are the learning outcomes? How can we connect that goal to specific expectations in our Course Curriculum? I like to provide examples of prior students' work. When writers hear each other's pitches, it stretches them to work harder. Examples of work at varied levels helps kids understand how to start. When a student is stuck about where to begin, advise them to just start anywhere. It also moves them to reach higher and try harder.

Having a new host each week brings in fresh energy, ideas, and enthusiasm. I see each new class unit as a new host, with each one representing a chance to start anew. The more genuine enthusiasm and clarity I begin with on the first day of a unit, the smoother it seems to go. Similarly, it can be a challenge to convince the new host of ideas for new sketches. **One strategy to earn confidence from students from day one is to tell them why they are learning and what tangible knowledge and skills they will gain.**

TUESDAY

"You write all Tuesday night and then they pick only thirty of the forty sketches. Then, they whittle that down to fourteen and then six more get cut. Only about eight or nine sketches make it to air. It was competitive... it just was the way it worked."
– Jon Lovitz [60]

The writers work all day and night creating sketches for the next day's read-through. Meanwhile, the host shoots a series of promos with one or two members of the cast. These promos will be posted on nbc.com and air on the network.

New technologies have not replaced hard work and deliberate practice. At *Saturday Night Live*, the cast and crew spend all Tuesday night writing and rewriting sketches for that week's show. They rarely, if ever, leave the 17th floor during the period of time when they're working on the initial individual and development phase of sketches for the next day. Lorne Michaels and his producers will tell writers and actors to go into one of the writer's offices and not come out until they have come up with sketches.

What I took from this to my teaching career, is the importance of emphasizing hard work, daily effort, and consistency as the essential learning habits of successful students. What a strong work ethic looks like in a classroom and during a student's home studying is not obvious to some teenagers. I sometimes reference *Saturday Night Live's* schedule when I speak with students about the importance of time management in their study habits during intense workloads.

I will show students how to break down their study time into twenty-minute chunks with five-to-ten-minute breaks over a concentrated period. During the study time, there are to be no distractions.

During the breaks, students are encouraged to do yoga stretches, eat something light, or take a power nap. The key is depth, not breadth. A recent article by Tim Metz on *Saentproductivity. com*showed the most productive professionals in organizations work for fifty-two minute intervals with seventeen-minute breaks. They are not the hardest workers; they are the smartest ones who don't do activities to the point of exhaustion. By pacing themselves they accomplish more in ten minutes than an overly stressed, burnt out colleague accomplishes in an hour.[61] The twenty minutes on/five-minute break is a teenage version of this.

Will Ferrell questioned the necessity of continuing the Tuesday night all-nighter. He did not see the point in carrying on a tradition that resulted in eventual enervation for some cast and crew members.

Focusing on a priority project for an evening is an effective way to teach students to zero in on one chunk of a project at a time. What does this have to do with group collaboration? Students need to come prepared to class by doing their own research at home. They can then present their ideas to their group.

The creation period should be separate from the editing time. Some of my students write one line and say, "Is this good?" This movement back-and-forth between creating and editing is less productive than writing the first draft quickly, without self-judgment. Once the first draft of a project is complete, the creator can give themselves space and distance from the task. Then, they can move on to the editing phase. On *Saturday Night Live*, the writers had only a short window over the course of a week to separate creating from editing, but the division still occurred.

WEDNESDAY

The cast, writers, crew, and the host gather in a conference room for a three-and-a-half-hour session. They read thirty-five to forty sketches out loud. Lorne Michaels plays the role of the narrator. After the read-through, the host gives his/her input on the sketches to Michaels, the head writers, and the production team. The number of sketches to be performed in the broadcast is narrowed down to around eleven. After the meeting, the cast and writers go into Lorne's office to look at the corkboard on his wall to see what sketches have been chosen.

The read-through is the first test to see what sketches will work for the audience and which ones fall flat. Lorne Michaels provides the final evaluation. Writers and cast members provide peer-to-peer feedback. Laughs were a good sign; silence was discouraging. It made each writer and cast member realize it was up to them to get themselves and their work on the show and fight to keep their job. One secret to a writer's longevity on the show was how they handled feedback and rejection of his/her sketches.

The read-through is equivalent to a student's rough draft of a paper. I make sure there are opportunities for students to do peer-to-peer read-throughs. Checklists provide guidance. Students receive class time to re-work the written component of an oral presentation. If the rough work is off base, the time to revise it is during the initial read-through. I tell students that young people should fail often when they are young to learn from their mistakes quickly and early.

When a student proposes a new idea or a radical approach to a topic, the teacher's response is always, "Yes. Do it. Go for it." SNL writers who have written something too conceptual or edgy or cleverly subversive can end up seeing their sketch excluded from the roster of that week's show. It was a private victory if fellow writers received a sketch well, even if it didn't make it to airtime. Knowing one was growing as a writer helped them survive the comedy equivalent of a dog-eat-dog world. This is an example of the growth mindset - seeing effort and improvement as a personal victory detached from outcome. Hard work and learning from mistakes usually lead to improvements. In the search for answers, students' curiosity can lead to better questions and new directions.

THURSDAY

The selected sketches are re-written to produce a final draft. Meanwhile, rehearsals begin for the non-sketch parts of the show. The sets and costumes for the week's sketches are designed and assembled.

Hemingway said, "The first draft of anything is s***." [62] This crass truism can be applied to the initial ideas of any assignment from English to Math. There's no such thing as writing, just re-writing. The *Saturday Night Live* creative process is no different. What starts out as a raw idea on Monday afternoon is transformed into a barely recognizable polished sketch within days of its conception. This evolution of an idea, through painstaking, tedious, roll-your-sleeve-up-park-your-seat-on-the-chair actually works.

The lesson here is students who are used to a world of instant, daily gratification need to experience what it takes to develop a skill. Academy-Award winning screenwriter of *Traffic*, Stephen Gaghan says, **"It takes time, patience, and giving yourself a break to not be a genius overnight."** [63]

An intriguing question to ask students during their revision process might be, "Is that the best you can do?" The students may interpret this as a challenge to push themselves further. Depriving teenagers of immediate acknowledgment can lead them to the intrinsic desire to stretch and develop on their own. Former Secretary of State, Henry Kissinger, asked this question three times to one of his aides. The young man broke down in frustration the third time he was asked. "Yes, it is the best I can do." At that point, Kissinger accepted the research he had requested. "Now, I will take a look at it." [64]

Students can provide suggestions to other group members' work based on a checklist provided by the teacher. The unsung heroes of *Saturday Night Live* are the costume and set departments.

They spring into motion to magically create different worlds and transform actors into characters like the President of the United States, or a caveman.This segmentation of responsibilities can apply to a productive student group, as well. **Define specific roles so each learner is clear on their part.**

My mentor, Jim Barry, had a simple solution to the problem of figuring out exactly what each student did on a group assignment. He asked each member to draw a pie chart indicating the amount of work they did with only a description of their contributions. By reporting in at the end of a group project, no member should feel they are betraying any other member. The teacher can then determine each person's contribution to the work.

FRIDAY

The rewriting of sketches continues. The process of blocking the scenes for the camera begins. The blocking is when the host and the actors walk through the set-up of each one. Actors go over where they will get their make-up done. De-facto booths have been set up to make costume changes between commercial breaks.

The blocking process can be applied to the classroom. In classes that require an intricate use of technology or pre-assembled classroom set-up, a rehearsal may be necessary. U2 does a run-through in the empty stadium the day before a concert. A TED speaker practices on the stage he'll speak on to make sure he hits the key points and makes sure he sticks to the eighteen-minute time limit. In a school presentation, it's helpful to do a run-through a period ahead of time if my room is available. If it's not, I rehearse the day before or during lunch hour. I find a practical way to do a run-through is to write the learning target and a point-by-point breakdown of the key components of the class. I have the technology up and ready to go and the window open for some fresh air before the students enter the room. I meet them at the door, greeting and guiding them to their places.

SATURDAY

Before every show, there is the dress rehearsal, in which all the sketches being considered for the final cut are aired in front of a live audience. This type of real world rehearsed practice takes the blocking run-through to another level. In order to be considered for the show, every performer and writer must treat the practice like the actual production until they are told that their sketch has been cut.

"I observed Lorne Michaels cut portions of a sketch or reorder the sequences. He was like a surgeon – very quick, very smart." – Host Gary Shandling on Michaels' process of selecting sketches.

Cast and crew are on their toes to perform at their best. This structure, as stressful as it is for the performers, pushes the cast and crew to visualize and execute the show as if it is the final. The show airs on Saturday night from 11:30 p.m. to 1:00 a.m., followed by the after party.

The more complex the classroom set-up, the more essential it is to have a dress rehearsal prior to the class. When I use technology, I see how long it takes for all of the technical details to work. I take notes on how long the computer takes to turn on, what may or may not pop up on the screen unexpectedly, how much time the Wi-Fi takes to load the images and what type of speakers I need to ensure students can hear the media correctly. I will test the sound of the speakers and seek out help from a student prior to the class to make sure I know which cords go where. My version of the dress rehearsal helps me to get a realistic grasp on the time chunks needed to execute each aspect of my lesson. This process goes beyond visualization. It irons out the parts that fall flat when they are practiced and in creating smooth transitions between the opening, the body and the conclusion of the lesson.

The Secret of Successful Group Bonding

When I first started teaching, I let students work together with whomever they wanted most of the time. It created an environment where peer-to-peer isolation of some students occurred. When I reflected on what was happening, I changed my approach. Now, I select the members of each group. This arrangement avoids cliques and cronyism. It also enables students who may not otherwise have gotten the chance to know each other to work together. Two teenagers previously unfamiliar with each other may form a mutual respect and make a new friend. In Broadway Video, BBN and*Saturday Night Live,* I felt myself instinctively seeking out a few allies to bond with.

When I didn't find these individuals right away, a sort of anxiety set in. I felt alienated and out-of-place. I think students feel the same way. If I choose the groups carefully, savvy partnerships increase the quality of their efforts and make their learning experience more meaningful. The challenges they face in tackling the assignment are more manageable with someone they look forward to working with.

I do my best to balance each group based on social intelligences and learning styles. There is not one ideal way to match groups perfectly. I get to know the students and adapt the groups throughout the year based on my observations. Each team member feels there is a task within the group that plays into their abilities and talents. This elevates their confidence that they are making a significant contribution. Ideally, a member of their group can support them with the tasks in which they are weaker. The result is a symbiotic partnership, not just a group of individuals performing separate tasks.

See Failure as a Challenge to Grow

Failure can lead to self-reflection and growth. Success can result in complacency and lack of drive. At *Saturday Night Live*, most of the star players had to go through weekly rejection. They had to put out new work in front of their peers every week. They were only as valuable to the show as their last at-bat, as the baseball saying goes. This kept the cast and crew on edge and created an air of competition, where only the thick-skinned persevered.

I try to reframe failure for students as an opportunity to grow and a challenge to push themselves to new heights. The hope is the students will learn resilience in that if something doesn't work out, it won't define them. It's just valuable information to learn from. Students can withdraw into a shell when their ideas are rejected by their peers. One way to pre-empt this is to have them define their vision at the beginning of a project. During every meeting, one student reads the group's "essential intent." [65] It reminds the group why they are doing this project – whether it's for an academic purpose or a charity committee. If every idea is filtered through the lens of this consensus vision, then individual ideas not accepted by the group can be recontextualized. This way, team members don't feel the rejection of their ideas is personal.

A former student e-mailed me devastated that a professional app developer had already created an app he thought was his original idea. I told him the important thing to do is to keep creating. I also told him not to put too much weight on one project being the be-all-and-end-all. I worked for two Toronto International Film Festivals and spoke with some extraordinary filmmakers. One of them was John Blair, the Academy-Award Documentary Winner for *Anne Frank Remembered*. He said he had twenty project ideas. Three went into production and only one was a success. I told this student that in finding out this app had already been created, he learned the process of coding and app creation that are two invaluable skills that will last much longer than a project he created in high school.

In the book, *Talent is Overrated*, Geoffrey Colvin writes about Amadeus or The Beatles failing early and often. They began imitating other artists before breaking through with an authentic voice. After years of toil and practice, they are heralded as overnight successes. [66]

Mike Myers recalls one of the secrets to Conan O'Brien's success, when they worked together as writers on *Saturday Night Live*. "He'd always give you great, positive encouragement, but he also had an eye on how to make something better."

Give young women and men encouragement and then offer particular ways they can improve. **From both my anecdotal observations in eleven years in the classroom and in reading educational studies that back it up, both boys and girls respond**

more favourably to specific encouragement of their effort, not on their outcome. Complimenting only positive outcomes may give a student the impression that your approval is conditional based on performance.

Constructive feedback works well when effort and positive aspects of the activity are acknowledged first. This approach lowers defenses and opens up students to see that you are fair and empathetic. **Negativity erects a wall; positive feedback builds a bridge.**

In his study of failure as a valuable form of feedback, journalist Shane Snow writes, "Crucially, experts tended to be able to turn off the part of their egos that took legitimate feedback personally when it came to their craft, and they were confident enough to parse helpful feedback from incorrect feedback. But when we do that, feedback becomes much more powerful."

Learning how to take feedback objectively is relevant for teachers because we find ourselves constantly being judged and evaluated by administrators, government officials, parents, students and colleagues. I feel that as a teacher, the more skilled I become at honestly reflecting on my mistakes without dwelling on them, the more impact I will have as a teacher and role model for my students.

Snow provides an example in his book, Shortcuts, from the world of comedy of how to extricate the lessons from negative feedback without being defensive or interpreting the statements about one's performance as offensive. "The Second City improv group where many Saturday Night Live stars such as Tina Fey, Dan Aykroyd and Seth Meyers received their training, teaches its students to take [failures] in stride, to become scientists who see audience reaction as commentary on the joke, not the jokester. To turn off the part of their brains that says 'I fail' when they get negative feedback."

The legendary improv group re-frames failure, defined as a fixed, unalterable result, in to feedback or information useful to help a person grow. This process is repeated "hundreds of times a week." The actors learn how to "fail fast" and how to re-frame the uncomfortable feedback as input – "without taking it personally," Snow observes.

In summarizing the ideas of psychiatrist and brain researcher Daniel Amen, on the subject of seeing failure as an opportunity to get better, author Brian Johnson writes:

"Daniel Amen talks about a similar idea in his new book Change Your Brain, Change Your Life where he says: 'Do you learn from your failures or ignore them? New brain-imaging research suggests that when some people fail their motivation centers become more active, making it more likely they will be able to learn from their experience. When others fail the brain's pain centers become more active—it literally hurts—making it more likely they will do whatever they can to avoid thinking about the episode, which means they are more likely to repeat the mistake. Learn from your mistakes and use them as stepping stones to success.' Dr. Amen tells us we need to get CURIOUS not furious." From a humourous perspective, it may also be a reminder to take what we do as educators seriously, but not ourselves.

Bring Back Alumni to Tell Their Stories

In my SOLE Student Leadership Seminar, I ask alumni to make actionable and inspiring presentations on the next steps they have taken out of university. In one instance, my former student, David Kornhauser, for whom I helped secure an internship, created a 7-step action-plan based on how to organize a human rights campaign. He developed this while interning for the Human Rights Action Center in D.C. Sometimes, students respond differently to an inspiring guest speaker than when they hear the same message you may have been giving them. One benefit of bringing back alumni is they understand the system in which the students are working. They can make direct connections to their experience when they were in school. This gives them a level of trust and credibility with students because they are seen as one of them.

In the late eighties and into the nineties, Lorne Michaels would invite writers from the first five years of *Saturday Night Live* to return to the show for a week. Former writer, Andy Beckerman said, "He didn't sense any tension and it was actually a great system because everyone came in knowing the show and knowing what Tuesday nights were like and what was expected after read-through and how Thursday nights worked and how rewriting worked."

The Power of Deadlines

Deadlines create a sense of urgency, cutting the rope, so there's no turning back. Right after I explain to my students what the assignment is and why the group is doing it, I make clear what the timeframe is for completion of the project. Deadlines are a critical part of bringing to mind the big picture. In a collaborative environment, it pushes participants to say, "Look, it's now or never, heightening their need to pull together to make their project happen." One way *Saturday Night Live* writers and actors met their emotionally exhausting deadlines was to stay in the same room until the work got done. Deadlines have the power to heighten the senses. Each participant is sharper and more focused.

> *"There was a bunker mentality. You know the siege of putting the show up each week. And so, ultimately, it was like college. It was a lot like the freshman year rooming experiences, where you don't necessarily get to pick your roommates, but you have to try and get along." David Mandel, former SNL writer*

Working in a group usually means a compromise. Five or so individuals, with different ideas, biases, agendas, and perspectives inevitably results in misunderstandings and wounded pride. Some members wanted to take over, control, and dominate the group. What I've learned is to fight almost no battles as a teacher with my students, their parents or administration. Every battle fought requires emotional energy that is draining and counter-productive. It takes discipline to walk away and to, "not just say the right thing in the right place, but far more difficult to leave unsaid the wrong thing in the tempting moment," [67] as Georges Augustus Henry Sala once said in most likely the right moment.

David Spade, former SNL actor said, "They say if you go with the flow, it's always better. That would be my recommendation to anyone going on the show: If you're going to go on, then just make fun of yourself and have a great time. **It is always endearing to watch someone make fun of themselves. To fight every possible sketch... is exhausting.**"

A deadline teaches students to deal with real-world situations. Work completed is better than half-finished potential that never sees the finish line. I always wondered about the cliché, "Eighty percent of life is showing up." I think it's also accurate to say, "Eighty percent of life is finishing a project on-time." Lorne Michaels said, **"We don't go on the air because the show's ready; we go on because it's eleven-thirty."**

On the day of a presentation, a few students inevitably are absent for various reasons. I make sure every student can present regardless of whether or not other members of the group are absent. I tell each student to bring their own USB with the slides or their own costume and notes. I sometimes quote former SNL star, Darrell Hammond, to students on the importance of preparation: "If you're hoarse, have the flu, didn't have time to prepare, didn't sleep well last night, feel depressed – too bad. It's eleven-thirty and it's live, so you've got to change your mental state."

How to Go from Sage on the Stage to Guide on the Side

A student on the fence can be swayed in favour of buying into an assignment fully when a teacher presents it in a way that models what pride and care look like in a classroom.

I tell students, like my mentor, Jim Barry told his students, to "take pride in their work." When teenagers work hard and immerse themselves into something that's memorable and meaningful, the process will increasingly matter as much to them as the product. Long-time producer on *Saturday Night Live*, Mike Shoemaker, explains the role of a producer on the show in a way teachers can directly learn from when overseeing group work in which certain assessment of learning outcomes need to be met.

"When you're a producer your job is talking to people and getting them to do things you want them to do and yet having them feel it's their choice and they're not being forced."

Tell the students why they are doing the project. Reference one or two specific expectations in the curriculum. Then, go right to both practical and emotional outcomes. Examples include achieving new skills they will learn through the process of creating this project. Tell them how they can gain confidence by stretching the possibility of what they thought they could do. Get them saying, "Yes," to every challenge instead of, "No, I can't."

I explain to them the expectations for the group project and, why they are doing it. I give them space to add or take away certain parts of the assignment, where appropriate, because these student-driven modifications add to their level of ownership of their work.

What happens if students do different projects or take diverse approaches? I tell them to work on their own but to find one element that is similar to the major group project.

"The plan of SNL is everyone – cast, writers, performers – they're all doing what they want to do and it's theirs and they own it, but at the same time, it is also what we want them to do. We have in some ways to make them feel it is theirs. We don't dictate things. **The show's like a stampede and I feel my job is to keep it going. When someone falls and is about to be trampled, you pick them up and dust them off and kind of send them on their way." – Co-Producer, Mike Shoemaker**

I've never liked group work. In Teachers' College, I found contributing creative, unconventional ideas to a group threatened some and turned off others. It made me hesitate to put ideas out there to the other group members if I felt they would shoot me a disapproving glare followed by an indifferent stare. So, I can relate to students who feel alienated by group work that doesn't take their learning styles into consideration prior to forming the groups. I realized that some class groups worked well and others were a disaster.

Why Do Some Groups Work Better than Others?

The trend seems to point to the importance of collaboration in order to solve complex, real-world problems. The thought being that trying to tackle a big problem as an individual is out-dated and counter-productive. I started reflecting on the way I compose groups in my class. It is not easy to create authentic and workable group projects. However, when you do assign group projects that work, it is classroom heaven.

Another kind of group work is making short films and TV commercials. Why is this type of joint project rewarding and enjoyable? The only way to make a good movie is to have a good team. A film production needs many talented people working together to create something much bigger than any one person can achieve.

There is the director (this is the teacher's role) whose vision and leadership guides the production like a conductor in an orchestra. The producer trouble-shoots all aspects of the production. The cinematographer is in charge of the look of the film. The writer's initial story provides the roadmap. The actors bring the words and story to life. The caterer makes sure the cast and crew have two meals a day plus snacks.

The people on the five short films I have directed consisted of many individuals I had met for the first time. I enlisted them from online film recruitment sites and through friends' recommendations. This combination of new collaborators with trusted friends who I had spent some time with working on previous films, seemed to work.

CHAPTER FOURTEEN SUMMARY

ACTION STEPS

GUIDE ON THE SIDE

☑ Productive brainstorming begins with individuals coming up with their own ideas they then bring to a group.

☑ Define precisely the learning goal or objective at the beginning of class. Along with clarifying the target during the first minutes of class, tell the students why they are doing this lesson today. What tangible skills will they learn? How does the experience connect to the bigger picture, the outcome of the unit? Why is this subject humorous and fascinating to you?

☑ Straightforward ways to do this include: writing it clearly on the board and providing examples of student work.

☑ 20-minute study intervals followed by 5-10-minute exercise breaks. Model productive chunking of study time by providing this amount of uninterrupted, structured time to complete brief assignments. Walk around the room making encouraging comments on their efforts, not on results.

☑ When a student proposes a new idea or unconventional approach to a topic, the teacher's response is, "Yes. Do it. Go for it!"

☑ I say to parents on the parent-teacher night at the beginning of the year to give your kids a break. Don't expect them to be geniuses overnight.

☑ A question to ask students during the writing revision process might be, "Is that the best you can do?" Say it in a non-judgmental, positive tone.

- ☑ To figure out exactly what each student did on a group assignment ask each person to draw a pie chart indicating the amount of work they did with a description of their contributions.
- ☑ Do a walk-through or rehearsal of classes that consist of complex technological set-ups ahead of time.
- ☑ When students get into groups for the first time in extra-curricular clubs, ask them to define their essential intent or vision as a team. At the beginning of each group meeting, one student reads the group's essential intent to stay focused on their vision.
- ☑ Ask students who feel like they failed, the lessons, knowledge or growth they experienced on the journey. If they have trouble coming up with lessons, help them find specific things they gained. Focus on their hard work and effort in their development. Zero in on personal growth, not fixed outcomes.
- ☑ Invite alumni who are 2-5 years out of school, to share stories about their challenges, setbacks and triumphs. It gives hope and adds credibility to their message because they traveled the same road.
- ☑ Set clear and fair deadlines on both short-term classwork and longer term assignments.
- ☑ When students are doing in-class work, give them time prompts like 15 minutes left, 10 minutes left. In groups, one member can be the timekeeper.
- ☑ Make sure each student is individually ready to present their portion of a group project, regardless if other students are absent at the last minute.

CHAPTER FIFTEEN

"What [is the teacher] doing physically to show them this is interesting?

– Speaker, Educator and Author, Michael Brandwein

WHAT TACTILE LEARNERS REALLY NEED

Use Improv Games to Reach Tactile Learners

Tactile, hands-on, or kinesthetic learners can be the most misunderstood students in class. Easily bored and physically restless, these students thrive when they are doing, building, creating, and moving. In a teacher-centered classroom environment in which students spend the majority of their time sitting in rows, these young men and women have trouble concentrating and focusing.

Studies from Columbia.edu [69] have shown in a typical lecture class students are attentive 40% of the time. Improv is a way to combat the inattentiveness that occurs during lectures. The suggestion is not to do improv for an entire class. Instead, it's to combine instructor-focused lectures, which appeal to auditory learners with more interactive, hands-on activities such as improv. It may help the tactile learners absorb the information both in the lectures and through movement with a far greater attentiveness rate. An improv activity has the power to bring to life or highlight a theme or concept taught during class.

I've experimented with improv in classrooms for a decade. Tactile learners, students with behavioural issues, international students, and ESL students respond well to "what I am doing physically to show them this is interesting," as author and education keynote speaker, Michael Brandwein, who gave the finest professional development seminar I've seen in my teaching career says, teachers can ask the question, **"What can I do in the first few moments of class to incite curiosity, take them by surprise, make my students wonder what's going on, and make them hungry?"** [70]

Improv and role-play can be your answer to this question. I've done both with students with behavioural and learning challenges in a split Grade 10/11 English class. They improvised a day in their life that we turned into a short documentary. I've tried it with Adult ESL students at City Adult Learning Centre in the Toronto District School Board. These Career and Civics students were from the Congo, Afghanistan, Sudan, Mexico, Iran, Tibet, Kenya, China, and Korea. We improvised real-world job interviews and various situations they may experience, in Toronto. I've tried it with Grade 12 students at Taylor's Canadian Pre-University Programme in the World History and Challenge and Change in Society classes I taught in Malaysia. I used improv to encourage the students to re-create Darwin's voyage to the Galapagos Islands. The students also put on a Great Depression Job Fair. They re-envisioned Napoleon as a modern French rap artist. As I saw how much fun and experiential this style of learning was for these learners, the role plays and improv continued weekly. In one assignment, an improv about Malaysian teen life turned into *The Breakfast Club* short films if it was re-cast with Malaysian high school students. We acted out famous psychological experiments and recreated Martin Luther King, Jr.'s famous speeches.

I've introduced improv at TanenbaumCHAT, the school I've taught at for the past seven years with Grade 9 English students. At the beginning of the novel, *The Curious Incident of the Dog in the Night Time*, we used the "Yes... and" improv game to explore absurd cultural sayings. The purpose was to empathize with the confusion felt by the main character, Christopher. In *A Midsummer Night's Dream*, I used the Status Improv Activity created by Keith Johnstone. From my diverse teaching experiences, improv and role-play is a no-lose scenario for the teacher.

Improv is a game-changing opener or a hook for any high school class. Do you want to capture your most challenging students' attention in the first sixty seconds? You may attempt improv at the very beginning of class to introduce a lesson theme or idea. If it works, it will be a big hit and engage your students in ways that both surprises and delights them. If it doesn't work as you would have hoped, it still has positive benefits. Your students will give you points for trying something new. At the end of it, they will be more alert and open. They will release restless energy through the activity.

Tactile learners can appear disengaged. They are really just bored and need to move. These signs include nervous movement of legs under the desks, twitching while sitting, and looking around constantly. Try a five-minute exercise break in the middle of the class. I rotate between doing yoga and throwing a soccer ball or football around the class. Another option is to encourage students to just stand up and walk around. I also give them permission to go to the back of the room during an instructor-centered lesson if they feel too constrained sitting at their desks, as long as they do not distract other students.

They make crucial decisions based on their instincts and comfort level. I've often discussed with students how life experiences teach you to trust your gut. I tell of a time of failing to trust my gut, below.

What's Your Lemon Juice Story?

When I was in Grade 8, several boys I desperately wanted to befriend invited me to hang out after school at one of their homes. I was thrilled to be included. The group of four boys went to the kitchen and helped themselves to drinks. I just wanted to fit in, so I poured myself what looked like a large glass of 7 Up. I took a sip and instantly spit up on the floor. It wasn't 7 Up at all; it was pure lemon juice.

One of the boys said, "That's disgusting?"

I winced at the sour taste and told them why I spit it out.

"Clean it up now," another said.

Embarrassed, I scrambled for a cloth of some kind. I got down on my hands and knees and cleaned up the mouthful I spit on the floor.

"Show us," another boy said.

I showed them the spot on the floor that was now cleaned up. I then started pouring the rest of the lemon juice down the sink.

"What are you doing?" one of the boys asked.

"I can't drink this," I said.

"You wasted a full glass of that stuff. It's expensive! If you ever want to hang out with us again, drink it now."

My heart was beating fast. I felt light headed. I gave in to the peer pressure and drank the lemon juice. I fought my gag reflex and forced it down in two gulps. Then, I ran immediately to the bathroom, fell down on my knees, and threw up.

While holding myself over the toilet bowl, I could hear the group of boys laughing at me on the other side of the door. When I eventually stopped, I quietly walked out the door without saying a word to them and took the long ride home on a series of connecting TTC public transit buses. I then walked into my house with a blank stare and my eyes down.

My mother asked me what was wrong. I shrugged, sighed and said, "Nothing."

She didn't let me off so easily. "What's wrong with your voice?" she asked.

I shrugged again and fought back tears. I told her the story. I didn't need her to tell me what I already knew. I let my instincts down and ignored my better sense. It was a painful lesson that conjures up strong visual images and physical discomfort to this day.

Students shake their head in bewilderment. Why would I drink the lemon juice? It humanizes me. It makes them feel they, too, are safe to make mistakes in my classroom environment. It teaches a lesson about not following your gut.

This story never fails to strike a chord with tactile learners. **The desire to socially connect is of paramount importance to a hands-on learner.** The description of the physical revulsion of the lemon juice helps them re-live this moment with me. The real-world situational story of peer-pressure is relatable to teens.

During an argument, tactile learners are most concerned with whether a teacher or their peers are sensitive to their feelings. It's meaningful to a tactile learner to share their feelings and experiences on a topic. Because their perceptions are often tied to these experiences, I acknowledge them for sharing their responses. I then take them aside and tell them they have the right to feel however they want to feel in that situation. This approach feeds a hands-on learner's need to be understood. I often notice an improvement in tactile learner's behaviour after these one-on-one conferences. I can address the appropriateness of the student's behaviour in that situation without demeaning their right to feel the way they do.

When a teacher asks a kinesthetic learner an important question, she/he will appreciate more time to search inside herself/himself for the answer. Their mind works like a building block deliberately stacking one piece of information on to the next. Inventors, like Thomas Edison, are often tactile learners. Hands-on learners are ever-increasingly misdiagnosed as having learning disabilities. Their depth of thought is like a still water that runs deep. Their thought processes slowly absorb the meaning of questions. When I am aware of this in a student, I make sure to allow sufficient wait time, which takes patience.

When I ask a question in class, I wait for up to fifteen seconds before calling on someone to answer. An interesting thing happens. Comprehensive thinkers, those who think fast, will quickly raise their hands during the first five seconds. However, if you wait a few seconds longer, at about the ten-second mark, people who rarely speak in class are more likely to put their hands up at this stage. These students may be your tactile learners.

When kinesthetic learners are given the time to absorb the question and respond, they can offer a new layer of perspective to your class discussion. The student will feel a connection to the subject matter, teacher, and their classmates.

Some hands-on learners are self-conscious and aware of their relationships with other students in the class and to the teacher. The hands-on learners' behaviour in class will depend on his/her comfort level.

A tactile learner wants to build solid relationships within a group. If he or she feels at ease with whom they're working with, then their best work will materialize. If the student feels out of place in the group, then the work will suffer. This student could be a productive mediator in managing conflicts that may arise with other group members. It's crucial for me to think where this student would best fit within collaborative settings in order to maximize his/her happiness and comfort level.

The hands-on learner may consider writing down key points rather than typing them into a document on their laptop for increased memory recall. Taking notes by hand leads to active listening and deciding what's key. In an article on the blog, VOX, Pam Mueller and Daniel Oppenheimer, the psychologists who conducted recent research on this topic believe "it's because students on laptops usually just mindlessly type everything a teacher says. **Those taking notes by hand, though, have to actively listen and decide what's important because they generally can't write fast enough to get everything down — which ultimately helps them learn."** [71]

I also provide handouts for at least 20% of the class, even on a paperless assignment. Tactile learners appreciate the option of having the physical piece of paper in their hand from which to learn.

In times of stress, the hands-on learner has trouble separating their feelings from what other people may be feeling. It is essential for the teacher to provide specific, constructive feedback that takes this student's emotions into consideration. Due to their sensitivity, remind the tactile learner to try not to take feedback too personally. Instead, I ask them to search for one lesson from each mistake.

To trigger a tactile learner's memory, it helps to generate experiences through movement. One strategy is to act out parts of a play rather than just read and analyze it in class. A friend and teaching mentor, Paul Comeau, called this, "getting a play to its feet."[72] Improvising a speech by a historical figure or putting students in an experiential learning environment in which they solve real-world problems in a collaborative setting are dramatically more effective than reading a text followed by answering questions in class to kinesthetic learners. The second way is to link an idea to a three-dimensional object. This strategy will also help the tactile learner absorb and apply knowledge more than being asked to memorize a series of facts that have no meaning to him/her.

Other strategies include:
- ☑ Frozen tableaus narrated by one student
- ☑ Play musical chairs in the middle of the room. Students have to answer questions if they are left standing.
- ☑ Opening or closing a student seminar with a choreographed dance. For this, you could recruit a dance instructor or colleague who can teach a fun, easy dance.
- ☑ Ways to Empathize with Tactile Learners
- ☑ Speak slowly and pause between main points.
- ☑ They take time to process information. Think of their minds as cumulative building blocks where one block is stacked on top of the other until all the pieces are in place.
- ☑ Their emotions significantly inform their reasoning and decision-making processes.
- ☑ Feeling if something is right or wrong guides their decisions.
- ☑ Give them time to settle into a new environment or situation.

Dislikes of the Tactile Learner

- ☑ Being interrupted
- ☑ Someone talking about them in a demeaning way
- ☑ Feeling overwhelmed with too many ideas or choices at once
- ☑ Stifling fun and creativity by overanalyzing
- ☑ Not having time for fun
- ☑ Not having time to connect with others
- ☑ Being rushed
- ☑ Don't like when lessons end abruptly

Challenges of the Tactile Learner

- ☑ Feeling hurt when they feel they are being left out
- ☑ When they don't feel comfortable in a relationship, they can be needy and demanding of attention.
- ☑ When they feel negativity in a relationship, they may withdraw physically and emotionally.
- ☑ When they have too many choices or complicated tasks, they avoid doing what needs to be done.
- ☑ Will do almost anything to avoid conflict
- ☑ Tend to become passive instead of standing up for themselves and voicing their opinion

Ways to Help the Tactile Learner

- ☑ Ask them: How can I best support you?
- ☑ Give them time to be in their own space.
- ☑ Offer guidance to keep moving forward.
- ☑ Don't overwhelm them with too many ideas at once. Provide them with dates. Break down projects into small, simple steps.
- ☑ Volunteer to become their support person and to be a team with them.
- ☑ Be patient in letting them get to the point.

Useful Questions to Ask the Tactile Learner

- ☑ How do you feel?
- ☑ What would make this activity/assignment/group project more comfortable for you?
- ☑ Does this fit for you?
- ☑ Can you relate to this?
- ☑ Does this work for you?

Effective Teaching Styles for Tactile Learners

☑ Having hands-on experience
☑ Working with a buddy
☑ Being creative and having fun
☑ Using worksheets

In a TEDx Talk, Improv teacher Dave Morris said, "Improv is the art of making things. **He goes on to say improv improves people's lives because life is improvised.** "Incorporating improv in a class helps students develop a growth mindset in the following ways:

1. Play – engaging in something just because you like it.

2. Let yourself fail. Failing does not make you a failure.

3. I failed. Okay. I'll just start again.

4. Listen. Listening is the willingness to change.

Yes...and – The Classic Improv Game Explained by Improv Actors

The lesson starts off with the context: Stay positive and active. Improv actor, Jim Annan said, "How many times does a kid hear 'no'? It just kind of ends it; it's final. With a 'yes and...' you're open to possibilities." Dave Morris adds, "By saying yes to everything, it opens you up to the opportunity and furthers the scene naturally. Play the game. Relax and have fun. 'No' equals safety, 'Yes' equals adventure."[73] Jim Annan continues, "A lot of improv is the guy who is not trying to steamroll his scene partner. He is the person who is listening, taking it all in, and reacting. He uses what the scene partner is giving him to further the scene, to the process." Additionally **Dave Morris says, "When students are listened to, they feel valued and appreciated and most likely to come up with new ideas in the future."**

Another activity teachers could adopt from improv is the development of listening skills. Jim says, "It's important in the first few seconds of an improvisation to tell who, what, and where.

There's no right or wrong." This initial interaction is a kind of warm-up that "takes listening on both partners' sides." Jim continues, "It's about being truly present, listening to the next line – and then coming up with a new idea. It's also about making other people look good. It's all about your partner making an offer and you accepting it."

When you say 'yes', you are accepting ideas. It also encourages a positive frame of mind, at once optimistic and good-natured. He goes on to say that when you say 'yes', you "open the door to possibility, discovery and progress." In another TEDx Talk on improv, Galen Emanuele said the *Yes... and* improv game gets people "thinking of how something can be done, not why it cannot be done."[74]

5 Improv Activities to Open or Close Any Class

1. **Yes... and...**

2. **See-Saw Status Games.** "A comedian is someone paid to lower his own or other people's status," described improvisation teacher, Keith Johnstone. "I go up and you go down." Two strangers meet in the street. Provide a topic of conversation that could be related to content in class or a situation that is related to characters studied in class.

3. One student is asked to play "high status," the other is asked to play "low status." Every word or gesture is meant to reflect their status in the interaction. This improvisation could also be done through status group photographs. Each student in the photograph is asked to take up a different level of status compared to the person standing beside them.

   An example is as follows: Walk into a dressing room and say, "I got the part" and everyone will congratulate you, but will feel lowered. Say, "They said I was too old" and people will cheer up. Kings and great lords used to surround themselves with dwarfs so that they could rise by the contrast. Some modern celebrities do the same. The exception to this is the see-saw principle.

It comes when you identify with the person being raised or lowered when you sit on his end of the see-saw. It also works well to teach empathy. Students alternate between raising themselves and lowering their partners in alternate sentences; and vice versa. [75]

The author, Johnstone suggests using Moliere's, A *Doctor in Spite of Himself* as an example.

Status Conversations - Students say something nice to the person beside them. Then, they say something nasty about their shoelaces. Ask the class what the effect of this was, which is different than what they expected.

4. ***Eye Contact Status Game*** - Everyone walks around the room saying, "Hello." Half the class holds eye contact for a couple of seconds while others try to break eye contact and then immediately glance back for a moment. Ask each student, how they felt when they were using high status or low-status eye contact. The teacher can add, "Speak with a still head" and "stand straighter." Then, give the opposite instruction to low status players. Once again, a student can be asked how this made him or her feel and how they perceived themselves and others from both groups.

5. Another instruction is to ask the high-status group to move smoothly and slowly while the low status group is to move with jerking motions. Additionally, high status sits back and makes herself or himself more spacious while low status points his toes inwards. In terms of language, students with high status can speak slightly slower, eliminating filler words like, um, and err, and "you know," while low status can add filler words like, um, err, and "you know," while speaking rapidly.

    Another alternative to this improv activity is to play high or low status to furniture or an object.

6. ***The Third Choice or Digging for the funny.*** – The first choice is obvious. The second choice is a little more interesting. The third choice is more creative; it's the gold. Comedian Ron Tite uses this activity to get people out of their comfort zone and to think beyond the surface level. A teacher could open a class with this

improv exercise to push students to develop layers of insight in answering a question.

7. A similar activity to this game is called, Things in a kitchen, as described by New York Times best-selling author and speaker, Michael Port.

    The top 3 responses are fork, knife, butter.

    Port says that, "to be memorable, say something no one else has thought of in a way that adds a lot of colour in your choice."

CHAPTER FIFTEEN SUMMARY

ACTION STEPS

WHAT TACTILE LEARNERS REALLY NEED

☑ Work on getting students to greet challenges with a 'yes', rather than 'I can't'. Remind them of the progress they've made up to this point in the year.

☑ Let students modify an assignment to make it more personalized giving them more ownership over their learning. There is always one common element or expectation, I allow for the delivery of the content based on students' learning styles.

☑ What can a teacher do in the first few moments of class to incite curiosity, take them by surprise, make your students wonder what's going on, and make them hungry?

☑ Improv is an effective opener for any high school class.

☑ Tactile learners sometimes make nervous movements like fidgeting at their desks and looking around constantly which means they need to move.

☑ Get students up at least once during class to accommodate the tactile learners. Yoga breaks at the halfway point are helpful to the tactile learner's need for movement while learning.

☑ To go one step further, give kinesthetic learners the option to walk around the back of the room.

☑ Visceral, emotional stories that deal with social issues relevant to students like peer pressure will capture the attention and connect with tactile learners.

☑ Give an additional ten seconds for tactile learners to answer a question in class. They may not always be the first ones to put up their hands, but when they do, they'll have something valuable and in-depth to add to the class discussion.

- ☑ Play close attention to which group you place tactile learners in as they are acutely aware of their relationship with other students.
- ☑ Encourage them to take notes by hand as their retention level will go up, and they'll absorb more than taking notes on a laptop.
- ☑ Take the tactile learners personal feelings into consideration when providing constructive feedback as they are more likely to interpret a teacher's comments personally.
- ☑ Tactile learners learn through movement. Acting out a scene in a play rather than just reading it as a class while they sit in their seats is an effective strategy to balance out straight analysis.
- ☑ Link ideas or themes to three-dimensional objects to further enhance hands-on learners' understanding.
- ☑ Speak a little slower, emphasizing and repeating key ideas.
- ☑ It takes tactile learners more time at the beginning of the year to adjust to a new classroom environment.
- ☑ Try to avoid interrupting a hands-on learner
- ☑ Giving them too many choices may result in procrastination. Keep choices simple and clear.
- ☑ Over-analysis will stifle their creativity.
- ☑ Provide time to be in their own space.
- ☑ Offer to become their support and guide in the class and within the school.
- ☑ Ask them questions like: How do you feel today? What would make this assignment or learning environment more comfortable for you?
- ☑ Give them time to connect with others in class.
- ☑ Don't rush them or lose patience.
- ☑ Even when a class is largely paperless, provide worksheets and hand-outs for 20% of the class.
- ☑ Improv games have the power to reach tactile learners. Such games include, "Yes…and", See-saw Status Game, Status

Conversations, Eye Contact Status Game and The Third Choice or Things in a Kitchen.

CHAPTER SIXTEEN

"A teacher should be like the air we breathe while group work is taking place – a necessary presence yet invisible."

— *Jamie Mason Cohen*

MODERN RULES OF STUDENT GROUP WORK

Keep the size of groups to four or less. Two students per group works well. They can contact each other at night after class hours and dialog back and forth.

Three student in a group also works as long as one of them doesn't feel excluded. If a teacher selects members of the group, this is less likely to occur.

A group of four is the most common formula for classroom group work. The desks conveniently fit together making a compact community. Using four students rather than two means much less class time is required for a presentation.

Don't let students pick their groups on an important group assignment.

When I taught in the public school system, a school psychologist said another student who was being bullied could not believe her teachers were not aware she felt alienated. **The psychologist said letting students choose groups made many of them feel as if they don't fit in or have very many friends.** The solution is to set up an inclusive classroom environment by choosing groups. Pair students who may compliment each others' learning styles and strengths. The opposite of this is a classroom environment that defaults into cliques, deliberate isolation, and exclusion of some students.

Put students together who have different learning styles when the assignment calls for multiple, complex tasks. This way of pairing is especially true for project learning assignments. It helps with differentiating learning through styles of thinking and increases confidence and self-esteem. If I observe that a group works well together on an assignment, I let them re-unite for future projects. It develops productive collaborative relationships. It also builds individual self-confidence and intrinsic motivation of feeling like a key contributor in a group.

On *Saturday Night Live*, writers were paired with cast members whom the producers thought might work well together, not necessarily with friends. Co-producer, Mike Shoemaker, pushed new writers to sit with a cast member and write something. "I'll put you with this new writer, Matt Murray; you sit in the room until you write it."

"We sat there for four hours and we wrote it," former cast member, Jimmy Fallon said.

During the first few weeks of school, Grade 9 students are most concerned with who is sitting beside them in class or whether or not they have someone to sit with during lunch. One way to encourage productivity and positive social interactions between students is to put thought into whom I am pairing with whom. **Once I see that a pairing works, I encourage these students to sit together in class. As Steven Martin said, "Lorne Michaels puts people together well. He will encourage partnerships."**

I remind students during the introduction of the group project that every participant should be able to present regardless of whether or not all group members are present. Everyone must be clear on exactly what he or she will present. Each student saves the entire content of the production on a separate USB or Google Drive.

They should also communicate if they will be absent at least 24 hours ahead of their group's scheduled presentation. Inevitably, at least one group will run into this problem; it's a dynamic learning moment to show students that the show must go on, in spite of obstacles like the absence of members of a team.

I make notes while students are presenting. It is difficult and time-consuming to remember the next day what students did. I make specific references to at least one positive contribution each group member has made. Teacher Jim Barry feels the teacher should give the students his full attention by being engaged and fully present with eye contact throughout the performance. I've tried this, and it doesn't work for me in terms of accurately assessing parts of their oral presentation but it may work for other teachers.

The compromise I have made is to make eye contact as much as I can. If I sense a student is feeling vulnerable by making some personal revelation or has a fear of public speaking, then I make sure I show them empathy through the way I listen. I usually start by looking up as each group member presents and smile. I write some notes, but I must be present in the moment of their presentation. I repeat this body language for each student as he or she presents.

I ask the class, "Who," not "Does anybody" have positive comments about something they liked in the presentation?" The distinction in the wording of the question is important. It assumes there are students in the audience who will notice something positive about their peers' performance. After the first group, the goal is to encourage a few students to raise their hands and give positive feedback. Once they know how it feels to hear supportive feedback from their peers and their teacher, it encourages them to contribute positive feedback for others.

I don't usually give negative feedback to students in front of their peers. Even though others may gain from the critique, some students feel embarrassed or picked on. There are obvious exceptions. If a student makes an inappropriate statement, I deal with it immediately. I make it about the offending student's behaviour, not about the individual.

I turn it into a learning moment. I never let it go without saying something to the class about the boundaries of acceptable and moral speech and action and that which is not. In my experience, students will gain respect and trust in the teacher. The individual who made the comment will be better for it. He or she will know that not only is the behaviour or words unacceptable, but he or she will think twice about saying or doing this again.

For major projects or end-of-unit tactile experiences, turn the making of groups by the teacher into an event. This type of lesson takes time to set up but pays off in terms of student excitement when they walk into the room. I wrote each student's name on a separate card from a deck, and taped it to the outside of the window beside the classroom door. On each card, there was a sticker that represented the assigned group.

When the students entered the class, they looked for and found their card and moved to the area where their group was instructed to meet. The cards became a physical piece of connection with the other group members. Additionally, it was a way to save a few minutes because whoever doesn't take the card is absent. It is also an original opening to the class. You can also explain your reasoning as to why you made the decisions you did to demonstrate your insights into their unique strengths.

A teacher should be like the air we breathe while group work is taking place — a necessary presence yet invisible. I divide my time circulating and sitting at the desk and watching with an open, non-judgmental look. I like to give students freedom and space to create. **A beneficial time to circulate is at the beginning in order to make more insecure group members feel that you are there to support them.**

At the start of a group project, students often have questions that require clarification for them to feel confident in moving forward. **I used to rush through questions at the beginning of class. It seemed as if these questions were off topic and taking away from class time. Now, I make sure to address each question briefly. It helps students feel confident, relieves their doubts and assists them in focusing on the task at hand.**

During my time with each group, I'm not just staring into space. I'm looking for students who are pushed to the periphery of the group. If I spot this, I address it. How do you notice this? Look for students who are quieter than usual, rolling their eyes at others comments, and are displaying a lack of motivation to engage in their particular task. These signs may not have to do with the assignment at hand, but it's better to inquire with the student one-on-one by asking how things are going with the group than ignore it.

Ways NOT to Brainstorm in Groups

Once the members of the group have some individual time to formulate their thoughts in their space, the group comes together and shares their ideas. At this time, each team member presents an idea. The other members provide critical feedback. They can ask questions, play devil's advocate, but never harshly judge.

This form of constructive critical response will move the project forward through beneficial tension. Why? Because it makes the student who came up with the idea prove, clarify and simplify his idea. If the idea falls flat, then the student learns that most ideas will not hold up to an intelligent group's scrutiny. It's part of life that a quantity of ideas leads to quality. If the idea passes the group's questioning, then the student will feel stretched and challenged.

CHAPTER SIXTEEN SUMMARY

ACTION STEPS

MODERN RULES OF STUDENT GROUP WORK

- ☑ Keep groups to 4 or less. 2 students in a group works well.
- ☑ Don't let students pick their groups on an important group assignment.
- ☑ Pair students together who have complimentary learning styles in which they can take on different tasks on a project.
- ☑ Remind students each member of the group must be able to present their part, regardless of who may be absent on the day.
- ☑ Immediately after an oral presentation, I give positive, specific spoken feedback. Followed by the favourable observations, I give critical feedback to students on paper or in a one-on-one conference.
- ☑ Turn the process of the teacher making groups into an event. You can put students in groups in creative ways. One example is to write their group names on the whiteboard with an 8.5 by 11 coloured piece of paper taped over each one. Then pull off each piece of paper revealing the groups in front of the class. You can then briefly explain your reasoning as to why you put students together to demonstrate your insights into their unique strengths. Next, tell them to find their groups and begin the assignment.

CHAPTER SEVENTEEN

"Conan would always give you great, positive encouragement, but he also had an eye on how to make something better."

Mike Myers on working with Conan O'Brien on Saturday Night Live

CREATE A CLASSROOM ENVIRONMENT IN WHICH GROUP CREATIVITY FLOURISHES

Brian Uzzi, a sociologist at Northwestern University, found that "musicals developed by a team of creative collaborators who had worked together many times before had a much higher chance of success than if a team of strangers worked together. They had a shorthand language. They also had a prior way of working together that would conserve energy.

This relationship helped them get off to a quick start. It made the group more likely to be successful in overcoming obstacles because of the relationships that had already weathered storms in past projects. When people who don't know each other work together, they will struggle to exchange ideas openly because of a lack of trust." [77]

The ideal group dynamic, according to Uzzi was where a majority of the participants knew each other. A few selected newcomers added fresh energy and perspectives to the project. These new faces also shook up the veteran group so they were not complacent.

Pixar Animation Studios on Creative Group Work

The founders of Pixar believed creativity comes through collaboration and its ability to get talented people from diverse backgrounds to work together. Pixar's founders believed the team is even more important than the idea. The team would find a way to make an average design work. However, if you had an average team, they would mess up a great idea. [78]

Pixar principal, Steve Jobs, believed the design of workspace impacts the culture of collaboration. Jobs asked, "What is the company's most important function?" The answer was the interaction of his employees. So, he created a big, open space for his employees always to be speaking with each other. A teacher can do the same by pushing all desks to the edges of a room prior to group work being assigned. It will instantly turn the room into a more hands-on, active workspace in which students engage with each other more naturally.

Much more productive peer-to-peer discussions happen when students are not tied to their desk but are given some freedom to move around. Some educators may think by giving students freedom from their pre-arranged desks, the teacher loses power. This freedom sends the message to the students that they are being given room to create, explore in a dynamic, unusual and playful workspace where expectations are still high, just in a different space.

Much depends on how disciplined the students are. If a teacher gives students the option of places to work such as on the ground outside the classroom doors, students can be more productive than if asked to stay in their regular seats. Expectations need to be made clear to what is required by the end of class. Additionally, the teacher can tell students the behaviour that is expected when given this kind of freedom. As a result, in the best cases, students come in with more energy and enthusiasm about their project than they had at the beginning of class. The key for teachers is to take a deep breath and relinquish some control. This strategy may be difficult for some teachers. **The paradox is the more trust and space I give my students, the more control I will have over guiding them to perform at their best.**

If teachers find this freedom given to different groups too difficult to oversee, then there can be what sociologist Ray Oldenburg refers to as, "third places" that are neither the class nor home. [79] I call these changes of environment micro-field trips. I borrowed this term from author, Alastair Humphreys who defined micro-adventures in his book, *Microadventures* as, "adventures that are close to home, cheap, simple, short, and yet very effective. A micro-adventure has the spirit (and therefore the benefits) of a big adventure." A micro-field trip is a surprise class excursion within the building to another space. Examples include putting on a scene from a Shakespearian play in the school's gardens, having a guest speaker on a big screen in the board room or doing a library scavenger hunt.

Depending on the assignment, it can also be productive if different group members drift into other groups to see and ask what they are doing. SOLEs or self-organized learning environments, popularized by Professor and TED Education prize winner, Sugata Mitra, are student-centered, flexible structured lessons. A SOLE sets up a friendly competitive atmosphere, peer-to-peer sharing of ideas that can serve as a jumping off point or model of possible ideas for the project. [80] *Quora.com* is an excellent site to be inspired or find questions and answers submitted from thoughtful people around the world on a variety of topics. If more than one group has similar ideas, then the groups are challenged to scrutinize their ideas to see what is uniquely valuable in their proposition.

I've heard teachers dismiss this approach for fear of the various groups copying each other's ideas. In the past few years, there have been incidents of widespread cheating on tests at top universities like Harvard. This is not the kind of note taking based on studying for a big test. If a teacher is monitoring the work, group drifting can be observed to make sure the informal meetings are focused on the task at hand. Some teenagers learn content in a clearer, straightforward way when they explain it to each other. When they share class notes or help each other understand the instructions, it can enhance their comprehension and absorption of the content.

Tom Allen, a professor of Organizational Studies at Massachusetts Institute of Technology (MIT), studied the communication interactions of engineers in the early seventies in large corporate spaces. After years of taking note of informal conversations in hallways, he found the likelihood is significantly higher for a person to communicate with a colleague who sits at a desk close by. Allen found the highest performing employees - those with the most useful ideas - were the ones who consistently engaged in the most interactions. In his book, *Managing the Flow of Technology*, Allen wrote, "Increasing the number of colleagues with whom an employee consults contributes independently to performance." [81] **This finding means for teachers that creative production by individual students has a high probability of increasing both quantity and quality when he or she is placed in the right group of collaborators.**

It also suggests if a teacher finds ways for students to interact with other learners outside official class perimeters, innovation can take shape both individually and within a group.

One simple, effective strategy a teacher can implement to encourage naturally this type of informal collaboration is a yoga break. In the middle of every class or just before the halfway mark, stop whatever you are doing in class, stand up, and lead a series of yoga stretches. This not only creates a fun, easygoing environment, it helps focus students, creates an entire team activity modelling positive group dynamics and results in more concentrated work after it's over. Once the two-minute yoga exercises are finished, let the students talk informally or move in the class for three minutes.

Far from a waste of time or letting the class go, it provides a structured timeframe for the students to interact, socialize and build relationships. It can result in students going the extra mile, when their usual pace would be just to make it to the finish line. Why is this? This form of break within class time takes away the tendency of teenagers to resist school authority or rules by providing a way to sublimate their energy and desire to socialize by giving them a real break. It also gives young people some breathing room and it provides them with some relief from the constant rules and timeframes that dominate their lives at school and home. It also gives them more autonomy over how they learn.

Yes, but some teachers may argue that giving a five-minute break in a fifty-minute class, is unrealistic given the amount of work expected to be completed by the end of the year in the curriculum. I would contend from practice that such breaks in classes from Grade 8 to Grade 12, increase productivity.

More teaching does not result in better learning. As the Minister of Education of Singapore, the 4th-highest ranked education system in the world put it, **"Teach Less, Learn More."** [82] What happens during these breaks? More students talk to other students within their group and in other groups, and this leads to new ideas that wouldn't have happened within the standard, formal process.

What will parents think of these breaks? When I announce during Parent-Teacher Introduction Night we will be doing yoga, stretching, or tai chi in most classes for some of the reasons mentioned, most parents smile and even stand up and do the stretching I ask them to do. Parents of former students whom I run into years later mention yoga in the classroom as something memorable for their son or daughter.

From my experiments with breaks in class, the energy in the class shifts to higher level when the class resumes. The momentary rest relaxes, de-stresses, and helps students focus on the goal at hand. Try it. It also gives the teacher a chance to observe social interactions in a new light.

This type of informal student assessment provides valuable anecdotal evidence on how students are managing socially. When a parent asks how their child is adjusting in class, they mean socially, as well as academically. **If a child feels uncomfortable socially in a class, it will have an adverse effect on their academic performance.** Additionally, it can cause stress and emotional pain that will eventually come out through outbursts, sickness, self-isolation or depression.

When it comes to different learning styles, opposites do not always attract. Sometimes, those who are too different, in the way they think, can be threatening to others. Once students have put their initial ideas on paper, the next step is critical analysis. Even though some people fear unfavourable feedback, it is the only way to move a project forward. I'm not referring to harsh or hurtful personal attacks disguised as criticism. I'm speaking of the informational, specific, project-based, helpful, constructive, balanced and empathetic comments that lacks a judgmental tone. It serves the purpose of improving the project and building trust among team members.

Some may argue that blunt honesty is the best approach with students. I disagree and quote a line from a source unknown, "Honesty without restraint is arrogance." [83] I think there is something to be said about the elegance of diplomacy. Burning a bridge with a team member results in distrust and resentment amongst the group, hurts working relations and ultimately the team.

The way Pixar structures constructive criticism may not be entirely viable for a classroom setting or appropriate for sensitive teenagers. But, it's still worth looking at their valuable self-analysis framework that has led to the production of some of the most successful animation films in Hollywood history. Every day at Pixar begins the same way: A group of animators and computer scientists gather in a screening room. Then the team begins analyzing the few seconds of film produced the day before, dissecting each frame. (There are twenty-four frames per second.) These meetings are not uncommon in creative companies. Similar sessions are conducted at companies such as Apple and Google. At Disney, Jon Lasseter observed that these meetings were efficient because everybody had the opportunity to learn from others' mistakes. These sessions also gave each person in the group the feeling of playing an essential role because it was each member's responsibility to catch errors. [84]

A group focused on finding every fault within the group's project goes against what I've been taught and have practiced for much of my teaching career. I always tried to withhold judgment during the creative process because it's counterproductive in the development or learning stage. I've altered my view, to a degree. I now believe students should work independently first in developing their ideas asking themselves at least three times, "Is this the best I can do?" After each round of ideas, students may take a break and come back with fresh ideas. Once the student has, within the timeframe provided, come up with their best Plan A, Plan B, and Plan C ideas, it is time to present these notions to the group. It is at this time, when constructive criticism and feedback on these thoughts should occur. Trust is either invested into the group dynamic or withdrawn. The feedback structure for students can be clearly set out to ensure that it is not too jarring or insensitive. Each student can be given a series of questions by the teacher with comment areas at the bottom.

The questions can contain simple phrases to be completed such as:

- ☑ What I like about your idea is _____.
- ☑ Followed by a critical idea:
- ☑ What I don't like about your idea is _____.
- ☑ What I think can be improved on this idea to make it better is _____.
- ☑ I think this idea would work for our group project because _____.
- ☑ I don't think this idea would work for our group project because _____.

When the students have finished their oral presentation, the teacher can focus on one to two positive things the student did in the presentation and invite other students to chime in with encouraging feedback. The critical observations should be given in writing only. Some teachers may argue that all students could benefit from the teacher's immediate critical and instructional insights. I agree that other students may benefit. The flip side is the student who is receiving feedback may be self-conscious, or insecure about how they are perceived by their peers. Their self-esteem may be damaged by well-meaning criticism given in this way.

Decades of research by Washington University psychologist, Keith Sawyer, has demonstrated basing brainstorming sessions around the premise that participants must provide positive feedback, only, just doesn't work. [85] Working independently and pooling ideas and then setting up a framework for each to give constructive feedback is more productive than group brainstorming sessions with only positive feedback.

Teachers can model for students how to provide helpful responses. This strategy can be done through a handout. The handout can include examples of clear, simple and straightforward phrases that demonstrate appropriate critical feedback. This sheet can also show the type of language and phrasing that is inappropriate, unnecessarily harsh, dismissive, rude or insensitive.

Brainstorming the traditional way is ineffective because of the lack of criticism and debate involved. Steve Jobs, at times, verbally degraded his staff and got legendary results. Excluding this strategy, teachers can learn from other Jobs' strategies in getting the most out of his/her teams. Jobs insisted on brief meetings, without PowerPoint, in which members of his creative team took turns poking holes, and looking for areas of improvement or imperfections in a new product design or model. The team would openly debate every aspect of the design. Each member of the team had to defend his/her decisions to Jobs, who interrogated each.

If students openly debated each idea presented in a group setting they would strengthen their communication skills and develop a toughness necessary for working in real-life corporate or entrepreneurial work environments.

This approach works when individuals start believing their flaws will be efficiently corrected by the group, so they're less worried about each idea being perfect. [86] It also leads to more honest and straightforward discussion. **In other words, we can only get right when we talk about what we got wrong.** Debate and criticism increase creativity in a group setting dramatically, whereas no criticism or only positive feedback inhibits growth of an idea and produces far less innovation.

Why does criticism, rather than blanket positive encouragement in group work, actually work? According to Charles Nemeth, a psychologist at the University of California-Berkeley who conducted studies on this subject, the findings show that our imaginations do not shut down in the face of conflict. It strengthens it and encourages us to engage fully with the work of others. We think about their concepts because we want to improve; it's their imperfection that makes us want to listen to them. When everybody is right - when all new ideas are equally useful, as is the case with the type of brainstorming sessions that have become so common in schools - we keep our thoughts to ourselves. There is no intrinsic motivation or productive competition to think about someone else's thoughts or different options. [87]

Another counter-productive result of brainstorming is that it is based on free-association — or express whatever you think of at the moment that's connected to the subject. Free-association can lead to clichés that never penetrate beneath the surface.

According to Nemeth, one counterintuitive answer is to start a group session with a point that the group members disagree on and argue about its merits or negative aspects. The initial debate will have a greater impact on getting the creative energy flowing than starting with areas of agreement within a group. It pushes the participants to stretch. They articulate their positions and put their positions in writing. The result is a solution based on another participant's relevant criticisms. It keeps each person on her/his toes. The group members are much sharper than sitting back in the couch in which they are getting along nicely but not getting much further than the day before.

It's crucial I set some boundaries and provide clear examples of suitable framing of constructive criticism for the students to follow. Paradoxically, it's healthy for sensitive students to learn to build their emotional resilience in order to deal with uncomfortable reviews. Hurt feelings may sometimes occur, but students will find it's never as bad as they feared. When they survive the imagined ferocity of the criticism that never came to pass, they feel more confident in their abilities and in their capacity to withstand challenging feedback.

Pixar has a system in place that makes sure criticism doesn't go too far; it's called "plussing." The goal of plussing is that whenever work is criticized, the criticism should contain a plus, a new idea that builds on the flaws in a productive manner. [89] In other words, the criticism is mixed with a new idea that allows the group to move immediately on, to start focusing not on the mistake but on how to fix it.

It works so well for Pixar because criticism feels like a surprise. It makes everyone in the group more willing to invent a plus, a new idea that moves the project forward.

Plussing has often resulted in the best solutions coming after the meeting as group members contemplate the criticism. Instead of productive debate and some growth happening just within the confines of the meeting itself, plussing ends up working for hours and days.

One Pixar animator said, "I'm not capable of surprising myself every day with some great new idea. That kind of magic can only come from the group". With plussing and peer feedback, an initial idea can be turned into something special during the revision process. [89]

CHAPTER SEVENTEEN SUMMARY

ACTION STEPS

CREATE A CLASSROOM ENVIRONMENT IN WHICH GROUP CREATIVITY FLOURISHES

- ☑ The ideal group dynamic is where the participants have previously worked well with each other. If student groups work well one time, you may consider continuing to put them with that group.
- ☑ A teacher can push all desks to the edges of a room prior to group work being assigned. It will instantly turn the room into a more hands-on, active workspace in which students engage with each other more naturally.
- ☑ More productive peer-to-peer discussions happen when students are not tied to their desk but are given some freedom to move around.
- ☑ Create third spaces. Take your students on micro-field trips around the school to put on Shakespearian scenes in the school's gardens or do library word scavenger hunts.
- ☑ *Quora* is a site that students can use to model intriguing and meaningful questions on a variety of topics in self-organized learning environments.
- ☑ Creative production by individual students has a high probability of increasing both quantity and quality when he or she is placed in the right group of collaborators.
- ☑ One way to encourage informal collaboration is to do a yoga or exercise break in the middle of each class.
- ☑ Structured, informal breaks within class time takes away the natural tendency of teenagers to resist school authority or rules. It provides a way to sublimate their energy and desire

to socialize by giving them a space to do so. It also gives them more autonomy over how they learn.

☑ A teacher can provide this series of questions to ensure a group project moves forward through constructive feedback.

☑ What I like about your idea is _____ .

☑ Followed by a critical idea:

☑ What I don't like about your idea is _____.

☑ What I think can be improved on this idea to make it better is _____.

☑ I think this idea would work for our group project because _____.

☑ I don't think this idea would work for our group project because _____.

☑ Pixar has a system in place that makes sure criticism doesn't go too far; it's called "plussing." The goal of plussing is that whenever work is criticized, the criticism should contain a plus, a new idea that builds on the flaws in a productive manner.

CHAPTER EIGHTEEN

"You believed in us, encouraged us no matter what, and truly brought new meaning and understanding to interactive learning. I found hidden talents I never thought I possessed."

— Taylor's Pre-University-College Student, Malaysia

MY MALAYSIAN TEACHING EXPERIENCE

How I Connected with My Malaysian Students Through Humour

At a once-a-year family holiday party, I spoke to my cousin who had just spent the past two years teaching with her husband at an elementary school in Columbia. I was fascinated by her experience. I had the desire to live and work overseas since coming back from New York and being at a crossroads in my life. They talked about hiking in the hills outside of Bogota where The Revolutionary Armed Forces of Columbia – People's Army (FARC) had been continually fighting the government.

They had heard the rebels did not kidnap foreign teachers because they thought they were good for the country, so they hiked without too much concern. They also took a trip to the Galapagos Islands in neighbouring Ecuador. Inspired by their story and nearing the end of a difficult yet growth-inducing nine months at Teachers' College, I looked into teaching overseas. My cousin and her husband had attended the annual international recruitment fair for Canadian teachers interested in teaching abroad. It cost $250 to attend the fair that took place over two days at Queen's University in Ontario. I paid the money online, sent in my resume with a headshot and made my way up to Kingston.

When I arrived, there were three notes waiting for me from various international schools who had read my resume and were interested in meeting me to interview for teaching jobs. The schools included: a well-known not-for-profit school in Monterrey, Mexico on the border with Texas and a two-room schoolhouse in Honduras. Located in the heart of the Mayan ruins, security guards drove teachers to and from the school to their homes. The final school I spoke with was located an hour outside of Kuala Lumpur, Malaysia. I was flattered to receive these notes, and so I made appointments with each of the representatives.

The Monterrey school official was a charming, slick fifty-something Canadian who had lived and worked in Mexico for over a decade. He was intrigued by my background working for *Saturday Night Live*. He thought the school, primarily consisting of female teachers would benefit from a young, creative male teacher. The teachers came in on Saturdays, roomed together and travelled on weekends together. It all sounded a bit too much. It's not a country I was passionate about seeing. The main reason I was intrigued in teaching abroad was to travel. I also wasn't sold on the idea of committing two full years to one school. It seemed like a considerable commitment on the spot. The school didn't make me an offer, but I was told to follow-up the next day.

The second school I spoke with was from Honduras. Located just outside a city with one of the highest murder rates in the world, I wasn't jumping at the opportunity. To be polite, I met with the representative because he had left more than one note. His pitch was humble, sincere and showed real interest in me coming to the school. The deal was a two-year contract that seemed a long time to spend in the middle of the Mayan jungle. The romantic in me had fantasies of teaching by day in a one-room schoolhouse and writing a sweeping epic about a thirty-something Canadian teacher exploring the Mayan ruins in the jungle on weekends. Not a bad motive for leaping into this adventure but not tempting enough to go.

The third interview was the one I had resisted the most. Kuala Lumpur? A Muslim country whose Prime Minister only a few years earlier had publicly stated that Jews rule the world. This is a country in which an Israeli passport is not welcome. Why on earth would I want to spend a year there?

I took the view that the opportunity you resist can be the one that fits best. The interview was a surprisingly positive experience. The interviewee, a former Superintendent in the Catholic School Board, asked challenging questions about my style of teaching and knew my resume inside-and-out. He asked me about how I knew a student was learning. He wanted to know how I'd integrate my media skills working in film and television into Malaysian classrooms unaccustomed to such techniques.

He asked me if I was interested in the surrounding countries like Thailand and Cambodia because I'd have the opportunity to travel cheaply during off weeks. He said all the right things to change my mind about teaching in Malaysia. I was animated, un-self-conscious, passionate, and even jumped up and demonstrated how a class with multiple learning styles would be set up. We warmly shook hands and ended an hour-long interview, which usually stopped after thirty minutes because another candidate was waiting. I also met with other representatives from Columbia and Belgium. I had dinner with a few teachers, who were at once eager and unconvinced of the claims made by various reps. I shared my three experiences with them and then headed to my hotel room. If schools were interested, they would put another note in your box the next day.

I got contract offers from Taylor's University-College in Subang-Jaya Malaysia and the elementary school from Honduras. I was happy to get more than one offer, but neither school ignited my curiosity because of where they were located. I took a moment and started thinking about the school in Malaysia.

I felt like the young doctor in the film, *The Last King of Scotland*, who is looking for an adventure. He makes his friend a bet that the first place his hand lands on a globe will be the destination he will set off for to work. His finger lands on Uganda, a country he has no knowledge of or desire to go to. But, he keeps his word and goes, resulting in a near-death confrontation that lands him as Idi Amin's personal physician.

I made a list of the positives and negatives of teaching in Malaysia. The positives included: it was only a one-year conditional contract unlike most of the schools that required two years. I was impressed by the professionalism and pedagogy of the representative for the school thinking that if he represented the quality of the administrative leadership I would be in good hands. Malaysia was in the heart of South-east Asia, a few hours plane ride from Cambodia, Thailand, and Burma -- three countries that were on my wish list of places to visit. The representative painted a picture of $50-week-end flights to these countries.

There was also a sense of exoticism about a country I knew nothing about. The only thing about Malaysia I had seen in the media was in Ben Stiller's *Zoolander*. He played a brainwashed American male model programmed to assassinate the Prime Minister of Malaysia during a fashion show. The negatives were that the school's representative's pitch seemed too good to be true.

I imagined myself like Tom Cruise in *The Firm* where he is sold on the perfect law firm with lots of perks only to discover it was a cover for a mafia-run corporation. The other reasons were the anti-Semitic reputation some Malaysian leaders had and the uncertainty of not knowing what to expect. After I had spoken by phone to my parents, I decided to accept. They were behind the decision. They thought it would be an intriguing travel adventure at this stage in my life. Plus, they agreed with me that it would be a much-needed change after Teachers' College. In Teachers' College, I was almost expelled. The first teacher I was placed with said to me, "You're trying to bring New York into a middle school, and it just won't work." I planned to have the Grade 4 class re-create Canada during the War of 1812. I wanted to turn the Grade 4 hallway into Laura Secord's early 19th century Canada. These nine and ten-year-olds were writing a script based on the days leading up to the war, and building professional sets, with tents and artificial grass. They would act alongside professional actors dressed as British soldiers and Canadian settlers.

The teacher sabotaged it and refused to let it happen after weeks of prep. I almost quit Teachers' College thinking, "Is this what I have to look forward to?" But, I thought back to Robin Williams' portrayal of John Keating, in *Dead Poets Society*, in which his new ideas were met with resistance. I survived my practicums and ended up in Malaysia.

I accepted the one-year position and was excited to leap into the unknown for a year. I only had a month to prepare for Malaysia following the graduation ceremony at Brock University in June. I had tried emailing teachers or administrators at the school several times. There was no reply. This issue was the first sign that something was a bit off.

Tip: Do not accept a contract with an international school until you speak with at least three teachers, who have worked there within the past two years. If I had done this, it would have impacted my decision. I relied on the smooth sales pitch of the representative who travelled back and forth to Malaysia at the expense of the school. I don't buy a book on Amazon for $15.00 before looking at the reviews nor do I book a vacation at a resort prior to seeing others' experiences. Why commit to a school before hearing other teachers' experiences first?

Don't give in to pressure to make a decision within 48 hours as I did. The representatives may tell you that they need to know before the job fair is done, and that position will be filled if you don't accept. That's okay. Never make a decision in an emotional state.

35 Essential Questions to ask a Previous Employee of the International School before Committing

1. What was your overall experience like?

2. Would you recommend teaching at this school to a colleague or friend?

3. What were the positive parts of working at this school and the negative parts of working there?

4. How were you paid? Was this an organized and transparent process or disorganized and unprofessional?

5. What is the housing like? Is it affordable to live well or does it eat up most of your income?

6. Are there any hidden parts of the contract I should know about? For example, do they expect you to work on week-ends to market the school or make speeches to middle-schoolers to sell them on the school?

7. Are the promises or claims the representatives make true, half-true or misleading in what they deliberately leave out? For example, if they show images or a slick website of high-end classrooms, that look new and contain cutting-edge technology does that reflect the classroom I will be teaching in?

8. What kind of people work at this school? (Ask yourself: - Are these the kind of people I could see myself being friends with or not?)

9. Is the staff supportive of each other or petty and threatened by new people? (I'd only ask this question to a teacher who no longer works there).

10. How much does it actually cost to travel on Air Asia (or the most popular economic airline in that part of the world) to neighbouring countries). The representative misled me and others into thinking that the lost leader cost, $50 – 100 U.S, was the average cost of flying from Malaysia to Thailand, Cambodia, Bali and even Burma. The actual cost was over $300 U.S. within only Malaysia! To travel to these other countries was enormous considering what I was told. Cambodia = approximately $800/ Bali = $500/ Thailand = $500/Burma = $800-$1000/Vietnam = $500. (Approximate prices in 2006)

11. What is the food like? Is it easy to find healthy, clean, reasonable local food? Locales have grown accustomed to extra-spicy food and have developed stomach lining of steel. Ask a teacher who has been there for a short amount of time from a food culture similar to yours. I memorized a Lonely Planet episode on Malaysia as my food bible. The video suggested Mamak stalls for

their delicious vegetarian food at a dollar a day. I ended up in a hospital from eating at certain Mamak stalls.

12. What is transportation like? How do you get around? Can you walk to the school safely or not? If not, do you take daily taxis? Does the school have a bus to pick you up daily? Do teachers carpool?

13. Can a teacher live comfortably on their teacher's salary?

14. Is it possible to travel a little and save a little or not?

15. Does the school supply resources or not? What are the resources the school does supply if any?

16. Does the school provide a plane ticket prior to leaving or do they expect you to pay for it upfront?

17. What is the principal or headmaster like to work for?

18. How many students are in an average class? What are the students like?

19. What is the air quality like? Is the area in which the school is based and where you will be living, a high pollution area? This is especially important if you have asthma like I do. Many parts of Southeast Asia have poor air quality and humid temperatures that make it difficult to breathe during the day.

20. If you were to know before accepting the job, what you know now, would you have accepted the job?

21. Is there any question I haven't asked you that I would ask if I worked there for a year?

I arrived in Malaysia after paying for a one-way plane ticket. The only guidance the school gave on this matter prior to leaving was just to say you're visiting. This seemed a little casual and up-in-the-air as they just hired us to work in a country 14,682 kilometers away.

When the plane landed, I strolled through the high-tech yet empty airport terminal with anticipation. One of the other teachers, Scott was in his late 30s, from Niagara Falls. Scott and I would form a friendship during our time in Malaysia. We became roommates, even though neither of us went into this wanting one. The only way a Canadian teacher could comfortably afford a decent rental by Toronto standards, would be to find a roommate.

Tip: In the first two weeks, I tried to make a friend amongst my colleagues. It can be lonely and exhausting teaching in a new country. **A colleague who understands what you're going through and who you can confide in about your experiences is an important bond to build.**

The search for a place to live: New teachers were connected with two local real estate agents through Taylor's. They took us from condo to condo within the general vicinity of the school. The only way we realized we would find a place that was not in a slightly dangerous, out-of-the-way area or had a run down, unkept immediate surroundings was to pay considerably more than we had budgeted for. After one week of looking, I decided to rent an expensive apartment located in the hotel strip at $1,600 U.S. a month. I spoke with Scott and suggested we split the rent. He agreed. Our place had a peaceful view overlooking a man-made pond. In the distance, you could see the local mosque. The Islamic call of prayer blared over the loud speakers at around 5:30 a.m. each morning. It would be my daily wake-up call. I'd then stumble outside on a cat litter bag used as a Zen cushion and meditate for about thirty minutes. Next, I headed off to the gym down the street housed in the Sheraton hotel. Just further up the street was a local Indian take-out restaurant called a Mamak stall. The food served was an aesthetically intriguing variety of vegetarian sauces to be dipped in pieces of flat bread called Roti Canai. I ate this for lunch, snack, and dinner for a week. I felt I was adjusting to the local culture I had seen in a Lonely Planet video to learn about Malaysian life.

The video made it seem as if these $2 seemingly healthy vegetarian meals were safe and suitable for the stomach of any traveler. I sat outside watching World Cup soccer games with locals and tourists. I was provided a hotel room to stay in by the college until the paperwork was complete for the condo. On my seventh day in Malaysia, I woke up on the hotel room bathroom floor with a nasty headache and blood dripping from my mouth. What happened?

A veteran teacher had called to ask if I wanted to go out with teachers. I pressed the call back number and mumbled I needed some help. The teacher eventually showed up at my place with his girlfriend. He seemed like it was an inconvenience to take me to the hospital down the street, but his girlfriend pushed for it. I was put on a stretcher, my stomach feeling like it was about to explode and called long distance. There was no answer, so I called a friend whose number came to me. I told him I was in the emergency room of a Malaysian hospital from food poisoning. He eventually tracked down my parents. They called one of my friend Scott, as my phone had died. Years later, that friend would say I'm the only person he knew who he was not surprised to have received such a call from a distant corner of the world.

I was admitted through emergency, and my stomach was pumped. The doctor in charge, a calm and kind forty something Malaysian man who studied at Waterloo University, just outside of Toronto, asked, "Who told you to eat that stuff?" I told him the TV travelogue show, Lonely Planet, said it was ideal for local travelers. He chuckled and shook his head.

He said, "There are no health regulations in many of those places. They probably recycle that stuff and leave it outside in the sun for weeks at a time."

Once you land in a new country, buy a fellow veteran teacher lunch. Ask them the following questions:

1. Where are the safe, busy restaurants or take-out places to eat nearby?

2. What are the restaurants to avoid?

3. Is the information you learned from travel websites accurate? Ask a local, too.

4. Ask what restaurants serve the kind of food that you like: For example, vegan, vegetarian, gluten-free, low-carb. This is a question that you may want to ask prior to arriving to ensure that there is some staple food in the country that you enjoy. Food is fundamental in helping a teacher get through gruelling hot days

teaching in non-air conditioned classrooms and unwinding at the end of a day. If the food is not compatible with your tastes or health issues, it will have a negative impact on your daily mood, physical strength and overall experience.

I sat in a bed in the hospital for five days. During that time, I lost about ten pounds from the unexpected full body cleanse the Mamak stall food had provided for me. The doctor said my stomach lining in one area had been highly irritated and stripped away from the mixture of spicy, spoiled food eaten in one-hundred-degree heat. The principal of the school came to the hospital concerned for my health in relation to whether I would recover fully to teach at the school. He told me the school had high hopes for what I brought to them and he wanted to do whatever he could to get me on my feet as school would be starting in one week. The school made sure I was taken care of regarding health insurance and anything I needed while I recovered.

I shared a hospital room with a local Malay boy; a curtain separated us. I ended up teaching the boy some conversational English. We became curiosities to one another. I became an acquaintance to the boy's father. Our friendship was short-lived but interesting. He bought me a black and orange button down shirt worn by Muslim Malays during weddings and important events. It reminded me of the shirts Mandela often wore. I even wore it during a Passover Seder. I never told him I was Jewish, which may have put an abrupt end to our friendship. He asked me on more than one occasion how much money I made, how much money my parents had, and hinted that he wanted to arrange a date for me with his single sister. At that point, I let the friendship fade.

Prior to teaching at Taylor's, I had received advice from one of my professors at Brock Teachers' College. She had attended a seminar in Malaysia a few years earlier and said the teaching culture was "quite different there." When I asked for more details, she just said, "Trust me." She said I should not jump into my unconventional creative teaching style right off the bat. The students will need time to adjust to it. She said I should begin in a more low-key traditional way.

I respected her advice and thanked her. She was probably right. As I had her thoughts in my head in the days leading up to the first day of class, I decided to be myself in the classroom and see what happens. This lesson would be confirmed the year after I returned from Malaysia in Jim Barry's Additional Qualifications course. He told me to smile when given advice about what or how to teach in my class, close the door and teach the way I want.

On the first day of class, the keys didn't work for the classroom, and no textbooks were given to me until the last minute. I was sweating profusely and constantly loosening my tie.

Tip: If possible, get to the classrooms a few days early so that you are familiar with the environment. Know which key goes where. Just like any well-prepared presentation, do a walk through ahead of time.

I had twenty-five students per class. I was teaching Grade 12 World History and three Grade 12 Challenge and Change in Society classes. I borrowed one of the teacher's sweat-stained hockey helmets, stick, and gloves for the first challenge and change class. He brought the equipment from Ontario to play in a local hockey league made up of ex-patriots working in Malaysia. They played on a shiny hockey rink at the local mall.

7 Ways Teachers Can Instantly Connect with International Students

1. **Create a Warm, and Fun Classroom Environment from Day 1.**
   I wanted the tone to be not boring, humour-filled, uncommon, curiosity –driven, intriguing, playful and inspiring. I dragged the hockey equipment to the third floor room. The double takes and glares I received from suspicious students and scoffing teachers made me doubt whether it was worth it to plunge ahead.

   During the opening class, I attempted to take attendance for 120 students whose names I couldn't pronounce properly. I put on the helmet, the hockey gloves and held the stick in the air with one hand. With the other hand, I declared, "I am

Canadian," in an imitation of the famous Molson Canadian beer commercial, "I am Canadian." I listed some fun ways I acted as a Canadian. I showed them I wasn't afraid to make myself look a little silly, have fun, and break the usual high status position of teachers in this school culture.

The students pulled out their cameras and starting clicking away and laughing. From this moment, I had them hooked. It was the beginning of working with an amazing group of young people. I tell my current students that Malaysian teenagers are amongst the most respectful, open and hardworking young people I have ever met. Most said, "thank-you," upon leaving each class. They acknowledge the teacher by parting the narrow, outdoor hallways as you walk past. I've found that students from one culture are interested in hearing about how other teenagers act in another culture. My students in Malaysia were the highlight of teaching overseas.

I got the students up and moving as much as possible. Rows have their place for individual learning of hard facts and tests. I experimented with group work at tables, friendly debates between groups of students spread out in corners of the classroom and creative use of the physical space and pace to match the day's lesson.

2. **Make it a Priority to Learn Each Student's Name within the First Month**

This may seem obvious but it was my priority. Learning names is essential to gaining students' trust. It made my international students feel I cared about each one of them. Sir Ken Robinson said, "[a teacher's] job is not to teach subjects; it is to teach students".

I did not think I was capable of learning one hundred and twenty Chinese, Malay and Indian names right away. Through a genuine desire to make those names a priority I learned the first and last name of every student within the first month. This small, personal triumph made it easier for me to connect with them. I introduced fun and novel activities in the classes beginning the first month of school and was greeted with openness and enthusiasm.

Every time you pronounce a student's name, even with your foreign accent, it will bring a smile to his/her face. Ripples of giggles will ensue throughout the class. This is a good thing. You will be known as the teacher who remembers names, which is a reputation worth having. To learn the names, I would try a few different strategies: I wrote down every name and visualized the student. I asked for passport photos on day one attached to a brief bio. I would associate the name with one of their hobbies that stood out to me. I would ask them to put name cards in front of them. I would picture their name on their forehead as I spoke to them. If I didn't know their name, I would ask them to remind me of it. I would create pictures of difficult names as like-sounding images.

I was constantly thinking about how I could make each class interactive and fun. Prior to the trip, I had consulted with two brilliant teachers from Crescent School, an independent boys' school in Toronto.

Tip: Before teaching a new subject, I ask veteran teachers what needs to be covered to satisfy standards set out in the curriculum. I make sure to cover this material over the period of teaching a new subject. Further, ask them what the core essential skills a student in this subject should have by the end of the course.

Before the meeting, I felt overwhelmed. I didn't know where to start or how to approach the material for a new subject. After just one ninety-minute meeting with these two stellar, experienced and innovative teachers, I had a starting point. Within three weeks, I had built a skeleton unit plan. I like to be organized and plan ahead but always leave room to adapt and change my approach, once I get to know the students, their strengths and their needs.

Grade 12 World History was a day-to-day experiment gone right. Everything seemed to be falling in to place, accept my health. Taking the master Zen teacher, Shunryu Suzuki's belief to heart, "Wherever you are, you are one with the clouds and one with the sun and the stars you see. You are one with everything." I gave everything to this class, I became one with this class. But I started burning out, so it was essential to start pacing myself. Instead of trying to hit a home run each day, hitting singles would suffice from time to time.

3. **Role Play to Make Real-World Lessons Stick**

My early progress in reaching my students came in introducing role-play. I used this approach to help students better understand and apply what they learned in the textbook. We explored the U.S. Civil Rights movement during the 1960s through re-enacting Martin Luther King's, "I Have a Dream" speech. We acted out psychological and anthropological experiments by Ivan Pavlov and Paul Ekman. We debated the value of Intrinsic vs. Extrinsic motivations. Some students spent the day in a home for students with disabilities, organized a student film festival to show their humorous films on teenage culture and performed a class choreographed 70's dance. Exam review was turned into class trivia in which the losing team had to do something harmlessly funny as voted on by the winners.

We did a French Revolution role-play in which students put Napoleon in various modern social situations that teenagers experience. They imagined how he would awkwardly respond. The students created his online dating profile and then proceeded to act out how he would nervously make small talk with one of his online matches on Skype, his future wife, Josephine.

Now, the class was not all improv or role-play. **A successful class has a balance between direct, teacher-centered learning and learner-centered activities.** For example, in World History, I first lectured on parts of the French Revolution. I then taught students the skill of annotating historical documents. We then looked at speeches given by Napoleon. After a firm foundation and context was put in place, students then did these fun activities by applying what they had learned.

In the Challenge and Change in Society course, we used role-play to re-create famous case studies. We came up with social experiments that we played out over the duration of the school week.

I realized the impact and influence role-play was having on the school. Some of my Canadian colleagues, as well as some local teachers, started incorporating role-play into their classes. My student teacher, William, a man with a Master's degree and a student of the Malaysian school system, didn't really connect with the idea of role-play in the classroom at first. By the end of the semester, he began incorporating role-play into his practicum lectures. I gave him feedback after each attempt. He became so confident in applying this approach to his classes that he chose to be judged on a class in which he incorporated role-play in front of the Principal of the school. After I returned to Toronto, this principal informed me that William was the most popular lecturer of Malaysian Studies, known for his interactive classes and signature role-play assignments.

4. Hands-on Creativity: Do and They Understand

We created a children's poetry book simplifying events that led to the French Revolution.

Students learned about 19th-century art by making original paintings in the school courtyard. They became unconventional art critics. They were to tell a two-minute story based on a classic painting. Then they were to create a frozen tableaux picture of what is happening just off screen. Finally, they were to write a song that represented the painting.

There was an assignment called, Parachuting into the 18th Century. Students re-created the sea voyage of Charles Darwin to the Galapagos Islands right in the classroom. One student brought in her snapping turtles that latched on to my thumb for a funny and painful five minutes. They turned off the lights in the class, blindfolded their classmates and filled the room with jungle-smelling incense and palm leaves. These kinds of hands-on, student-driven projects in which all the senses were engaged were encouraged and expected.

There was the Russian Revolution Live Museum Tour in which students simulated key events and personalities of the Russian Revolution, including costumes and setting.

Students made Graffiti Boards. In small groups, they drew and painted symbols, summaries, and poems to apply key parts of different political philosophies. The young men and women then explained their Graffiti Boards to the rest of the class. We hung the boards in our room and referenced it throughout the term.

In World History, students brought in tents to represent the Great Depression in the United States and made a bunker from desks turned on their sides.

5. Students produced Short, Humorous Videos Based on Local Teenage Life

In Challenge and Change in Society, students interpreted the 1980s film, *The Breakfast Club* from a Malaysian teenage perspective. The assignment for my Challenge and Change in Society students was to watch the movie as a class. I gave minimal instruction, and then asked them to get into groups of five to make *The Breakfast Club* from the teenage Malaysian point-of-view.

The teenagers went above and beyond what I asked of them. They came in on weekends, which was unheard of for a non-priority subject like Challenge and Change in Society. They stayed late after school to film on the school's grounds. They worked hard despite having no prior training in filming with video cameras or smart phones. Some of their parents questioned why they were spending so much time on a subject they didn't consider to be essential for their child's future.

They constructed culturally insightful, hilarious short films that had shades of Charlie Chaplin, modern action-adventures, and over-the-top romantic genre comedies. The students in both classes wanted to share their media creations with a wider audience. I reserved a university auditorium for what I was told was the first high school Malaysian Student Film Festival of its kind. The auditorium was packed with hundreds of students, family and friends. The students showed their films in front of their peers and parents. They received awards presented like an Academy-Awards ceremony that didn't take itself too seriously.

6. Have Students Write and Perform Original Songs

One way to break down cultural and language barriers is to have students write songs. I had my students write a rant called, "I am Malaysian," after I modelled, "I am Canadian." I stood on my desk on Day One and exclaimed what makes me Canadian. They wrote theme songs for their Malaysian *The Breakfast Club* films, songs about Vincent Van Gogh's art, and a rap song from Napoleon's point-of-view. These assignments got the whole class involved, laughing and learning.

7. **Create Exam Review Competitions with Fun Consequences**

Exam time is stressful everywhere. Instead of the typical review, we found ways to make it an event. Students didn't want to leave class during review time. I had them create questions they thought would be on the exam in groups. Once they completed the questions, I typed them up and handed them to the class. The groups competed against each other in a Jeopardy-style review for part one. One consequence for getting an answer wrong was to be squirted with a water gun on your feet from one of the other teams. The alternative consequence was to stand at the front of the school for five minutes during lunch. With a big smile, my students looked passing strangers in the eye and said, "Welcome to Starbucks" and other random lines chosen by the winning group. It worked. The students associated studying for their final exams in my class as a challenge and as play. It turned learning into a fun yet productive adventure. And, it wasn't all play. The final marks on the exam exceeded the class average over the course of the year.

An Unhumourous, Yet Fascinating Experiential Project that Almost Got Me Kicked Out of Malaysia

The most controversial and meaningful project I assigned was a documentary on the Holocaust from Malaysians' perspective. Even though students had the option of a number of world history topics, three groups chose this one. I noticed in the history books taught in school that there were two pages devoted to World War II out of a book of nearly three hundred pages. There was no direct reference to, nor even a paragraph devoted to the six million Jews and other groups of people including: Poles, Russians, Gypsies, homosexual persons and those murdered by the Nazis and their collaborators. In the assignment, students were to interview a varied group of Malaysian citizens about their knowledge of the Holocaust and do a critical analysis on how it was taught in schools.

On the list to be considered as interview topics included: fellow students, journalists, students from Muslim schools, Malaysian educators, imams, priests, Buddhist monks, professors, and parents. One day, I got a message from the Taylor's University-College principal to come and see him. If you were not called down to the principal, it was a sign he was happy with your teaching. It was the first time I was called to his office. My heart raced as I hurried down after an early afternoon class. He smiled and asked how I was feeling.

He continued, "I got a phone call today from a Minister in Malaysia's Education office about a project his nephew was assigned. He wants to speak with you."

Students had options to do projects that included: a graphic novel about Mao's Communist Cultural Revolution, a Live Museum Tour of the Russian Revolution filled with PowerPoint visuals and hand-crafted objects meant to represent key moments. Three of the five groups chose to do the Holocaust documentary.

"Someone in the Ministry of Education wants to speak with me?"

"Yes," the principal said the minister wanted to know why a teacher from our programme had given his students an assignment on the Holocaust.

I told the principal about the independent study options. It was in the curriculum to cover World War II.

The principal nodded. "Okay, just checking," he said.

It wouldn't be the last time the Holocaust documentary would come up. I found out how the former Minister in the Malaysian Education Department learned of the project in the first place.

One of the students doing the documentary did what the project guidelines asked. He interviewed Malaysian citizens from different walks of life. He decided to ask his family member, a former high-level official in the Malaysian Education Ministry, about whether he believed in the Holocaust or not. His uncle's response was, "Who is your teacher?" The student told him I was a Canadian instructor with a unique style teaching him World History. The uncle then said he thought Malaysians should be learning about "Malaysian history" and how world history related to them. This response was fascinating to me considering all Malaysians must take a mandatory course in Malaysian history.

The uncle then asked the student if the teacher was "Jewish."

He said he didn't know.

"What's his last name?" the former Minister asked his nephew.

"We call him, Mr. J, but his last name is Cohen," my student responded.

"Cohen," the Minister repeated.

He apparently walked over to his bookcase where he produced an almanac full of world surnames. He flipped through the book to "C" and located "Cohen."

"Cohen is a Jewish name," he said.

"No, I really don't think so, the student said. "It says right here they were high priests in Judaism during ancient times. The only other name he could be is Irish if his name was spelled Cohn."

The student reported the gist of this back to me after I met with our principal. I thought to myself that I could be the first Canadian teacher kicked out of Malaysia for giving a history project on the Holocaust. Nothing transpired. I wasn't booted out of Malaysia. This experience was a contradiction to my experience with Malaysian students and Malaysian friends I had met like, Helen and the doctor who treated me when I was ill. Malaysian students were intelligent, warm, deferential, brilliant, open, and possessing latent creativity that blossomed when they were encouraged to be innovative. The student whose uncle questioned the assignment was a compassionate, unconventional thinker. He is now a high school teacher. He credits his father, a professor, and me as his inspirations for going into teaching.

The Holocaust documentaries were mesmerizing and a little shocking in parts. The student reassured his uncle to re-consider his concerns on the project. He even convinced him to speak briefly on camera about his views on the Holocaust, which demonstrated empathy for the Jewish victims. This student's group interviewed over twenty Malaysians, from students to Muslim community leaders and journalists. They discovered there was an attitude of tolerance and sympathy for what they knew about the Holocaust. The most revealing part of the documentary to me was their critical analysis of Malaysian history textbooks they grew up studying.

On camera, the students flipped through their Grade 10 Malaysian textbook in which several pages were devoted to a protest demonstration in Malaysia during the 1960s. In contrast, the Holocaust was only mentioned once on two lines. Another group of secular Muslim girls who didn't always hand work in, worked hard on their documentary, but their focus became a challenging teaching moment.

Their documentary footage and point-of-view were taken primarily from Hamas's website. Their argument equated Israel's treatment of Palestinians to the treatment of Jews by the Nazis. I walked a fine line between providing immediate feedback in complimenting the girls' significant time and effort spent putting the project together and addressing the biases and unreliability of their sources. The audience of students watched carefully how I responded and provided feedback. I wanted to offer these students with specific ways to improve. What I didn't want was for them to feel that the teacher was criticizing them personally or embarrassing them in front of their peers. Finally, I wanted them to learn how to ask questions to deem the accuracy of sources in online research.

Teachers in Malaysia were referred to as "lecturers." That's what most did. Lecturing in a loud, monotone, humourless tone for a class was common practice. Teaching to the year-end standardized test was the norm. Humour or role-play didn't seem to have a place in the classroom. The students took many notes. They memorized exactly what the teacher told them to. They took a huge, one-dimensional standardized exam at the end of the year. Depending how they did on this end-of-year standardized test would determine which universities they were accepted to. The program I taught in was the only one of the three educational programs that didn't teach to the standardized test.

Instead of teaching to the test, I let my imagination run wilder than it ever had. I tried every creative idea I could think of. Roleplaying was so effective with these 18-19-year-olds because it gave them a liberating, empathetic and playful way to learn history and understand the psychology of peoples in different cultures and distant eras. In every other class, I did some kind of role-play, dance, experiment, or mini-project that kept the students laughing, on the edge of their seats, relaxed, and focused. My best classes were on the edge of creative chaos. If you would walk by my room, often students would be sitting on desks, talking, joking, brainstorming, and not tied to their seats. I aimed to create an environment in which every class provided young women and men with the opportunity to discover their strengths and develop a curiosity and passion for learning.

How to Get Students to Love Learning on Their Own

The answer to this is twofold: the first is to inspire your students to act and take responsibility for their work by providing a 'why' at the beginning of a lesson. The more thought that goes into creating a meaningful and empowering 'why' will lead to a 'what' and a 'how'. The second part is through the development of a creative, growth-mindset space from day one. A learning environment that is playful yet focused, with strategically placed times to exercise and rest within the class will contribute to intrinsic motivation. How? Students will feel the teacher is taking their holistic needs into consideration.

Students who are self-driven will do their homework during swim meet breaks. They feel a quiet pride and passion for competing against themselves. Young people who are motivated by their passion for the subject may be partially compelled to get high marks but push themselves because they see growth in their learning. They are not working hard solely for the teacher's approval, but want to do well to show the teacher just how much this class means to them. In a way, it's a thank-you to the teacher for triggering a spark to learn and excel on a level they didn't realize they were capable of until they walked into the class.

At the end of the semester, the students in each class presented me with group video scrapbooks of their time in the class. While most classes at the Canadian Pre-University Programme had only a handful of students on the last official day before exams, my class was packed. Along with my students, several teens from other classes stayed after theirs were complete, to watch the films and see what our class was all about.

As I watched the videos, it was clear to me why I teach. It moved me to experience a feeling of how exhausting, yet rewarding it is to give and to serve others as a teacher.

(Click here for Year-end Tribute videos showing our classroom environment by my Taylor's Students)

41 Things I Learned About Myself in Teaching in Malaysia

1. Usually, it is the breaking point when breakthroughs happen.
2. Don't react to minor jabs. Have no buttons to push. Just laugh. Breathe. Walk away. Never look back.
3. Acknowledge and then let go of every absurd action around me.
4. Breathe and pause before answering.
5. Don't say too much. It's always best to say less.
6. Keep instructions brief.
7. Don't let my guard down at the very end when I'm enervated. That's when I tend to make careless emotionally-driven mistakes.
8. Smile.
9. Meditate every morning—30 minutes—if possible.
10. Specialize in one subject – don't overextend myself.
11. Don't justify everything to students. Don't oversell. They'll see the value in it or they won't.

12. Don't tell other teachers how hard you work on a classroom project.

13. Promise less, deliver more than expectations.

14. Never complain or criticize publicly.

15. Be humble.

16. Uphold professionalism, but not self-importance. This too shall pass; let go of ideas and thoughts. Turn the page. Don't turn anthills into Mt. Everest.

17. Be totally committed to giving of myself, of making people feel special without expectation of being liked in return or getting a nice "tribute."

18. Focus on listening. Be open. Available. Non-judgmental. Let people ask questions. Be thoughtful and sparse with advice.

19. Let people discover answers to their problems.

20. Be independent of the good opinion of students. Even if many are positive about the class, it is not good to teach or act to being liked.

21. I don't have to win anyone over. I don't have anything to prove or a reputation to live up to. Just do the best I can in every moment and be appropriate.

22. For tests – do a mix of multiple-choice, short answer, true and false, and one essay question. Less marking, less stress.

23. Write for one hour every day.

24. Write a daily journal after work (15 minutes per day).

25. Incorporate the following movies: *The Breakfast Club, Pump Up the Volume, Scared Straight, City of God, Bus 172, American Graffiti, Gandhi, Ghosts of Rwanda,* Ingmar Bergman's *Persona.*

26. Do what I'm doing. Don't force anything. Just be the best I am while I'm doing it – teaching. "Teacher to the last" – Morrie from the book, *Tuesdays With Morrie.*

27. Keep refining and developing public speaking ability.

28. It's good for these kids to see I am vulnerable, down-to-earth, human, fallible, emotional, self-doubting, and unclear about big things. If I come down to reality once the emotions have settled, and they change their views of me, so be it. Everything changes, including fickle young opinions. Walt Whitman wrote, "I exist as I am, that is enough, If no other in the world be aware I sit content, And if each and all be aware I sit content."

29. I cannot control what other people think of me, or how their mind may change their perceptions. It is exhausting trying to live up to an image or perception.

30. Stop doubting every action. Should I keep my mouth shut – and let them keep that perfect image of me?

31. Stop being so hard on myself. Stop trying to be perfect in every moment. No one is. It's not fair to me. It's ego. It's pride. It's not radical humility. Be radically humble.

32. Look out to learn something from them. Look to be in the moment. Look out for the best they have within. Look to just be present.

33. Sometimes things work out, sometimes they don't. Accept both, pick up the pieces and move on.

34. Don't overreact to someone's negative opinion of my work. Just take a breath, accept it, and move on.

35. Whether people think I'm great or terrible, they're both right.

36. What I think of myself is all that matters. By accepting another person's opinion of me, I am saying what another person's random ideas and perceptions are in the moment own and define who I am. Is that true? Heck no. I know myself. I define who I am. Not a stranger. No one. Only me. My opinion – especially my thoughts can be wrong. Sometimes it's best to go outside, meditate, and let go of incorrect views.

37. Recognize when my melancholy moods bias my thoughts and are disguised as truth.

38. Be honest, but don't answer questions for students such as age, why I left New York, or questions about dating.

39. Answer the "Why did you leave New York for Malaysia?" question by asking, "I'm here… how can I serve you?"

40. Use the magical word: "inappropriate" to any unsuitable question or comment to me or between classmates.

41. Don't be sarcastic with individual kids. Or most of the time with a class. Sarcasm just isn't productive.

Testimonials from My Malaysian Students

"Thank you for realizing the potential in all of us and actually providing us an outlet to realize what we're capable of."

"You believed in us, encouraged us no matter what, and truly brought new meaning and understanding to interactive learning."

"History has never been so much fun."

"It was an amazing experience. I not only had fun, but I also gained knowledge."

"This is the first History class where a teacher let us do painting and linked it with history."

"This class was my favourite subject this semester and the most interesting not only what I learned but by who taught it and who I learned it with."

"History has been brought back to life."

"I realized for once I didn't have to memorize anything at all. Everything was laid out in my head. Because I felt like I was experiencing history itself."

CHAPTER EIGHTEEN SUMMARY

ACTION STEPS

HOW I CONNECTED WITH MY MALAYSIAN STUDENTS THROUGH HUMOUR

☑ Do not accept a contract with an international school until you speak with at least three teachers who have worked there within the past two years.

  Ask questions to current teachers at the school such as:
  a. What was your overall experience like?
  b. Would you recommend teaching at this school to a colleague or friend?
  c. What were the positive parts of working at the school and the negative parts?
  d. How were you paid? Was this an organized and transparent process or disorganized and unprofessional?
  e. What is the housing like? Is it affordable to live well or does it eat up most of your income?

☑ In the first two weeks, make an effort to befriend a colleague.

☑ Once you land in a new country, buy a fellow veteran teacher lunch. Ask them the following questions:
  a. Where are the safe, busy restaurants or take-out places to eat nearby?
  b. What are the restaurants to avoid?
  c. What restaurants serve the kind of food you like?

☑ Smile and nod when given advice about what or how to teach your class and then close the door and teach the way you want.

☑ If possible, arrive at your classrooms a few days early so that you are familiar with the environment. Know which keys go where.

☑ Create an empathetic, easy-going and open classroom environment from Day 1.

☑ Make it a priority to learn each student's name within the first month.

☑ Before teaching a new subject, ask veteran teachers what needs to be covered to satisfy curriculum standards. Ask what the essential core skills a student in this subject should have by the end of the course.

☑ Do role play to make real-world lessons stick.

☑ Get your students producing inspired, unconventional work by inventing project-based, personalized assignments.

☑ Encourage students to make short, humourous videos based on local teenage life.

☑ Have students write and perform original songs.

☑ Develop fun exam review challenges with silly consequences.

☑ Telling a student in front of her or his peers what they need to work on is not as successful in helping her or him grow as conferencing one-on-one with the student.

Build an intrinsically motivated classroom culture by:

☑ Providing a meaningful "why" at the beginning of a lesson.

☑ Building moments for students to get up and move.

☑ Modelling for students that growth comes from making excellent mistakes.

☑ Designing assignments that tap into multiple learning styles.

CHAPTER NINETEEN

"Stephen Douglas had called [Lincoln] twofaced, that he was trying to be appealing to both sides and both wings of his own party or to the whole populace. Lincoln said during a debate, "Judge Douglas, do you think if I had two faces that I'd be wearing this one."

— Dr. James Cornelius on Abraham Lincoln

HOW TO APPLY ABRAHAM LINCOLN'S USE OF HUMOUR TO REACH STUDENTS

Jamie: We're with Dr. James Cornelius, the Curator of the Abraham Lincoln Presidential Library and Museum located in Springfield, Illinois.

One thing, James, I was surprised when I watched Steven Spielberg's 2012 film, *Lincoln*, just how witty Lincoln was. He displayed a sense of humour in very tense moments with his political allies, when he was debating his opponents, and when he was speaking with constituents. He also showed a touching playful side with his son. Was this portrayal of Lincoln's lighter side accurate based on the historical facts?

James: It was accurate. As far as we know from a variety of testimony left to us by several people who Lincoln knew pretty well, lots of people in both Illinois and in Washington explained how Lincoln told stories and jokes. Not all of them were humorous, a number of them were, but I think they had a couple of different purposes, depending on the situation for Lincoln. Sometimes it was just to lighten the mood and he did famously say that he had to laugh sometimes amidst all of this horrible tension and death of the Civil War, otherwise he would break, and he would die.

It seems that several of his cabinet and colleagues agreed with that or more or less welcomed the respite, that there were a couple who really did not find it appropriate at the time, if they were just about to discuss what to do concerning the latest military loss, that Lincoln wanted to tell a joke that was oftentimes completely unrelated to the situation.

Jamie: So, to take a step back, how would you define humour during Lincoln's time?

James: Well, the type of humour he used, I guess you could say falls into two straight categories and maybe it's three. The two are rustic, and that includes everything from stories about farmers having troubles with pigs or cows or their own uneducated or uninformed or unsophisticated ways to bawdy and ethnic humour that is not, in some cases, considered polite these days. Certainly not in mixed company and Lincoln never did that in mixed company, but the man's world he lived in as a circuit attorney in Illinois is what he used as the basis for and as the audience for a lot of his jokes.

Then, category two essentially is what you could call parables. This does probably enter his mind as a youngster reading the Bible pretty thoroughly, he could quote long passages of the Bible from memory and did, and that was not unique in his day, when, in general, people had more reason to and more practice to commit things to memory, whether political speeches or sermons they heard at church or conversations with family that had to be repeated to others later on.

But, he could repeat these stories and understood that Jesus spoke in parables sometimes about how one situation was like another situation and that Old Testament prophets referred back to the early teachings of their people, for example, in terms of laws of their society and behaviour and practice that were suitable or fit examples to guide us.

Lincoln did a lot of this. It was one way to simplify what seemed like very complex issues.

Jamie: Did he ever use humour in his parables or to simplify complex issues that you can think of?

James: Well, yes. I can think of an example, and he did this once with his boys at home and then tailored it again for a critical issue when he was president, which is to say—and maybe you've heard this one before, I like to quote it because it works for all age groups.

If you picture a dog and you count the dog's tail as a leg, then how many legs does the dog have altogether? His boys would say, and his cabinet members would say, "Well, five, if you count the leg as a tail also, because it's kind of the same shape." Lincoln would say, "No, a dog has four legs. Calling the tail a leg doesn't make it a leg. Calling the slaves free in the Emancipation Proclamation doesn't make them free, at least in the long term, because it's a war-time measure," which Lincoln issued as a military Commander in Chief during war time. It would have no effect in peacetime.

Calling them free also will require the cooperation of a lot of people around them and to some extent the behaviour, the actions—the beliefs maybe even—of the slave, himself or herself, too. It's not good enough to say this is my private property right here, this is my pig, this is my farm, if no one around you agrees that it's yours, they take it from you, they break it, they steal it.

In the same way, the slaves, the freed people were not recognized as free by some people around them for a long time, and of course a whole succession of laws have been passed and a whole succession of a generation's behaviours and attitudes has changed as a result of those laws, but also the passage of time, other people's ideas and conversation.

That's a good story because it shows that Lincoln had this pretty simple ability to move from what was a little joke for his kids about language, calling something X when it's not Y, then you move it up to the abstract level and the legal and the social level for a major political problem for us.

Jamie: Not exactly on those lines, but in the general vicinity, did Lincoln ever use humour to balance power? What I mean by that is did he ever use humour to lower his status in the eyes of common folk, the electorates, even some of his colleagues in order to make himself either relatable or approachable?

James: You mean, sort of humble himself amongst others?

Jamie: Yes.

James: Oh, yes, frequently, that was one of his most common types of humour. It could just be a passing remark. I think this one comes up in the Spielberg film, but it's attested to very well in his pre-presidential years, too, that supposedly he once got into a carriage, a stagecoach, we'd call it, going from one town to another, and there was a rather proper older lady sitting in it already and she looked at him and said, "Good heavens, sir! You are the ugliest man I have ever seen." Lincoln said, "Well, I'm sorry, madam, but there's nothing I could do about that." She said, "Well, I suppose that's right, but you could at least stay home."

He told this to a convention of newspaper editors from this part of the state in 1856, during the John C. Fremont versus James Buchanan presidential campaign and it got recorded in a couple of small-town newspapers as almost exactly identical stories so that we're pretty sure that that's about as he said it. There are other versions of it that come up during his presidential years, slightly different, about who says it to him and where it happens, but the point is he knew he was ugly. He said at another time during his debates with Stephen Douglas, that Douglas had called him twofaced, that he was trying to be appealing to both sides and both wings of his own party or to the whole populace. He said, "Judge Douglas, do you think if I had two faces that I'd be wearing this one?"

This always breaks the crowd up really well and it humbles him. It reduces the intellectual tone of the conversation by a fair bit and that's one thing that people really disliked about him—not many people—but that he was in some respect anti-intellectual.

There's the case in which he was about to announce his decision concerning emancipation to the Cabinet and he started the Cabinet meeting by reading from a volume of humorous essays, the rustic type, by a guy named Artemis Ward. It was a pen name. He was more like a Garrison Keillor, or Dave Barry humourists in our era today, in which Artemis Ward wrote about a hick from Utica, New York, who was angry about some blasphemous, anti-Christian artwork that had recently been displayed somewhere and he stumbles through his self-righteous approach to this problem and mispronounces words and misunderstands history and doesn't understand art.

Lincoln thinks this is all really funny and three or four of the cabinet members are guffawing away and others are sitting there stone faced. Then Lincoln puts it down and says, "Well, today's business is this new policy of emancipation that I've decided upon."

Jamie: This is an example of how Lincoln would try to lower the tension of the meeting before dealing with serious issues that were about to be discussed.

James: Yes, exactly. What he was trying to do was soften them up a little bit, prepare them for a serious discussion to come.

Jamie: From what I understand from this example, he's also using a very specific and deliberate type of humour to lighten the tone. He's creating an environment when he senses that that's the right approach to get his point across.

James: Right. There are lots of different ways or different reasons he did it. Sometimes he was just cracking jokes for no real reason. He didn't think of it as wasting time. He didn't really have that Puritan's sense of using every minute productively, although he was himself quite productive and got a lot of work accomplished.

But, he didn't work at the pace of let's say what Edwin Stanton did or Salmon P. Chase. There's a different sort of background. The reason he could tell these stories, for the most part, was that majority of his cabinet members, like himself, had been attorneys. One was a newspaper editor originally, and they knew what the life of the rural people was like. Their own upbringing had been moderately humble in most cases. Not all of them, Montgomery Blair, his Postmaster General, grew up quite wealthy in the Washington, D.C. area and Edwin Stanton became a very wealthy lawyer, but he sure didn't start out that way. He had some hardships early in life. William Seward, Secretary of State, grew up moderately comfortable, but lived in a pretty small town in a rural county upstate New York.

So, they all understood this kind of person, back in the day when something around seventy percent of the population of the U.S. was categorized in the Census Bureau definitions as living in rural areas.

The simple, unsophisticated, honest, hard-working people with their simple, unsophisticated problems, like stray dogs, sick cows, horses that wouldn't trot when you wanted them to trot, travelling salesmen. All of these things were common coin to nearly all of them.

There just wasn't the sensitivity that really is quite new, it's really only about roughly thirty years old in our country today, about jesting after people's ethnic origins or their accents. Lincoln was a great mimic as a kid and this is actually correlated with good memory and good public speaking later on. People who are good mimics, who can remember the way the preacher sounded or the salesman and capture his accent and his peculiar expressions and then get up on a tree stump and exaggerate them for the neighbourhood kids later and get a good, long laugh, made Lincoln really popular. People appreciated that.

Even on his last day of life, we learned only about four years ago, he told a joke that was recorded in the diary of one cabinet member's wife because she actually recorded it right after dinner when her husband came home and told her the joke. The other people who wrote letters and kept diaries, of course all forgot about it by 10:15 p.m., when they'd heard the president had been shot at Ford's Theater.

But the joke is they were talking about whether Jefferson Davis and the other confederate leaders should be captured and imprisoned. Lincoln said, "No, I hope Jeff Davis can be treated like Paddy's flea. The poor Irishman, Paddy, who's got a flea all over his body and he just can't catch it. Finally, one day he reaches under his shirt and he grabs it and he pulls it out and it's not there. It's got away again." Lincoln wanted Jeff Davis to be treated that way, let him go. Let him sneak away like Paddy's flea.

Everybody recognized the problem of bed bugs and fleas because nearly all residences had them—I'm not sure about Montgomery Blair's—but Lincoln had bed bugs and fleas for the first fifty years of his life and he was thinking about it all the time and he makes a joke out of the poor Irishman because that's the most available "poor immigrant" group around whose plight everyone understands and at a certain level, they can all relate to it.

There are two or three other times when he told jokes about poor Irishman because the accent is funny and because their situation is identifiable and it's not all that different from everybody else's situation.

Jamie: Is that a way he used humour to educate the electorate, or crowds on certain issues?

James: It might be. It shows both sympathy for the plight of the poor Irishman, or the poor anybody. It brings you down, it humbles you a little bit, makes them know that you understand the problem of fleas.

I don't know if you'd say that it educates them so much as entertains them and politics was the greatest source of entertainment in the 19th century. That's why the Lincoln-Douglas debates were so famous and remain of interest, to get the chance to go see a couple of well-spoken men, who are very well informed, who come to your little town and talk for three hours straight about the issues of the day, with a fair amount of misrepresentation of your opponent's position or a fair amount of exaggeration, or certainly repetition, too.

In other words, making jokes about the Democrats and what Stephen Douglas's people believe played right into Lincoln's needs, politically, to set the Democrats off as extreme, immoral, wrong, profligate, whatever it is you choose, and that works. So, it's a form of education, even if you might call it exaggeration.

Jamie: Aside from the twofaced comment you mentioned Lincoln used during the famous Douglas debates, were there any other instances where he used humour in the debates in order to persuade?

James: Yes, certainly there are. Sometimes it isn't exactly humour, it's more simplistic. There's a case in which he used what might be introductory algebra, call it what you will—if A can enslave B, and does so because he finds it to be in his interests, then why can't B enslave A if he can persuade everybody that it's in his interests?

In other words, why shouldn't a black man enslave a white man if he can convince enough people nearby that it's in the interest of both of them for the situation to arise?

The absurdity of that simple logic is amusing enough. It's not a belly laugh, but it's humorous because it's ridiculous. What Lincoln is showing is the ridiculousness of a law that defines people by race, which is really driven by their own economic interest.

There are other cases like that in which he would turn a simple situation around to its reverse. If A, well, then naturally B. There's a case—not in Lincoln-Douglas, but earlier, I think it was 1840—he was debating a guy named Jessie Thomas when William Henry Harrison and Martin Van Buren were in the presidential race and Jessie Thomas was moderately well-dressed. He was a well-to-do man and he stood up on the platform and was talking about how the Democratic party was the party of the common man, the common people. Lincoln managed to sneak up behind Thomas, while he was speaking, and unbutton Thomas' front coat button and it flew open, because Thomas was a big, round guy, to reveal that he was wearing a silk vest and he had a gold watch chain hanging out of it. Lincoln said, "Common dress, Mr. Thomas?" This just breaks up the crowd.

That's a case in which he didn't even need to speak, though he used that punch line after everybody had seen that this guy was not what he appeared to be.

Jamie: What is the greatest lesson you've taken from Lincoln's life?

James: Well, he was remarkably diligent in teaching himself what he wanted to learn and this is true of everybody at a certain level, but Lincoln was notable for being really good at it in completely different things. He wanted to become a lawyer, so he borrowed law books from people because he couldn't afford them and he read them and he read them again, he memorized them, just as he had read the Bible and memorized it when he was a kid.

Then, he taught himself surveying, lots and lots of tables of numbers. He taught himself mathematics by doing problems out of the back of a book.

When he realized Euclid's geometry was something most educated men who became congressmen learned in school, he borrowed somebody's Euclid geometry to understand how proofs are made in order to make his spoken arguments more logically coherent. The proofs of geometry are the same as the proofs of rhetoric.

When he needed to understand military strategy, which he barely had any personal experience with, he checked out a book from the Library of Congress written by General Halleck, who was called "Old Brains," the smartest general in the army, about military strategy's history, and he read it. He got to the point where he understood certain tactics and strategy better than some of the generals did. He studied maps. He was always good with maps because he had been a surveyor and he understood where the attacks should come at a couple points and he actually directed such an attack from a boat at Norfolk, Virginia, in 1862.

Lincoln is certainly our last president to have done that, sort of in the way that Winston Churchill did it once in a small way during World War II. He actually directed the attack because he understood the tactics and the strategy and the physical lay of the land.

This is something everyone can do—get the books and read them. That's what he recommended to young men who asked him how you become a great lawyer. "How do I become a great lawyer like you, Mr. Lincoln?" He says, "It's very hard work and it's pretty boring. Get the works, read them, and read them again."

That's what is remarkable about Lincoln, that he did that in so many different fields. It's a lesson to us all.

CHAPTER NINTEEN SUMMARY

ACTION STEPS

HOW TO APPLY ABRAHAM LINCOLN'S USE OF HUMOUR TO REACH STUDENTS

- ☑ Abraham Lincoln told jokes unrelated to the situation at hand to lighten the mood during tense cabinet meetings.
- ☑ Lincoln told parables interweaving his personal history with historical references.
- ☑ He used these stories, some of them humourous to simplify the complex issues of the day.
- ☑ He practiced taking a little joke for his children and applying it to a broader social context.
- ☑ He used humour to make fun of himself or agreeing with certain disparaging remarks used against him by his opponents. This tactic always broke up the crowd and disarmed his challengers' attacks on him.
- ☑ Lincoln would attempt to soften up bitter cabinet members by acting a little silly and off-the-wall with impersonations or in his tone of voice. The idea was to shift the tone of the conversation to prepare the group for a serious discussion to come.
- ☑ Lincoln did not think of telling jokes or humourous parables during productive meetings as a waste of time. He thought of it as a way to relate to those he worked closely with as well as connect with the common folk.
- ☑ One of Lincoln's favourite ways to use humour was to mimic common archetypes of the day like how the traveling preacher or the traveling salesman sounded.

- ☑ A cabinet member's wife recorded a joke the President made on the last full day of his life.
- ☑ He used humour to show sympathy for those who were disadvantaged by society. It was another way he used humour to bring himself down and make the economically disadvantaged know that he understood their problems.
- ☑ He expressed humour to entertain the audiences during the great Lincoln-Douglas debates.
- ☑ He demonstrated the absurdity of an irrational law like slavery with simple logic. It wasn't meant to get a belly laugh, but it's humourous because it's ridiculous.
- ☑ He pointed out the inconsistencies of his opponent where the reverse was true. During one debate, a well-to-do opponent was talking about how the Democratic Party was the party of the ordinary man. However, this candidate was wearing a silk vest with a gold watch chain hanging out of it. Lincoln called this out by sneaking up beside him as he spoke, saying to the crowd, "Common dress, Mr. Thomas?" His humour made the most of surprise and sudden shifts in perception.
- ☑ He changed his humour to suit the audience with whom he was speaking. He didn't use the same stories for all situations. He adapted his parables, jokes, and impersonations to relate to his audience.
- ☑ Lincoln was remarkably diligent in teaching himself what he wanted to learn. He wanted to become a lawyer, so he borrowed law books from people because he couldn't afford them, and he read them again and memorized them. Then he taught himself surveying and mathematics out of the back of a book.

CHAPTER TWENTY

"It's very important to roll up your sleeves and go, I'm learning, I don't have to be a genius right off the bat."

Screenwriter, Stephen Gaghan

HOW STEPHEN GAGHAN WENT FROM CLASS CLOWN TO ACADEMY AWARD WINNING SCREENWRITER

How questions and interviews can lead students to epic levels of discovery

Disclaimer: The following interview with Academy Award winning screenwriter Stephen Gaghan may only be relevant to an English teacher who wants to teach screenwriting and shares this with his or her students to show them the challenges of a successful screenwriter and his suggestions. How does it relate to teachers of other subjects? I have found that the art of the interview and asking thought-provoking questions is a significant skill to teach students. Mainly, it teaches students how to ask big, meaningful questions, to think independently through in-depth preparation prior to interviewing a person, how to build rapport, listen, converse, think on your feet, improvise, connect with another person, and how to research and accumulate details for writing, both fiction and non-fiction.

It's a skill that could be used in classes such as: English (W6 – Who/ what/ when/ where/ why/ how, asking questions within the learning framework of a self-organized learning environment, Hero's Journey interview of seniors), law (debate), history (analyze significant historical figures through their interviews), modern issues or politics, (Skype interview with expert on the topic in class), sociology (case studies), challenge and change in society (experiments), modern western civilizations (role-play interviewing a subject in a biography), drama (play, role play), media studies (podcasting, analyze different interview techniques, bias in media questioning), art (interview great artists to learn their process and techniques) and film (documentary). I have found that practicing my interview skills has also made me empathetic and helpful to students who come to me for additional support in dealing with the challenges of high school life. I am more present and think more quickly on my feet, focusing on how I can provide helpful feedback through questioning rather than trying to solve the problem for them.

Here is a webinar I gave on creating self-organized learning environments, which includes the type of issues that impact students to go on an intellectual journey of discovery on a topic. I include different forms of questioning, including examples of interviewing experts or mentors on a theme of study. (http://www.slideshare.net/DigitalJLearn/the-simple-effective-way-to-use-soles-self-organized-learning-environmentsindependently research)

This short YouTube video by body language expert Mark Bowden shows a useful strategy for how teachers can actively listen to students during a one-to-one conversation.

Listening Better, A Body Language Skill by Mark Bowden (https://www.youtube.com/watch?v=JKVa9CfdtAI)

Legendary comedian Jerry Seinfeld masterfully gets a range of public figures to open up about themselves. He mixes witty questions with serious topics brought up in a respectful way. He sets the tone of the interview with a curious and amused frame of mind, shows a genuine interest in learning about the person he is interviewing and never seems to take himself too seriously. He gives and takes in opening up about his life when the moment calls for it. He also shows that doing an activity with the person you are interviewing (if the situation allows for it) is an excellent way to put someone at ease in asking them questions about themselves or their work.

Comedian Jerry Seinfeld interviews President Barack Obama http://comediansincarsgettingcoffee.com/president-barack-obama-just-tell-him-you-re-the-president

One of the three most dynamic teachers of my high school days, the late Julian Craft, who taught my grade 12 Modern Western Civilizations, assigned us a historical figure to interview in which we provided the questions and the answers. Mr. Craft chose for me the biography Made in Japan, about the life of Sony founder Akio Morita. I didn't know how to approach the imagined interview at first, but I started doing research on post-World War Two Japan and Japanese business practices. I realized the assignment had more to do with teaching us the value of preparation and close reading, than the interview itself.

In my Grade 9 English Hero's Journey unit, I provide students with a sample of questions (offered in the Resources section of this book) when interviewing senior citizens about their lives. I teach them the kind of questions it is appropriate to ask (about their childhood, their favorite memories, their mentors) and questions that they may consider avoiding unless the interviewee brings it up first (about death, religion, etc.) Asking and answering questions in an interview situation is a skill that can be developed and practiced in any classroom and applied to the world beyond, whether it's being interviewed for a job, making small talk with a new friend at school or writing an introductory e-mail to reach out to a future mentor.

"The secret to asking great questions is avoiding generalities or broad philosophical inquiries," New York Times reporter Jodi Kantor wrote in a Quora.com thread. She also suggests not to use hypotheticals. Do your homework, she adds. Be specific and concrete.

Questions not to Ask:
-no hypotheticals
-no 'yes' or 'no'
-Know your audience. Don't get too personal right away. Start with something lighter.
Instead of asking people if they have desirable attributes, ask them

to tell a story about a time they exhibited one of the attributes for which you're selecting. (Tynan)
Don't ask someone if they react well to a crisis; ask them to tell you about a crisis that they resolved successfully. (Tynan)

Questions to Ask:
-Open-Ended: How? What? Where? When? Why? Who?
-How you ask a question is important. "Tell me about the time when…/tell me a story about…" -Alex Blumberg, producer, This American Life
-Think of questions as prompts to get someone started
-"What were the steps?" (Blumberg)
-"If the old you could see the new you, what would you say?" (Blumberg)
-If someone answers a question and gives an answer that seems meaningful to them but you don't understand what they mean, ask, "What do you make of that?" (Blumberg)
-Sometimes less is more. Let there be slightly prolonged silences (count to 10) and stay in the pocket, to use the football term. People will often fill those silences with golden revelations. (Referenced from *blog.creativelive.com*: *4 Unexpectedly Great Interview Questions to Ask Anyone*)

From *Quora*, the site I reference to spark questions:
-"What's the most unexpected thing you've learned along the way?"
-"If you could call yourself five years ago and had 30 seconds, what would you say?"
-"What is the best piece of advice you have been given?"
-"What is the best question anyone has ever asked you? And how did you answer?"
-"How will you make the world a better place than when you came into it?"
-"What do you want to be remembered for?"
-"Are you doing what you thought you would be doing when you were growing up?"

-"Someone gets a text message from you, and for whatever reason they're not sure it's actually you. They're worried that someone may have stolen your phone. What could they ask to make sure it's really you?"
-"Are you lucky?"
-"What would you do if you were homeless?"
-"What has been your main motivation in life so far?"
-"What does being successful mean to you?"
-"What room in your house resonates most with you?"
-"What important truth do very few people agree with you on?" (Peter Thiel in *Zero to One*)
-"If you had to drop everything right now and write a novel, what would it be?" (visakanv.com)

MY INTERVIEW WITH STEPHEN GAGHAN

I did this interview with Academy Award-winning Screenwriter, Stephen Gaghan during the time I worked for Broadway Video. I interviewed leading screenwriters and filmmakers about how they got started in the business and what advice they had for creative students. I used my credentials of working for Lorne Michaels' companies to get in the door.

I included parts of this never-before-seen interview in this book because it has inspired me on countless occasions over the past fifteen years. It's as relevant today as it was then. Stephen Gaghan is self-deprecatingly humourous, brutally honest, humble, real, and thoughtful in his answers. We spoke about his early troubles in high school when he drove a go cart through the front door of the school. This led to a suspension and near expulsion.

He told me about his struggles to break into the business, what makes a good mentor and advice he has for students starting off on their path. I called him to congratulate him on his Academy Award win for the screenplay of, *Traffic*, that he received after our interview. He called me back and said that the interview he did with me, "was the best interview that he gave, out of over a hundred, including Charlie Rose and USA Today." This was one of the highlights during my time in New York. **When students ask me how they can meet mentors, one approach is to find a way to interview them.**

Jamie: What was the turning point in your career?

Stephen Gaghan: I knew my stuff stunk and something really interesting happened to me once. I'm friends with Charlie Kaufman, and he read a script of mine and then we got together and he gave me notes on it. In Hollywood, the easiest thing in the world is to say, "Hey your script is pretty good." It's harder for someone to read something and say, "You know it doesn't really work and let me tell you why." Clearly, he knew what he was doing at such a different level that it blew my mind.

Jamie: What other screenwriters have you learned from? What did you learn about yourself as a screenwriter from them?

Stephen Gaghan: Michael Tolkin. The guy who wrote: *The Player.* I sort of realised at this point, "Oh, my God, I really don't know what I'm doing, and then I could have easily quit at that point, even though I already had written five feature film scripts and ten TV scripts. Instead, it really made me want to get better, and then I really started working at it, and I really began concentrating.

Jamie: What do you know now that you wished you knew when you were starting out?

Stephen Gaghan: Totally easy. It's to give yourself a break on the first draft. Get a first draft done. Don't put so much pressure on yourself for that first thing to be brilliant or to be perfect. The thing is it's so important to finish something. It's very easy to get caught up by knowing in your brain that you want to write a script as good as say, Charlie Kaufman. But in your execution, if you have any honesty at all you look at your stuff and say, '"Look at how this isn't working and this isn't working and it's easy to start pulling your hair out and think you're a miserable, lousy fraud and I should just go back to Kentucky and sell cars.

Jamie: Is that where you're from?

Stephen Gaghan: I'm from Louisville, Kentucky.

Jamie: You got kicked out of school, right?

Stephen Gaghan: I got expelled from Kentucky Country Day for driving a go-cart through the administration building.

Jamie: How long did it take you to get to this point in your career?

Stephen Gaghan: I've been doing this now pretty much all the time for nine years, and I published short stories beforehand and did journalism. It takes a really long time to get an art form under your belt. Very difficult. It's very important to roll up your sleeves and go, "I'm learning. I don't have to be a genius right off the bat."

Jamie: What were some obstacles you faced along the way?

Stephen Gaghan: On the way to getting to work with people like Edward Zwick, I had run-ins with a lot of people who really didn't know what they were doing.

And another time, I was pitching over the telephone to Baywatch Nights, and the guy running Baywatch Nights was so condescending to me. He was like, "How did you get my number?" And it's humiliating, and your ego just gets destroyed. You think, I've worked for Paris Review; I've published short fiction in the Literary Quarterly- what am I doing here? But that's all ego because the fact is what someone once told me, and I really believe it- "When you're ready success will happen." When they told me that, it infuriated me as you can imagine. In fact, it's probably true that through all these rejections and continually writing more stuff, I got better. And then the day comes when you finally get in a room in TV with someone like Steven Bochco who really knows what he's doing, and in the movie world where you get to work with really good people. There's effort to get there. Maybe some people get really lucky and they get there right away but I had a lot of travails along the way.

Jamie: What are you working on now?

Stephen Gaghan: I'm doing a production re-write on *Black Hawk Down* for Ridley Scott and Jerry Bruckheimer, and they're just so smart. And the guys they work with are really smart and they know what they're doing, and their instincts are so good. Things move more quickly and there's not a lot of ego.

Jamie: What makes a great script?

Stephen Gaghan: Voice is really important. You read a script and it has a voice, and it has a point of view. Your characters talk in ways that feel real, not like you've heard before. You're looking for things that have a certain amount of energy and forward momentum. Good scripts take you into a world that feels real but you're not familiar with, and the best writers do that and it looks effortless. And even though it usually looks effortless, the draft you're reading is like the hundredth draft.

Jamie: What are a few questions you ask yourself before starting a script?

Stephen Gaghan: Please God, let me become rich and famous (laughs). I think about all the retribution I'm gonna get on the people who doubted me – no, I'm kidding again. It's a good question. I'm not sure. I think it's different every time. There's so much fear; it's pretty nerve-racking. You don't have anything in your head, you feel like a phoney.

Jamie: But Stephen, I can't believe after what you've accomplished, you can be so humble.

Stephen Gaghan: Totally calculated this humility. I've been trained by Public Relations Executives. No, I'm kidding. It's just that you feel nervous and it's humbling. You don't have all the answers and so it's easy to try to contemplate that you've got to figure out all these things and you're not sure you're gonna do a good job of it so if you're honest at all, you go, "I'm really nervous," and if I've done anything in the past that people have liked, thoughts starts to add up like, "God, I don't want to let these people down. I don't want to let myself down." You have to put all of that away, that's all ego stuff. You're just there and honestly try to show up and do a day's work as hard as you can. And then once you get into a story, it usually takes a life of itself and you finish something. There's just no greater feeling because you can see that finish line and you just start sprinting towards it and it's just a remarkable feeling.

Jamie: How important is a literary foundation for an aspiring screenwriter?

Stephen Gaghan: I came out of a background of reading a lot of books, watching TV. I saw many movies but I read more. Writing a script is writing, and reading a book is reading writing, and I think it is very helpful to have devoured stories, and I read thousands of books. In my case, it was very important.

Jamie: What immediate actions should an aspiring filmmaker take and what should he/she keep in mind on the road to success in this business?

Stephen Gaghan: I think they should start writing an original script the second they read the answer to this question. Turn off the TV; put down the paper, and type FADE IN. Start from there. Keep trying because once you create a good script it's yours and you control it. It will open every door and you'll get a crack at directing it, you'll get a crack at having a career. But, it all starts with the script and if you want to direct or even produce, the effort it will take for you to write a good script will teach you so much about dramatic art. I recommend to everybody to sit down and do it.

I mean, Steven Spielberg wrote his first script. Steven Soderbergh wrote his first script. Ingmar Bergman, Federico Fellini, Jean-Luc Godard, and Francois Truffaut - you name anybody you like as a filmmaker and they started out writing a screenplay. I think that if it's good enough for Spielberg, Soderbergh, Bergman, Fellini, Godard, and Truffaut, it's probably good enough for you and me.

CHAPTER TWENTY SUMMARY

ACTION STEPS

HOW STEPHEN GAGHAN WENT FROM CLASS CLOWN TO ACADEMY AWARD WINNING SCREENWRITER

- ☑ When students ask me how they can meet people or mentors in the field, they wish to pursue, one approach is to find a way to interview them.
- ☑ It's harder for someone to read something you've written and say, "You know it doesn't really work and let me tell you why." This kind of feedback helps your writing get to the next level.
- ☑ Give yourself a break on your first draft. Get a first draft done. Don't put so much pressure on yourself for that first thing to be brilliant or to be perfect. It's so important to finish something.
- ☑ It takes a long time to get an art form under your belt. It's crucial to roll up your sleeves and go, "I'm learning, I don't have to be a genius right off the bat."
- ☑ Voice is critical in writing. It has a point of view. Your characters talk in ways that feel real, not like you've heard before. Good writing takes you into a world that seems real, but you're unfamiliar with. And even though good writers make it look effortless, the draft you're reading is like the hundredth draft.
- ☑ I think it's very helpful to have devoured a lot of stories, and I read thousands of books to become a good writer.
- ☑ Examples of interviewing experts or mentors on a theme of study. (http://www.slideshare.net/DigitalJLearn/the-

simple-effective-way-to-use-soles-self-organized-learning-environmentsindependently research)

☑ This short Youtube video by body language expert Mark Bowden shows teachers how to actively listen to students during a one-to-one discussion so that students feel heard.

☑ Listening Better, A Body Language skill by Mark Bowden (https://www.youtube.com/watch?v=JKVa9CfdtAI)

☑ **Questions not to ask:**

- No hypotheticals
- No 'yes' or 'no.'
- Know your audience. Don't get too personal right away. Start with something lighter.
- Instead of asking people if they have desirable attributes, ask them to tell a story about a time they exhibited one of the attributes for which you're selecting. (Tynan)

☑ **Questions to ask:**

- Open-Ended: Why? Who? When? What? How?
- How you ask a question is important, "tell me about the time when..."(Alex Blumberg, Podcast producer)
- Think of questions as prompts to get someone started
- "What were the steps"
- "If the old you could see the new you, what would you say?"
- If someone answers a question and gives an answer that seems meaningful to them but you don't understand what they mean to ask, "What do you make of that?"
- Let there be slightly prolonged silences. (all questions referenced from an interview with producer Alex Blumberg on Creative Live)

CHAPTER TWENTY-ONE

88 LESSONS FROM *MY FIRST YEAR OF HIGH SCHOOL TEACHING*

COMMENTS (Excerpts from an actual report card I wrote)

"If I was a social anthropologist, I would have a field day calculating every facial expression Jen expresses over the course of an exam. There is the, 'I don't feel well today' sigh, the 'I'm in no shape to do this because I drove my brother somewhere yesterday and am exhausted' pout, and the, 'Do I really need to answer every single one of these questions considering I already got into university?' glare. I walked out of the English exam feeling like I did two hours of Ashtanga yoga due to the complete exhaustion of watching Jen get through this ordeal.

Jen must remember one essential thing for next year: first year university is an overwhelming, exciting, scary, fun, roller-coaster for everyone, so she cannot, under any circumstances, doubt herself or talk herself into not being up to the task."

In an office-building floor converted into a makeshift school in mid-town Toronto, a few floors under the Pakistani Consulate and adjacent to a tranquil pond, there was a former alternative high school called, Freemont. My sister, who had interviewed for a teaching position at this school suggested I send in my resume. I got a call shortly after that, interviewed with the Principal and Owner of the school, Sean Meggeson. I had less than 24 hours to prep for four separate classes.

I was asked to take over from another teacher. With no formal high school teaching experience at the time, it was a trial by fire. Sean told me if I didn't capture their attention by convincingly explaining a complex legal term in a way this class would accept, they would instantly reject me. Some of the ways I have discussed to incorporate humour into the classroom, were developed over the course of my year at Freemont. I experimented with improvisation, story-telling, and personalizing exams with inside jokes. I encouraged tactile learners to take exercise breaks during class, had a Friday afternoon flag football game and got students to make films about their lives.

I found my way through Grade 12 Law, Grade 10-11 English and Grade 10 Drama, often learning the material the night before I had to teach. Every day was an adventure figuring out how to deal with students who were intelligent, manipulative, always testing me yet fun to teach with a potpourri of behavioral challenges. I'm thankful to Sean Meggeson for giving me this opportunity. Freemont taught me humour can help make an instant connection and draw in the most reluctant learners.

After the last day of my year teaching at Freemont, I wrote a list of mistakes, omissions, slips, blunders, miscalculations, oversights, gaffes and lessons I ploughed through during my first year.

Here they are.

1. Catch students doing something right.

2. Focus on the top of the mountain, not on those trying to drag me down.

3. Always rise above gossip and negative talk about other people.

4. Never speak negatively about another person. It feels stressful and painful afterwards.

5. When questioned by a know-it-all student: 1) Ignore it 2) Ask a question back 3) Keep cool.

6. Don't leave marking until the last minute.

7. It's easier to start strict and ease up, than the other way. I'm still discovering that balance.

8. Call students on negative behaviour right at the moment.

9. The first student who misbehaves is sent out of the class for five minutes.

10. The first five minutes should be a simple, fun exercise to create momentum.

11. Sometimes, no matter what I do will have no effect on a kid with deep issues, or on drugs.

12. Keep some distance from students.

13. Don't answer inappropriate questions.

14. Keep using, 'inappropriate' to inappropriate questions, comments, non-sequiturs.

15. Give more immediate mark feedback for students. It is a constructive kind of encouragement.

16. Make more fun competitions within class.

17. Football or another kind of game in the middle of class calms students and is a good bonding exercise.

18. Pause. Breathe. Smile.

19. Always speak to students' interests.

20. When a student asks, "How old are you?" Answer: Not appropriate question to ask a teacher.

21. Don't show the process or go into too much detail how you got there. Just show results.

22. Don't praise myself publicly.

23. Never react in anger to students. Appropriate response: I understand you're upset about this. Let the student feel that I have heard them all the way through. Repeat back what they are upset about. Do not judge their feelings.

24. Don't swear.

25. The 'Human Rights Day' was an extraordinary lesson in bringing history into the classroom; a lesson of real strength, and the perseverance of the human spirit through the most unimaginable horrors. I really can accomplish interesting things in a creative, effective way.

26. I never would have had such a moving, satisfying life experience, if I was sitting at home in front of the computer.

27. Taking consistent action creates positive emotion.

28. In every situation in which I am dealing with challenging people, I am given the opportunity to practise ten years' worth of Dale Carnegie, Tony Robbins, and Wayne Dyer.

29. When a student displays disrespect, laziness, lack of gratitude, or anger, try to remember when they have been productive, positive, and respectful.

30. Display of outward anger is a result of inner pain, neglect, frustration and fear.

31. Being 'too nice' means being someone's chump, and allowing myself to be taken advantage of.

32. Deal with difficult, irrational people in the future by ignoring them, laughing at their comments and never engaging in an argument with them. Never.

33. Teaching develops communication skills in front of a group, develops persuasion techniques, makes me conscious of how I sell myself and my ideas to a group of people, forces me to discipline my life into a productive structure, makes me practice conflict- resolution skills.

34. The habit of working every day can and will be used to my advantage in creating new and better writing and art.

35. I've discovered that when planning lessons, using creativity and out of the box thinking my students are highly motivated and attendance is increased.

36. Keeping physically fit and maintaining my personal hobbies, interests and friendships gives me the energy and motivation to reach my full potential.

37. Sting, Paddy Doyle, Richard Bolt, Mark Knopfler were all teachers while they were working on their first significant creative works.

38. I like to work with kids of all ages. Sharing my knowledge and life lessons with them gives me great pleasure.

39. Once I'm in a zone in one area, confidence shifts to all areas of my life.

40. If you have a difficult student, have a five-minute meeting every week or two to touch base and discuss the states of the issue and give feedback.

41. Catch teachers/staff doing good things — especially praise publicly after a successful event.

42. Don't play favourites.

43. Be the best at whatever I am doing at that moment in my life.

44. I am an inspirational educator, and even though I have other interests I am pursuing, I should celebrate and be thankful for this gift.

45. Keep your head about you when everyone is losing theirs and blaming it on you. Kipling's line could be applied to teaching.

46. Always be aware of tone of voice – firm, confident, speak up without losing control or composure. Match the other person's tone and level and then bring it down to a civil level.

47. When I consistently send loving kindness and generosity without blame, it is difficult for people to stay abusive, defensive.

48. I don't have to answer every question or any question.

49. Never expect gratitude from students or the boss.

50. Don't take on, absorb or react to a students' or staff member's issues.

51. Ignore a student who demands to be the center of attention.

52. Don't explain marks. Don't overexplain or justify why we're doing something in class.

53. A good day-to-day matra is: Silence is simple, clear, stress free and always appropriate in comparison to gossip or expressing anger.

54. Don't give students the answer right away. Let them work for it.

55. Don't complain. Just do things based on my own inner moral compass and values.

56. Give students a list of what is due every so often.

57. Never speak negatively about anyone in the school at any level.

58. Don't be eager to point out my own trivial mistake unless it is brought up.

59. Don't go into every detail of a conversation. Give the general idea. Less is more.

60. Don't carry the baggage of yesterday into today's class.

61. Don't take anyone in a school environment's judgements too seriously.

62. Don't concern myself with anything other than the present.

63. Criticism is inevitable — especially directed towards the successful and the standouts.

64. Don't let students trap me or back me into a corner or successfully hit weak spots by reacting to them, or engaging at their level, or showing anger. The best thing to do is laugh, ignore, ask a flurry of questions back at them and change the subject in the process, and if none of that works send them out of the class.

65. Start stricter, and then ease up. It doesn't work the other way.

66. Bend to be fair, but don't cave in to be popular or else they will push down the wall.

67. I would not have had the opportunity to read *Hamlet*, and 100 *Years of Solitude*, and an excuse for teaching and practicing morning pages writing exercises with my students from, *A Writers' Journey*.

68. If you want to learn something, teach it.

69. I absorbed several books on CD on my joyous rides to and from work including *1984*, *Life of Pi*, Public Speaking, Wayne Dyer, The Old Testament, *One-Minute Manager*.

70. Call students on inappropriate comments or actions immediately, but don't overreact, and be careful not to point out some and not others. Be consistent and fair.

71. Don't let a few students dominate and monopolize the class. The way to stop this is by proactively engaging other students into

discussions, ignoring inappropriate, minor attention-seeking comments and actions, and asking them to work outside of the class if they can't work in the class environment.

72. Be approachable.

73. Don't tell specific details of my personal life. General is fine, but too many details makes students feel that they are your friends. Being friendly is good, being buddies creates more stress than it is worth.

74. Smile more.

75. Breathe more.

76. Every work environment has a place of silence, serenity, and peace. At Freemont it was the spot, in the trees, facing the water.

77. The lesson of Joseph — his life took an unexpected negative turn when he was sold into slavery by his jealous brothers, but he ended up being in the right place in the right time to be discovered by Pharaoh as the leader of the land. The lesson here is teaching is getting me closer to my creative goals — by teaching the fundamentals of writing, by forcing myself to confront my fear of speaking in front of people, by engaging my mind on many levels, my strengthening emotional, and mental and intellectual faculties.

78. I watched many films I wanted to see and incorporated them into the course.

79. I can't please everyone — nor do I really want to.

80. I learned not to underestimate the impact I have had:
    - Student: "My English teacher Jamie said I have talent for writing. Nobody ever said that to me before."
    - Student's mom: "You're like a hero to my son, and these kids."
    - Student: "I have so much respect for you, I talk about you all the time. Are you proud of me? I don't want to disappoint you."
    - Student: "We love you."
    - Student's mom: "You have no idea the difference you've

made in his life."

81. If I were a boss, I would meet with my employees individually at least once every two weeks and ask: Is there anything on your mind that you'd like to discuss? Problems? Good things? Solutions to fix things you see as potential problems? I would also catch employees doing the right things with casual praise. I would not focus on a teacher's minor mistakes.

82. Never lose it. Always be calm, cool, and outwardly balanced. Do this through breathing, focusing on the spot of the uncomfortable, negative emotion, take a break if necessary, and jump immediately into something else in order to get my mind off the issue.

83. If I focus entirely on giving — communicating, answering a question, and listening, I won't have time to concern myself with being self-conscious and worried about how students will perceive me.

84. The best way to deal with a school inspector, or someone in a position of power who is judging is to just listen, be agreeable, take criticism gracefully, acknowledging their words, thanking them for their feedback, and asking a few general questions to further procure insights. You never know..., there may be some.

85. Even when you give 100% of your energy to being the best teacher you can be, it's important to have outside interests that keep you well rounded and balanced.

86. I have the power to impact positively every new environment I'm in.

87. Don't try to be popular. The more I try, the more it backfires.

88. Teachers, bosses or leaders who aim for popularity never receive it.

CONCLUSION

I can't remember who won the Academy Award in any year, but I can remember the years of my favourite teachers.

Do you remember the years of your favourite teachers? For me, it was 1980 (Ms. Allen), 1984 (Ms. Davies), 1986 (Mr. Bordonelli), 1987 (Mr. Pelech and Mr. Ward), 1990 (the fictional John Keating in Dead Poets Society), 1992 (Mr. Davies), 1993 (Mr. Kraft), 2000 (Mariano Del Rosario), and 2006 (Jim Barry) and 2014 (Bart Baggett). Even though I majored in Film Studies and made short films, I can't name the Academy-Award winner for any of those years. However, I can remember my favourite teachers without hesitation. One trait all of these teachers had in common was the way they integrated humour into the class. The definition of humour, as we've discussed in this book has many facets that go well beyond making students laugh.

Ms. Allen inspired in me a curiosity for what lies beneath the surface of rocks. She focused on effort, not grades and learning, not mistakes. This planted the seeds of project-based, experiential learning I use to this day. Ms. Davies gave me the space to explore my own sense of humour, culminating in a performance of "Read It," my "Weird Al" Yankovic's homage to Michael Jackson's, "Beat It." Yes, I wore one red glove and a studded faux leather jacket with gel in my curly hair. Mr. Pelech made storytelling into an art and a reward for working hard after a major test. If he had a certain tie on, it meant he would tell one of his epic real-life stories like the sky diving incident. Mr. Ward once ripped up my entire history test, after I got a little too comfortable by giving him a sarcastic response. I was in shock. So was the class. The next day he came to class with the paper meticulously taped together and marked. John Keating played by the incomparable, Robin Williams, was animated, passionate, novel, believed in students before they believed in themselves and playfully imitated them. He put them in uncommon educational environments and challenged them to carpe diem. Artist and Art Teacher, Mariano del Rosario created a non-judgmental, open and easy-going learning climate and encouraged us every step of the way in his New York art class.

Jim Barry acted out Shakespeare and *Phantom of the Opera* on a chair in front of the class. He interspersed an improvisational, brilliant wit into classroom discussions. He reinforced in me the thought that teaching truly is an adventure and created timeless, unconventional assignments that I use to this day.

The title of this book may be slightly misleading. Everything I learned about the power of humour, I learned at *Saturday Night Live*. *Saturday Night Live* taught me how to integrate my experiences from the world of comedy into the world of teaching. Nevertheless, it is the teachers of my life that have made all the difference in the world. At the end of a class, if your students are laughing, they're most likely learning.

Here's to the frontline teachers who keep their students laughing and learning.

GET FREE DOWNLOADABLE TEACHERS' RESOURCES
AND WORKSHEETS BELOW THAT WILL HELP YOU:

Winner of the *TED-Huff Post* International
Teaching Award, The SOLE Challenge

INSPIRE CURIOSITY AND WONDER IN YOUR STUDENTS

The Simple and Practical High School
Teacher's Guide to Create Self Organized
Learning Environments (SOLES)

Jamie Mason Cohen

DOWNLOAD

www.jamiemasoncohen.com/resources

- Create Simple Self-Organized Learning Environments (SOLES) Your Students Will Love in Just 5 Minutes

- Gain immediate access to a SOLE Lesson Plan Template that you can use today! Get your students asking meaningful questions about the subject you're teaching (with over 20 Examples!)

- Improve engagement by 50% in just one class by creating a teen-centered learning environment that reaches your most challenging students.

Review request

Good reviews are important to the success of a book on Kindle.

If you enjoyed this book or if you found it useful, I'd be very grateful if you'd post an honest review. Your support really does matter and it really does make a difference. I do read all the reviews so I can get your feedback.

If you'd leave a review then all you need to do is go the review section on the book's **Amazon Page**. You'll see a big button that says, "Write a customer review" – click that and you're good to go.

Thanks again for your support.

Yours in good humour,

PART 3: RESOURCES

Jamie Mason Cohen's Teacher Resources

www.jamiemasoncohen.com/resources/

GET EASY TO USE, FREE LESSON PLANS, UNCONVENTIONAL
STRATEGIES AND PRACTICAL VIDEO EXAMPLES

Learn things like 'How to incorporate humour into your learning
environment to build trust-filled relationships with your students'
and 'How to contribute to learners feeling happier, more emotionally
content and achieving better results'

MY LESSONS, UNIT LINKS, ARTICLES AND IDEAS

TED- Huff Post, "SOLE Challenge" Award Winning Unit on Genius – "Siddhartha":

- http://genius.com/Mr-cohen-unit-overview-and-guidelines-annotated
- http://genius.com/2825096/Mr-cohen-hermann-hesses-chapter-1-the-brahmins-son/In-the-shade-of-the-house-in-the-sunshine-of-the-riverbank-near-the-boats

Part 1: How to effortlessly combine Digital annotation, Flipped Teaching, Multiple Learning Strategies and a Self-Organized-Learning-Environment into any elementary, high school or university unit.

- http://www.youtube.com/h?v=iJME5ebhiqQ&list=PLTAqkbpf AGJM5VJVq_1w8WHbxxlxu291u&index=2

Part 2: How to effortlessly combine Digital annotation, Flipped Teaching, Multiple Learning Strategies and a Self-Organized-Learning-Environment into any elementary, high school or university unit.

- http://www.youtube.com/h?v=jtl8ozmZ7Ao&list=PLTAqkbpfA GJM5VJVq_1w8WHbxxlxu291u&index=3

Part 3: How to effortlessly combine Digital annotation, Flipped Teaching, Multiple Learning Strategies and a Self-Organized-Learning-Environment into any elementary, high school or university unit.

- http://www.youtube.com/h?v=3ni3vX5fW7g&list=PLTAqkbpfA GJM5VJVq_1w8WHbxxlxu291u&index=4

Flip Teaching Introduction to Siddhartha Novel Study:

- http://www.youtube.com/channel/UCgmmWIwVrtNba-4PBTw4LcQ

Flip Teaching #1:

- http://www.youtube.com/watch?v=5b-OZiBcx7Y&list=PLTAqk bpfAGJOzhLKeE33ittY1KiEbLaf5&index=3

Flip Teaching #2:

- http://www.youtube.com/watch?v=aR-UW7sw58o&index=6&l ist=PLTAqkbpfAGJOzhLKeE33ittY1KiEbLaf5

Flip Teaching Interview #3:

- http://www.youtube.com/h?v=EZay4mfeYsc&list=PLTAqkbpfA GJOzhLKeE33ittY1KiEbLaf5&index=10

Flip Teaching Interview #4:

- http://www.youtube.com/h?v=CI0EHARH2UM&index=11&list =PLTAqkbpfAGJOzhLKeE33ittY1KiEbLaf5

Flip Teaching Podcast:

- http://www.youtube.com/h?v=P6OFUOQslaQ&list=PLTAqkbp fAGJOzhLKeE33ittY1KiEbLaf5&index=7

Poetry Brain blog article on 18 Ways To Engage Your Students:

- http://poetry.rapgenius.com/Mr-cohen-18-ways-to-engage-your-students-by-teaching-less-and-learning-more-with-rap-genius-lyrics
- http://professionallyspeaking.oct.ca/september_2015/ENG_ PS03_2015.pdf

Feature Article on this SOLE Unit in OCT's Professionally Speaking, September 2015 edition (page 59)

SOLE Collaboration with 'The Art of Learning'

- http://theartoflearningproject.org/educate/category/ programs/featured/

The Power of Media in the Classroom.

Here is a documentary my students in my first year of students created on 1 day in their life. This was at a Toronto District School Board school in an economically disadvantaged community of downtown Toronto.

- http://www.youtube.com/h?v=OipzydOBdxM&index=2&list=PLTAqkbpfAGJO4Fxd1WgdbzxUnUt3f0Uwt

At the end of the semester of the Canadian Pre-University Program High School classes I taught in Malaysia, I asked the students to create short videos of their experience

Malaysian Classroom Environment#1:

- http://www.youtube.com/h?v=ggV7JoTLpb8&list=PLTAqkbpfAGJNlICV1qZKUht5uAnreNvLs

Malaysian Classroom Environment#2:

- http://www.youtube.com/watch?v=Yn6_glSI&list=PLTAqkbpfAGJNlICV1qZKUht5uAnreNvLs&index=2

Malaysian Classroom Environment #3:

- http://www.youtube.com/h?v=SoQUrhqIze0&list=PLTAqkbpfAGJNlICV1qZKUht5uAnreNvLs&index=3

Self-Organized Learning Environment Introduction with Publisher Louis Jebb and panel via Skype in England.

Nenad Bach: How to Create a Self-Organized-Learning Environment with a Guest Speaker via SKYPE:

- http://www.youtube.com/watch?v=UiidKbxUnS4

SOLE with New Technologies

- http://www.youtube.com/watch?v=9FNjEtkJ8Jo&list=PLTAqkbpfAGJOOrGAfNcA3dtNGA5M--HOR&index=1

Self Organized Learning Environment Webinar

- http://www.youtube.com/watch?v=NeyQj3_NumE&list=PLTAqkbpfAGJOzhLKeE33ittY1KiEbLaf5

Self-Organized Learning Environment Step by Step Article Guide

- https://www.linkedin.com/profile/view?id=287722728&trk=spm_pic

SOLE Collaboration with 'The Art of Learning'

- http://theartoflearningproject.org/educate/category/ programs/featured/

How to Incorporate One of your Passions into the Classroom

I'm a Certified Handwriting Expert. I find moments in class to incorporate handwriting analysis into the class to connect with my students. I analyze positive traits in students' writing in front of of the class and show students how to consciously changing certain letters will positively change certain mental habits and beliefs.

See my upcoming book, "Handwriting Analysis for High School Teachers"

- http://www.youtube.com/h?v=JWmafBBMHSk&list=PLTAqkb pfAGJM5VJVq_1w8WHbxxlxu291u

If I go on a trip to an intriguing place, I video tape it, show parts of it to my students and incorporate it into an upcoming unit theme.

Chronicles of Siem Reap: This was a trip I made to Cambodia to premiere my short film, "The Barber of Kigali". I was an Ambassador of the Arts for the Canadian Government

- http://www.youtube.com/h?v=vUWlYmH5Plg&list=PLTAqkbpf AGJO4Fxd1WgdbzxUnUt3f0Uwt&index=4

Tips for the 21st First Classroom

- http://www.youtube.com/watch?v=ppvkNF5XOlI&list=PLTAqk bpfAGJOOrGAfNcA3dtNGA5M--HOR&index=2

Prepped and Polished Podcast Interview:

- http://preppedandpolished.com/jamie-cohen-life-in-the-21st-century-classroom/

ACKNOWLEDGEMENTS

To my good friend and teaching mentor, Jim Barry, who guided me to close the classroom door and teach my way. Whenever I'm not sure what to do or how to deal with students, I think, "What would Jim do?" Thank you for your generous and meticulous edit of this book and for always making yourself available and open to collaborating.

To Lorne Michaels, for giving me the chance to live and work in New York. This book would not be possible without the opportunity you gave me.

To my good friend and mentor, Jack Healey, Executive Director of Human Rights Action Center, whose actions reverberate across nations. His example of generosity of spirit and his indefatigable commitment shine through the causes he chooses and those which chose him.

To Cristina McGinniss and Jack Sullivan, my mentors at Broadway Video and SNL in New York, who did the work to help me get to Broadway Video and provided ongoing encouragement and wisdom during my four years.

To my lawyer, Alison Fitz-Perry -- I would never been permitted to work in New York for 4 years if it wasn't for the work you did on my behalf.

To Alan Davies, my Grade 12 English teacher, who modeled the kind of student-driven, challenging, creative learning environment I aspire to make for my students. It wasn't about the marks; it was about the learning. You were the real Professor Keating (from Dead Poets Society) to me.

To the late Julian Craft, my high school Modern Western Civilizations teacher, who made me want to speak as he did, so eloquently and effortlessly in front of a room full of students. His real-life lessons speak to me twenty-two years later about the importance of bringing the world into the classroom.

To the late Robin Williams, whose magical, awe-inspiring portrayal of the teacher, John Keating, in Dead Poets Society, planted the seed in my sixteen-year-old mind and heart to become a teacher.

To the late Frank McCourt, whose success as a teacher first and then an author later in life, inspired me to write this book. When I questioned why I chose this path during Teachers' College, I attended his reading of his autobiography, "Teacher Man." After that night, I took a deep sigh of relief, smiled, and knew I was headed in the right direction.

To Bart Baggett, my friend and teacher, whose books and methods made me believe I could write a pretty good book and reach the right audience. They say when the student is ready, the teacher will appear. This has been the case with Bart.

To Sean Meggeson, who took a shot in hiring me for my first teaching job and gave me the freedom to try some unorthodox strategies like having our class do a documentary on one of the student's parents' marriage and rewarding student effort on Friday afternoon by playing flag football on the field out back. Some of the teaching methods I would develop over my career began at Freemont Academy under your watch.

To Brooke Hodgins, who was a magnanimous teaching mentor during my first classroom experience as a Teacher's Assistant at West Toronto Collegiate. You trusted me with your class for a few mornings a week to teach the students how to write and create a short docudrama. You were always supportive and a willing and wise collaborator.

To Mariano Del Rosario, who showed me how to teach in a way that focuses on giving students freedom to explore through non-judgmental encouraging experiential learning and to believe in their instincts and choices.

To Rabbi Chezi Zionce, who was the first teacher to show me how humour can help children learn about a subject he/she didn't think he/she would be interested in.

To Mr. Bordinali, whose visionary project-based learning environment was ahead of its time. He had us practice real world skills and integrated compassion, creativity, and a love of learning in ways that informed my teaching twenty years later.

To Mr. Pelech, for his brilliant storytelling and wry sense of humour mixed with making annotation fun in Grade 7.

To Ms. Allen, who made me love learning how to count and discover the joy of hobbies like exploring rocks and collecting foreign coins as a six-year-old.

To Mr. Ward, who made me laugh every class through self-deprecating humour, spot-on imitations, and doing the unexpected.

To Ms. Davies, my Grade 4 teacher, who had the gift of making me want to work hard to improve and feel safe to be creative like my rendition of Michael Jackson's, Beat It, as "Read It."

To Coach Brad Selwood, for showing me the power of walking your talk and for teaching me through your example the idea of actions speaking so loudly it doesn't matter what you say. And, to the late Coach Troy May, who radiated humility and kindness. He was respected and loved by all players and is dearly remembered.

To Clyde and George, my first baseball coaches, who taught me the joy of playing for the sake of the game and to celebrate effort and being on a team. I couldn't wait to come to every practice and game because of the atmosphere the two of you created.

To Howie Bernie, thank you for showing me the value of community service and for creating a "Zen garden-like," in the iconic Leaside baseball diamond where I learned lessons that I've applied to my life and teaching.

To Mel Sperling for creating the type of teen-empowered sports team environment I would adapt for the extra-curricular activities I oversee.

To Nenad Bach, whose friendship, creative collaborations across simultaneous three continents, and support has been invaluable to my growth both personally and creatively. Our Self-Organized Learning Environment music classroom projects were amongst the most rewarding classes I've ever taught.

To Jimmy Gary, Jr., whose friendship, infectious positive energy, wisdom, and generosity left my students in awe and feeling inspired every time he stepped into my classroom as a guest teacher of life lessons.

To Marcus S., a.k.a. the handshake guy – "who meets what you need to succeed", for encouraging me to share my New York story and for always asking what he can do to support my projects. You've been present through each stage of my road back from New York and I'm grateful. The best press I've received is a result of your efforts and belief.

To Louis Jebb, whose friendship and projects created together on the modern hero's journey stretched my perspective of what's possible in a classroom.

To Grant Reimer, who gave me a chance to teach when I had some doubts. My experiences at Northern Secondary School, teaching Adults Creative Writing and Screenwriting, gave me confidence as a teacher and inspired me to writing this book, ten years later.

To Nick DeNinno, my friend and former colleague at Broadway Video and Saturday Night Live. To my other colleagues at Broadway Video who were generous and kind including Hilla Narov and Scott Barr.

To Steve W. Davis, for helping to shape the subtitle of this book to make sure it finds its intended audience.

To Randy Robles, my friend and roommate during my first year in New York and in university, who was always the funniest and coolest guy in the room.

To Steven Lewis, a lawyer then, who generously gave me his time and mentorship at a period when I was just starting out with little I could offer of value in return.

To Steven Moore and to Christine Jones for your extraordinary courage in the midst of life's challenges.

To Danny, Oren, Ronnie and Jeff Farbman, Natalie, Renata and Safta Helena.

Sean McCann, Jeremiah McCann, Mike Wasselin, Dr. Brian Alliston, Sheila Cohen, Charles Willerding, Ryan Ellis, Tom Petersil, Dan Eisenberg, Jeremy Goldman, Dr. John Snelgrove, Sam Desimone, Mr. and Mrs. Max Hahn, Frank, Rose and Raquel, Marc Champion, Michael Williams from Gugaleto, Dermod Judge, Surin Toor, Timmins Bissonnette, Melissa Hopkins, Meri Har-Gil, Jean-Loick Michaux, the Handwriting University Mastermind Group Members and Glendale Reyes.

To my friends, Emil Beheshti, Tom Rhodes, Dan Trommater, and Jim Annan for taking the time to share their mind - practical and fascinating insights into what teachers can learn from comedians and performers.

To Mark Bowden for your friendship, mentorship, inspiration and support.

To Scott Watson, Helen Gill, Frank Meagher and the warm, open, and amazing students who made my time in Malaysia a valuable and memorable teaching experience and adventure.

To Stephen Gaghan, and Dr. James Cornelius for sharing your unique and masterful insights.

To my New York friends who helped make my time there so memorable: Chaos Night Club owner, Tony, Musician, Doorman and Club Owner, Mike D., Promoter, Aramis, Oscar, Victor, Tony, Carol, Mariano and to my fellow painters at The Art Students' League of New York and Yuisa.

To Adam Chaim and Nick Maes, for being good friends, and brother-in-arms in our crazy projects.

To Frieda Woznicka, former TanenbaumCHAT Principal, who gave me the opportunity to teach at TanenbaumCHAT, Former VP, Ray Buchowski, a wise and insightful mentor and friend, who made me laugh every time I walked into his office unannounced. Graham Mawson, who called me the "crazy creative" and was always an innovative, intelligent, supportive and enthusiastic colleague to bounce ideas off of, friends and colleagues, Chayyim Kaduri, Linda Newstead, Shimon Weis, Deborah Lampert, Avi Grossman, Principal, Renee Cohen, and Principal Jonathan Levy and all my colleagues at TanenbaumCHAT, who have been an invaluable part of my growth as a teacher and learner the past seven years.

To my friend, Dean Dirk Daenen, who provided a world-class environment, an epic dinner amongst fascinating people, and gave me the chance to speak at his seamlessly run, TEDxUBIWiltz in Luxembourg.

To Josie, for all you do for our family and for giving me time every day over the past eighteen months to make this vision a reality.

To Sir Ken Robinson, whose books, example and TED Talks inspire me each year to find new creative ways to reach my students.

To Trevor Kahn, for recommending me eight years ago for my teaching job at TanenbaumCHAT.

To the following authors, thought leaders, people and organizations who have inspired my teaching and profoundly impacted my life over the past decade: Sugata Mitra, The TED "Sole Challenge" Committee, The Team Behind Genius, Joseph Campbell, Raoul Wallenberg, Victor Frankl, Wendel, Fred, and Suki, Patrick Sharangabo, Romeo Dallaire, Daniel Pink, Robert L. DeBruyn, Jack L. Larson, Richard Feynman, Thich Nhat Hanh, Joko Beck, Carol Dweck, Henry David Thoreau, Herman Hesse, Gandhi, Aung San Suu Kyi, Dr. Rick Hodes, the late Wayne Dyer, Dale Carnegie, the Stanford d. school, Paul Eckman, Joel Osteen, Pema Chodron, Lao Tzu, Stephen Mitchell, Anthony Robbins, Dale Carnegie, Michelle Providence, Michael Wesch, Jonathan Sprinkles and his amazing team at Presentation Power, Danny Brassell, Christopher Vogler, Stephen Mitchell, Hans Hoffman, Jasper Johns, Robert Rauschenberg, Don Miguel Ruiz, George Bernard Shaw, Leo Babauta, Tim Ferriss, Mary from Saskatoon, Luke Richardson, Jin Jang, Paul Comeau, Jim Norgate, Greg De Koker, Mr. B, Roland Joffe, Sydney Lumet, Free The Children and the incredible Me to We team members, Kalla Richards-Finnie, Michaela Evans and Katie Yigitoz, The Art of Learning, the JW Foundation and Nelson Mandela.

To Editor, Marley Gibson for your encouragement and editing.

To Book Interior Designer, Meg Sylvia for helping me realize the visual vision for this book.

To digital book designer Mehboob Sam for your meticulous and professional work.

To Cover Designer Zeljka Kojic for a pitch-perfect design.

To John Tighe, for your guidance in helping me launch the book and filling in the gaps to assist me through the sticking points.

To all the parents who have trusted me to guide their kids; I don't take this responsibility lightly.

To the students, I've taught from whom I've learned more than they could ever learn from me.

NOTES

INTRODUCTION

1. Frank McCourt, Teacher Man, Scribner, 2005.

   http://www.amazon.ca/Teacher-Man-Memoir-Frank-McCourt/dp/0743243781

   The author, Frank McCourt recalls his award-winning teaching career in the New York public school system. I quoted a line from his book in my introduction because it summed up the various roles teachers play.

DEFINING HUMOUR: A CONTEXTUAL PRELUDE

Laszlo Feleki, "The Science of Humour", A Random Walk in Science, public library, 1973

https://www.brainpickings.org/2014/04/16/random-walk-in-science-humor/

Lee Siegel, New York Times Sunday Edition, "Welcome to the Age of the Unfunny Joke."

http://www.nytimes.com/2015/09/20/opinion/sunday/welcome-to-the-age-of-the-unfunny-joke.html?_r=0

Ethan Hawke, The Hottest State, 1996

CHAPTER 1

SOLE Student Leadership Breakdance Video:

Audience participation angle by Glendale Reyes

Dance teacher: Shawn Ocampo (MoonRunners)

Female dance lead: Stefanie Caldeira (Soul Rebels)

BBOYS: Ethan, Payam, Patrick, Jim Kwik, Superhero You, Segment on Remembering Names

https://www.youtube.com/watch?v=sCN9Z8hLdfY

CHAPTER 2

Quotation by Sir Ken Robinson given in a speech

CHAPTER 3: MARY'S ANGEL ON 9/11

2. Louis Armstrong, "I'll String Along With You lyrics" Lyrics by Al Dubin and Harry Warren, WP Music Corp.

http://www.lyricsfreak.com/l/louis+armstrong/ill+string+along+with+you_20810604.html

This is the song Mary, sang in the car to me on the road back Toronto on 9/11. The lyrics were essential in conveying the story to my students of the instant friendship developed between Mary and I on that fateful day in history where our paths crossed.

3. Megan Garber, "How Comedians Became Public Intellectuals," The Atlantic, 2015.

http://www.theatlantic.com/entertainment/archive/2015/05/how-comedians-became-public-intellectuals/394277/

4. Jerome G. Delaney, "How High School Students Perceive Effective Teachers", Faculty of Education, Memorial University of Newfoundland.

http://www.mun.ca/educ/faculty/mwatch/Delaney%20Morning%20Watch%20Article%20on%20Effective%20Teachers'%20Characteristics%20Study.pdf

5. Cindi May, "The Secret of Better Meetings: Fun", Scientific American, 2013.

http://www.scientificamerican.com/article/the-secret-of-better-meetings-fun/

6. Interview with Jim Barry, "The Rookie and The Veteran Video Series" by Jamie Mason Cohen, 2011

7. Robert L. DeBruyn and Jack L. Larson, You Can Handle Them All: A Discipline Model for Handling 124 Student Behaviors at School and at Home, Master Teacher, 2nd edition, 2009.

   http://www.amazon.ca/s/?ie=UTF8&keywords=you+can+handle+them+all&tag=googcana-20&index=aps&hvadid=6089294817&hvpos=1t2&hvexid=&hvnetw=g&hvrand=17163029217589813743-&hvpone=&hvptwo=&hvqmt=b&hvdev=c&ref=pd_sl_6xz0qky1fk_b

8. Interview with Tom Rhodes by Jamie Mason Cohen, 2015.

9. Henry David Thoreau, Walden, Ticknor and Fields, 1854.

   http://thoreau.eserver.org/walden00.html

10. Rebecca Leung, Ed Bradley, "Dylan Looks Back," CBS News, 2004.

    http://www.cbsnews.com/news/dylan-looks-back/

    Bob Dylan talks to Ed Bradley in his first interview in 19 years.

11. The Wizard of Oz, dir. Victor Fleming (1939).

    http://www.bestbuy.ca/en-CA/product/wizard-of-oz-bilingual-75th-anniversary-edition-3d-blu-ray-blu-ray-disc/m2207406.aspx?cmp=pla-movies__tv_shows

12. Jonathan Sprinkles, http://presentationpowerbootcamp.com.

13. Ramit Sethi, "I Will Teach You To Be Rich" blog, 2015.

    http://www.iwillteachyoutoberich.com/blog/ramits-definitive-guide-to-building-your-network-with-scripts/

    Joke about the snail attributed to Bernie Sahlins by Ted Cohen

    Brian Setser, "The Teacherpreneur Opportunity".

    https://www.linkedin.com/pulse/20141116212936-23485324-the-teacherpreneur-opportunity

Professionally Speaking, Dec. 2015

http://professionallyspeaking.oct.ca

Superhuman Social Skills: A Guide to Being Likeable, Winning Friends, and Building Your Social Circle, 2015

Michael Port and Amy Mead, Heroic Public Speaking Online Course, Creative Live,

https://www.creativelive.com/courses/heroic-public-speaking-michael-port-amy-mead

http://www.amazon.com/Superhuman-Social-Skills-Likeable-Building-ebook/dp/B015QA1250/ref=asap_bc?ie=UTF8

Michael Port: Steal the Show podcast, Dec.31, 2015

CHAPTER 4

14. David Buckingham, Media Education: Literacy, Learning and Contemporary Culture, Chapter 10, "Politics, Pleasure and Play", Polity Press, 2007.

https://books.google.ca/books?id=7RANAAAAQBA
J&pg=PT206&lpg=PT206&dq=%22+politics,+plea
sure+and+play%22+education+media&source=b
l&ots=p3eaOJ5-Nf&sig=TgLKYN6rFZqHu-vLqpzUJ-
LPMw6g&hl=en&sa=X&ved=0CCMQ6AEwAWoVChMImt-G_
J7ixgIVkUGSCh35VgNF#v=onepage&q=%22%20politics%2C%20
pleasure%20and%20play%22%20education%20media&f=false

Michael Wesch, Anti-Teaching: Confronting the Crisis of Significance/Canadian Education Association, Vol. 48 (2).

http://www.cea-ace.ca/sites/default/files/EdCan-2008-v48-n2-Wesch.pdf

Jackie Robinson's epitaph on his gravestone

CHAPTER 5

15. Brian Tracey, Goals! How to Get Everything You Want -- Faster Than You Ever Thought Possible, Berrett-Koehler Publishers; 2nd Revised Edition, 2010.

   https://books.google.ca/books?id=YCl-I6IeYNMC& printsec=frontcover&dq=brian+tracey+-+goal+se tting&hl=en&sa=X&ved=0CC0Q6AEwAGoVChMI4_ n5wKPixgIVxBOSCh2XgQgQ#v=onepage&q&f=false

16. Dr. Wayne Dyer, Wishes Fulfilled: Mastering the Art of Manifesting, Hay House, 2012.

   https://books.google.ca/books?id=pFgwdphq-uUC&printsec=fr ontcover&dq=wayne+dyer+visualization&hl=en&sa=X&ved=0CC MQ6AEwAWoVChMI69z26KPixgIVzhmSCh2GTAQT#v=onepage&q &f=false

17. Quotes by Friedrich Nietzsche.

   https://books.google.ca/books?id=aZ93gG44dGcC&pg=PA22 &dq=nietzsche+-+he+who+has+a+why+can+bear+with+alm ost+any+how&hl=en&sa=X&ved=0CEEQ6AEwBmoVChMIpoj U3qLixgIVig2SCh1C6QBo#v=onepage&q=nietzsche%20-%20 he%20who%20has%20a%20why%20can%20bear%20with%20 almost%20any%20how&f=false

   Josh Waitzkin, The Art of Learning: An Inner Journey to Optimal Performance, Simon and Schuster, 2008.

   http://www.amazon.ca/Art-Learning-Journey-Optimal- Performance/dp/0743277465/ref=sr_1_1?ie=UTF8&qid=1452381 909&sr=8-1&keywords=the+art+of+learning

   Katy Wells and the JWF Team, The Teacher's Guide to The Art of Learning: Resilience, 2015

   http://theartoflearningproject.org/wp-content/ uploads/2014/12/Resilience_Teacher_Guide.pdf

   Jon Kabat-Zinn, Full Catastrophe Living, Bantam Books, 2013

http://www.amazon.ca/Full-Catastrophe-Living-Revised-Edition/dp/0345536932

MBSR Toronto Course run by Roy Hintsa

You Can Be Funny: Award Winning Comedian Ron Tite STEAL THE SHOW with Michael Port

https://www.acast.com/stealtheshowwithmichaelport/059-you-can-be-funny-award-winning-comedian-ron-tite-shares-secrets-of-the-comedy-masters

Douglas Stone and Sheila Heen, Thanks for the Feedback: The Science and Art of Receiving Feedback Well, Penguin, 2014

Norman Cousins, Anatomy of an Illness as Perceived by the Patient, 2005

http://www.amazon.com/Anatomy-Illness-Perceived-Twentieth-Anniversary/dp/0393326845

Craig Kielburger, Marc Kielburger, Shelley Page, The World Needs Your Kid: Raising Children Who Care and Contribute, Greystone Books, 2010

http://www.amazon.ca/The-World-Needs-Your-Kid/dp/155365918X

Me To We Educator Volunteer-Service Education Trips

http://www.metowe.com/school-trips/

CHAPTER 6

18. "Steve Jobs Stanford Commencement Speech", Stanford University, 2005.

    https://www.youtube.com/watch?v=D1R-jKKp3NA

19. Martin O'Malley, Justin Thompson, "Prime ministers and Presidents," CBC News Online, November 22, 2003.

    http://www.cbc.ca/canadaus/pms_presidents1.html

Brenda Miller and Suzanne Paoula, Tell It Slant: Writing and Shaping Creative Nonfiction: Chapter 9, "The Personal Essay", McGraw Hill, 2005.

http://www.amazon.com/Tell-It-Slant-Creative-Nonfiction/dp/0072512784

CHAPTER 7

20. Michael Crichton, Travels, Vintage Departures Press, 2014.

    http://www.michaelcrichton.com/travels/

CHAPTER 8

21. SETH GODIN, THE DIP, PENGUIN GROUP, 2007.

    http://www.amazon.com/The-Dip-Little-Teaches-Stick/dp/1591841666

22. Walter Isaacson, Jobs, Simon & Schuster, 2011.

    http://www.amazon.ca/Steve-Jobs-Walter-Isaacson/dp/1451648545

CHAPTER 9

23. Chogyam Trungpa, The Collected Works of Chogyam Trungpa: Volume Eight: Great Eastern Sun, Shambhala Press, 2004.

    https://books.google.ca/books?id=tF6giSBifqYC&pg=PA133&lpg=PA133&dq=chogyam+trungpa+-+%22a+tiger+in+its+prime+moves+slowly+but+heedfully+through+the+jungle&source=bl&ots=EkASZ0sa-B&sig=KtyS6pmZGS1eyF0EYrjswbvLZvc&hl=en&sa=X&ved=0CB4Q6AEwAGoVChMItY387KjixglVgQ2SCh3a4gDX#v=onepage&q=chogyam%20trungpa%20-%20%22a%20tiger%20in%20its%20prime%20moves%20slowly%20but%20heedfully%20through%20the%20jungle&f=false

CHAPTER 11

24. Jiro Dreams of Sushi, dir. David Geld (2011).

   http://www.magpictures.com/jirodreamsofsushi/

25. Nathan Myhrvold, Bill Gates, Peter Rinearson,The Road Ahead, Viking Penguin,1995

   http://www.amazon.com/The-Road-Ahead-Bill-Gates/dp/0670859133

CHAPTER 12

   http://presentationpowerbootcamp.com

   http://handwritinguniversity.com

CHAPTER 13

26. James W. Neuliep, "An Examination of the content of high school teachers' humor in the classroom and the development of an inductively derived taxonomy of classroom humor," Communication Education. (October), vol. 40:343-355, 1991.

27. Robert L. DeBruyn and Jack L. Larson, You Can Handle Them All: A Discipline Model for Handling 124 Student Behaviors at School and at Home, Master Teacher, 2nd edition, 2009.

   http://www.amazon.ca/s/?ie=UTF8&keywords=you+can+handle+them+all&tag=googcana-20&index=aps&hvadid=6089294817&hvpos=1t2&hvexid=&hvnetw=g&hvrand=17163029217589813743-&hvpone=&hvptwo=&hvqmt=b&hvdev=c&ref=pd_sl_6xz0qky1fk_b

28. Interview with Mark Bowden by Jamie Mason Cohen, 2015.

29. Keith Johnstone, Impro: Improvisation and the Theatre, Routledge, 2012.

http://www.amazon.ca/Impro-Improvisation-Theatre-Keith-Johnstone/dp/0878301178

30. Sir Ken Robninson with Lou Aronica, Creative Schools: The Grassroots Revolution That's Transforming Education, Viking, 2015.

http://www.amazon.ca/Creative-Schools-Grassroots-Revolution-Transforming/dp/0670016713

31. Sugata Mitra, (SOLE) Toolkit, www.ted.com, 2013.

http://www.ted.com/prize/sole_toolkit.

32. Interview with Dan Trommater by Jamie Mason Cohen, 2015.

33. A quotation attributed to stand-up comedian, Jack Milner according as referenced by Mark Bowden.

34. Interview with Tom Rhodes by Jamie Mason Cohen, 2015.

35. Interview with Emil Beheshti by Jamie Mason Cohen, 2015.

36. Voltaire and the Triumph of the Enlightenment (Great Courses,The Teaching Company) Audio CD 2001 by Alan Charles Kors.

This online lesson was referenced by Tom Rhodes.

http://www.amazon.com/Voltaire-Triumph-Enlightenment-Courses-Teaching/dp/159803149X

37. Using Humor in Branded Content by Meryl Ayres, Wistia blog, 2015.

http://wistia.com/blog/using-humor-branded-content

38. Jon Favreau quoted on The Tim Ferriss Podcast, 2015.

39. Amanda Palmer, The Art of Asking, Ted Talk, 2013.

http://www.ted.com/talks/amanda_palmer_the_art_of_asking?language=en

40. Daniel H. Pink, A Whole New Mind: Why Right-Brainers Will Rule the Future, Riverhead Books, 2006

http://www.amazon.ca/Whole-New-Mind-Right-Brainers-Future/dp/1594481717

41. Mihalyi Csikszentmihalyi quoted in A Whole New Mind: Why Right-Brainers Will Rule the Future, Riverhead Books, 2006.

42. Fabio Sala, "Take the Lead: Full-Throttle Engagement Powered by Coaching Everyday," Harvard Business Review, 2003.

https://books.google.ca/s?id=WfXeAAAAQBAJ&pg=PT223&lpg=PT223&dq=Fabio+Sala,+Harvard+Business+Review,+%22humor+reduces+hostility%22&source=bl&ots=8hvx0uz6_c&sig=Z1klb9-su-A46LeA2cwElKq8jXY&hl=en&sa=X&ved=0CCAQ6AEwAWoVChMI7rat6sLixglVkBmSCh0juQY3#v=onepage&q=Fabio%20Sala%2C%20Harvard%20Business%20Review%2C%20%22humor%20reduces%20hostility%22&f=false

43. Interview with Jim Annan by Jamie Mason Cohen, 2015.

44. Robert R. Provine, Laughter: A Scientific Investigation, Penguin Books, 2001.

http://www.amazon.ca/Laughter-Scientific-Investigation-Robert-Provine/dp/0141002255

45. Quoted Dr. Lee Berk of the American Physiological Society, in www.sciencedaily.com, April 10, 2008.

http://www.sciencedaily.com/releases/2008/04/080407114617.htm

46. Dr. Kataria, Laughter: The Best Medicine as quoted in, Raffi Khatchadourian's, "The Laughing Guru, Madan Kataria's prescription for total well-being, New Yorker, 2010.

http://www.newyorker.com/magazine/2010/08/30/the-laughing-guru

47. www.laughteryoga.org.

48. www.tinyrl.com/6t7ff.

49. The Lemelson Center's Invention at Play | Lemelson
   Foundation.

   www.inventionatplay.org

50. Jim Barry and Jamie Cohen, Upcoming, The Rookie and The
   Veteran e-book, 2016.

51. John Gray, Ph.D interview with Brendon Burchard, Experts
   Academy, 2013.

   www.brendonburchard.com

52. Dr. Wayne Dyer, Erroneous Zones, Harper Collins, 1991 Edition.

   http://www.amazon.ca/Your-Erroneous-Zones-Wayne-Dyer/
   dp/0060919760

53. Joel Osteen, Every Day A Friday, Faithwords, 2011.

   http://www.amazon.ca/Your-Erroneous-Zones-Wayne-Dyer/
   dp/0060919760

CHAPTER 14

offCamera with Sam Jones Podcast Interview with Martin Short,
Nov. 27, 2013

58. Stephen Tropiano, Saturday Night Live FAQ: Everything Left to
   Know About Television's Longest Running Comedy Paperback,
   Applause Theatre and Cinema, 2013.

   http://www.amazon.ca/Saturday-Night-Live-FAQ-Televisions/
   dp/1557839514 (This quotation has been moved to Chapter 18)

59. Mikael Cho, "The Myth of the Brainstorming Session," The Next
   Web, 2013.

   http://thenextweb.com/entrepreneur/2013/11/03/myth-
   brainstorming-session-best-ideas-dont-always-come-meetings/

60. Michael Diehl and Wolfgang Stoebe, "Productivity Loss In Brainstorming Groups: Toward the Solution of a Riddle in the Journal of Personality and Social Psychology," 1987, Vol. 53, No. 3, 497 – 509.

http://mario.gsia.cmu.edu/micro_2007/readings/Diehl_Productivity%20loss.pdf

61. Tom Shales, James Andrew Miller, Live From New York: An Uncensored History Of Saturday Night Live Paperback, Back Bay Books, 2003.

http://www.amazon.ca/Live-From-New-York-Uncensored/dp/0316735655

62. Tim Metz, "Three Work Rhythms: Which One Suits You?" Linkedin, 2015 reprinted from Saentproductivity.com

https://www.linkedin.com/pulse/three-work-rhythms-which-one-suits-you-tim-metz

63. 10 Quotes and Life Lessons From Ernest Hemingway, Vincent Nguyen, 2013.

http://www.selfstairway.com/hemingway/

64. Interview with Stephen Gaghan by Jamie Mason Cohen, 2000.

65. Robert, Greene, 48 Laws of Power, Viking Press, 1998.

http://www.amazon.ca/The-Laws-Power-Robert-Greene/dp/0140280197

66. Greg McKeown, Essentialism: The Disciplined Pursuit of Less, Crown Business Group, 2014.

http://www.amazon.ca/s/ref=nb_sb_noss_2?url=search-alias%3Dstripbooks&field-keywords=essentiailism

67. Geoffrey Colvin, Talent is Overrated: What Really Separates World Class Performers From Everybody Else, Portfolio, 2010.

http://www.amazon.ca/s/ref=nb_sb_noss_2?url=search-alias%3Dstripbooks&field-keywords=talent+is+overrated&rh=n%3A916520%2Ck%3Atalent+is+overrated

68. Quotation attributed to Georges Augustus Henry Sala.

http://www.giga-usa.com/quotes/authors/george_augustus_sala_a001.htm

Dave Morris Quotation from his talk at TEDxVictoria, 2012

Shane Snow, Shortcuts,2014

http://www.amazon.ca/Smartcuts-Hackers-Innovators-Accelerate-Business/dp/0062302450

Daniel Amen, Change Your Brain, Change Your Life, 2015

http://www.amazon.ca/Change-Your-Brain-Revised-Expanded/dp/110190464X/ref=dp_ob_title_bk

Brain Johnson, Failure as Feedback podcast episode

https://brianjohnson.me/microclass-tag/feedback/

CHAPTER 15

69. Syd Field, Four Screenplays: Studies in the American Screenplay. Quotation attributed to Michael Blake, Delta, 1994.

http://www.amazon.com/Four-Screenplays-Studies-American-Screenplay/dp/0440504902

70. www.columbia.edu

71. Michael Brandwein, http://www.michaelbrandwein.com.

72. Pam Mueller, Daniel Oppenheimer, Joseph Stromberg, "Why you should take notes by hand – not on a laptop,"

VOX blog, 2015.

http://www.vox.com/2014/6/4/5776804/note-taking-by-hand-versus-laptop

73. Discussion with educator, Paul Como by Jamie Mason Cohen, 2006.

74. Dave Morris, The Way of Improvisation, TEDxVictoria, 2013.

75. Galen Emanuele, Improv to be a Better Human Being, TEDxBellingham, 2012.

76. Keith Johnstone, Impro: Improvisation and the Theatre, Routledge, 2012.

    http://www.amazon.ca/Impro-Improvisation-Theatre-Keith-Johnstone/dp/0878301178

77. Author unknown, The Harold Improv Game, Improv Encyclopaedia.

    http://improvencyclopedia.org/games/Harold.html

CHAPTER 17

78. Jonah Lehrer, "The new rules of creativity: nine mind hacks to boost your brain," Wired, 2012.

    http://www.wired.co.uk/magazine/archive/2012/05/features/the-new-rules-of-creativity/page/3

79. Jonah Lehrer, Imagine, Houghton Mifflin, 2012.

    Disclaimer: Parts of this author's book have been proven to be unreliable. I wrote this chapter before these revelations came out. I decided to keep quotations and sections referenced from his book that were not proven to be false as I think the anecdotes, research and ideas add value to the main themes.

    http://www.amazon.com/Imagine-Creativity-Works-Jonah-Lehrer/dp/B007QRI1UQ

80. Ray Oldenberg, The Great Good Place: Cafes, Coffee Shops, Bookstores, Bars, Hair Salons, and Other Hangouts at the Heart of a Community, De Capo Press, 1999.

http://www.amazon.ca/The-Great-Good-Place-Bookstores/dp/1569246815

Bruce Mau, The Manifesto Project,

http://www.manifestoproject.it/bruce-mau/

81. Sugata Mitra, Build a School in the Cloud, TED Talks, 2013.

https://www.ted.com/talks/sugata_mitra_build_a_school_in_the_cloud?language=en

82. Thomas J. Allen, Managing the Flow of Technology: Technology Transfer and the Dissemination of Technological Information Within the R&D Organization, MIT Press, 1984.

http://www.amazon.com/Managing-Flow-Technology-Dissemination-Technological/dp/0262510278

83. Quotation attributed to the Singapore Ministry of Education.

84. Jonah Lehrer, Imagine, Houghton Mifflin, 2012.

http://www.amazon.com/Imagine-Creativity-Works-Jonah-Lehrer/dp/B007QRI1UQ

85. Quotation attributed to an unknown source.

86. Jonah Lehrer, "The Power of Q," Imagine, Houghton Mifflin, 2012.

http://www.amazon.com/Imagine-Creativity-Works-Jonah-Lehrer/dp/B007QRI1UQ

87. Jonah Lehrer, "The Power of Q,"Imagine, Houghton Mifflin, 2012.

http://www.amazon.com/Imagine-Creativity-Works-Jonah-Lehrer/dp/B007QRI1UQ

88. Ray Williams quoting Keith Sawyer, Washington University psychologist, Psychology Today, 2012.

https://www.psychologytoday.com/blog/wired-success/201204/why-brainstorming-doesnt-improve-productivity-or-creativity

89. Jonah Lehrer, "The Power of Q," Imagine, Houghton Mifflin, 2012.

http://www.amazon.com/Imagine-Creativity-Works-Jonah-Lehrer/dp/B007QRI1UQ

90. Research conducted by Charlan Nemeth, Psychologist at the University of California-Berkeley, 99U.

http://99u.com/articles/7224/why-fighting-for-our-ideas-makes-them-better

91. Jonah Lehrer, "The Power of Q,"Imagine, Houghton Mifflin, 2012.

http://www.amazon.com/Imagine-Creativity-Works-Jonah-Lehrer/dp/B007QRI1UQ

92. Jonah Lehrer, "The Power of Q,"Imagine, Houghton Mifflin, 2012.

http://www.amazon.com/Imagine-Creativity-Works-Jonah-Lehrer/dp/B007QRI1UQ

Alastair Humphreys, Microadventures. William Collins, 2014.

http://www.alastairhumphreys.com/books/microadventures/

CHAPTER 18

93. The Last King of Scotland, dir. Kevin Macdonald, 2006.

http://www.imdb.com/title/tt0455590/

94. Sir Ken Robninson with Lou Aronica, Creative Schools: The Grassroots Revolution That's Transforming Education, Viking, 2015.

http://www.amazon.ca/Creative-Schools-Grassroots-Revolution-Transforming/dp/0670016713

95. Sir Ken Robninson with Lou Aronica, Creative Schools: The Grassroots Revolution That's Transforming Education, Viking, 2015.

http://www.amazon.ca/Creative-Schools-Grassroots-Revolution-Transforming/dp/0670016713

96. Shunryu Suzuki, Zen Mind, Beginner's Mind, Shambhala, 2011.

http://www.amazon.ca/s/ref=nb_sb_noss_2?url=search-alias%3Dstripbooks&field-keywords=zen+mind+beginner%27s+mind

97. Jeff Thompson, "Is Nonverbal Communication a Numbers Game?" Psychology Today, 2011.

https://www.psychologytoday.com/blog/beyond-words/201109/is-nonverbal-communication-numbers-game

98. Mitch Albom, Tuesdays with Morrie, Broadway Books, 1997.

http://www.amazon.ca/Tuesdays-Morrie-Young-Greatest-Lesson/dp/076790592X

CHAPTER 19

99. Lincoln, dir. Steven Spielberg, 2012.

http://www.imdb.com/title/tt0443272/

100. Interview with Dr. James Cornelius by Jamie Mason Cohen, 2015.

CHAPTER 20

101. Interview with Stephen Gaghan by Jamie Mason Cohen, 2000

Quora thread on interview questions, 2015

www.quora.com

Hanna Brooks Olsen, blog.creativelive.com, "4 Unexpectedly Great Interview Questions to Ask Anyone", 2014

http://blog.creativelive.com/great-interview-questions/

Jerry Seinfeld, Comedians in cars getting coffee, Episode interviewing President Barak Obama, 2015 http://comediansincarsgettingcoffee.com/president-barack-obama-just-tell-him-you-re-the-president

Tynan, Social Skills, 2015

http://www.amazon.ca/Superhuman-Social-Skills-Likeable-Building-ebook/dp/B015QA1250

Mark Bowden, Listening Better, A Body Language skill by Mark Bowden Youtube training video at the University of Toronto (https://www.youtube.com/watch?v=JKVa9CfdtAI)

Peter Thiel and Blake Masters, Zero To Launch, 2014

http://www.amazon.ca/Zero-One-Notes-Startups-Future/dp/0804139296

Alex Blumberg quoted in the Creative Live blog posted above.

Taking LIVE FROM YOUR CLASS Beyond the Page

To inquire about a possible speaking engagement, please contact Cohen Soul Productions Inc. at jamiecoheneducator@gmail.com.

Live From Your Class – Keynote

A fun, engaging talk on how high-school teachers can incorporate humour into their classrooms. When they're laughing, they're learning.

You'll learn how to:

- Use humour to grab your students' attention within the first 60 seconds

- Effectively deal with the class clown and solve other classroom management problems without them stressing you out

- Effortlessly tell a story with humour and connect it to your lesson which enhances students' understanding of the content

- Create an easy-going, creative and fun learning environment

- Discover the humour in boring material

- 3 Resources to encourage humour through play

- The #1 humourous strategy to reach tactile learners.

Inspire Curosity And Wonder In Your Students Using A Sole – Keynote

As the Winner of the TED-Huffington Post International Teaching Award, The SOLE Challenge, Jamie will show teachers and administrators how to set up a self-organized learning environment to get 100% engagement.

What Your Signature Says About Your Success

Jamie will explore this question and you'll learn:

- 7 success traits you may have in common with leaders like Oprah and Richard Branson.

- What essential characteristics to look for in a business partner or employee in their handwriting.

- How to simply change one thing in your handwriting to impact your future goals.

- How handwriting analysis can be a fun, easy and powerful way for you to connect with anyone in this room in less than 5 minutes.

This actionable, entertaining and engaging hands-on talk will be given by Certified Handwriting Expert and TED speaker, Jamie Mason Cohen.

The Sole Student Leadership Seminar – Workshop

How can students become exceptional leaders in their school community and beyond?

Going into its 3rd year, this seminar teaches students practical, real-world skills in a personalized, unconventional and student-centered learning environment called a SOLE (Self Organized Learning Environment). By Jamie Mason Cohen, Director, Student-Activities, TanenbaumCHAT and Teacher

Students will learn how to:

- Create a compelling vision for their club, committee or event
- Build a step-by-step plan to follow through on their team's goals
- Communicate their message like professional presenters
- Discover how they can have a positive impact on their community
- Raise their confidence and their resilience to follow through

Past Facilitators include TED speakers, best-selling authors, magicians, body language experts, triathletes, entrepreneurs, a Hollywood actress, Handwriting Analysis Experts and a Saturday Night Live Producer.

Examples of Jamie Mason Cohen's Professional Speaking Engagements and Seminars can be seen below:

Jamie Mason Cohen's TEDx Talk, Luxembourg

https://www.youtube.com/watch?v=JWmafBBMHSk

Jamie Mason Cohen's Keynote at RAVSAK Education Conference, Los Angeles

https://www.youtube.com/watch?v=3ni3vX5fW7g

SOLE Student Leadership Seminar

https://www.youtube.com/watch?v=0Y3Nk9nuXXI

Manufactured by Amazon.ca
Bolton, ON